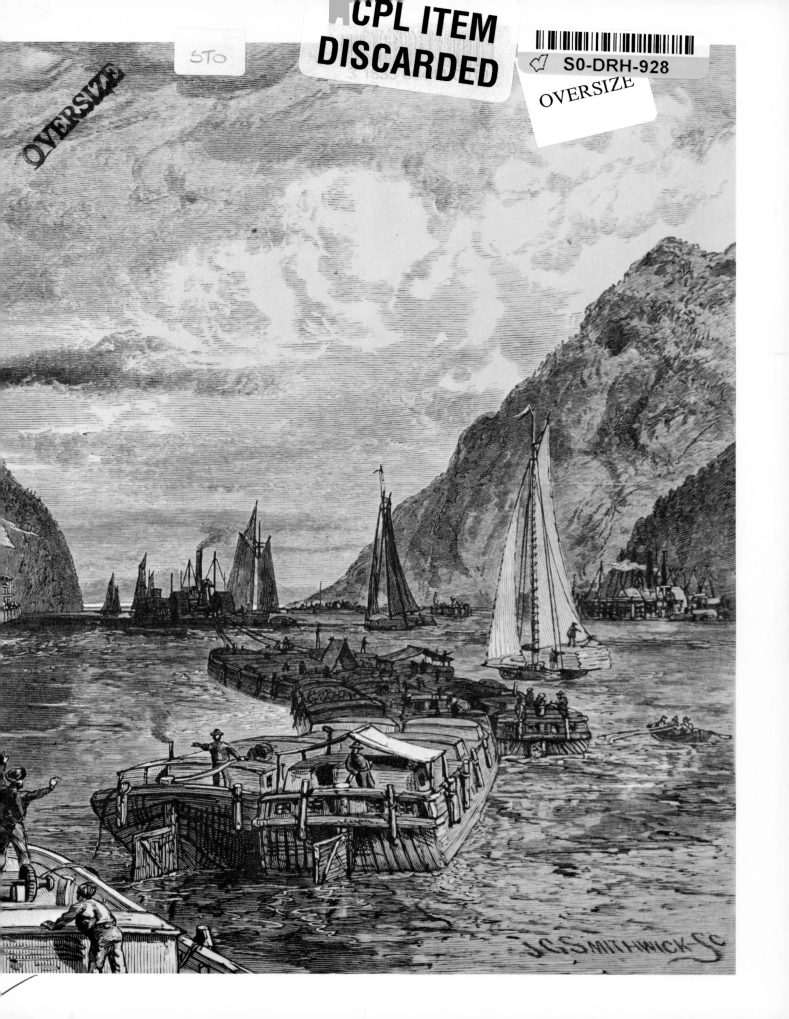

J.G.SMITHWICK SC

4·5·73

The MARY POWELL

In this painting by William G. Muller, the southbound *Mary Powell* steams through the Highlands of the Hudson in 1888, with Storm King Mountain looming up in the background.

The MARY POWELL

A history of the beautiful side-wheel
steamer called "Queen of the Hudson"

by DONALD C. RINGWALD

BERKELEY Howell-North Books CALIFORNIA

THE MARY POWELL

Printed and bound in the United States of America

Library of Congress Catalog Card No. 72-89714

ISBN 0-8310-7090-0

THE ENDSHEETS

In this popular lithograph by A. R. Waud, the *Mary Powell* in 1873 or 1874 is steaming down through the Highlands of the Hudson amongst a formidable array of sloops, schooners and tows. The northern gateway to the Highlands is marked by Storm King on the left and Breakneck on the right.

Published by Howell-North Books
1050 Parker Street, Berkeley, California 94710

Table of Contents

1744773

Acknowledgments

This book grew from a magazine article on the *Mary Powell* which I wrote for *The American Neptune* and which was published in two installments in 1954. At the time Ernest S. Dodge was managing editor and I appreciate his subsequent permission, on behalf of *The American Neptune,* to use that article as a base on which to build the present work.

For their usual liberality in such matters, I am grateful as always for the unlimited selection from the large collections of Hudson River steamboat material assembled by my old friends, Captain William O. Benson, Roger W. Mabie, William H. Ewen, Sr., and Herman F. Boyle. I must, of course, also mention the late Elwin M. Eldredge, who helped with the article mentioned above and whose collection, now in the Mariners Museum, provided additional material for this book. John L. Lochhead, the librarian at the museum, rendered his customary unlimited help in tracking down suitable pictures in the Eldredge and other collections.

Since the Hudson River Day Line held control of the Mary Powell Steamboat Company for many years, there is considerable material on the latter organization in the two Hudson River Day Line Collections — one in the New-York Historical Society library and the other in the reference library of the Steamship Historical Society of America, Inc. For expediting my considerable research in these collections, I give sincere thanks to James Gregory, librarian at the New-York Historical Society, and Mrs. Alice S. Wilson, Steamship Historical Society librarian. James T. Wilson, past president of the latter organization, also assisted by doing further library research for me.

Likewise, at the National Archives in Washington, Miss Jane F. Smith and Kenneth R. Hall helped immeasurably to speed my work there.

When the manuscript was completed, C. Bradford Mitchell, Roger W. Mabie, Captain William O. Benson and William King Covell read it critically and have my gratitude for many helpful suggestions.

For the painting reproduced on the jacket and frontispiece, I am indebted to one of America's finest maritime artists, William G. Muller, who also did the painting for the jacket of *Hudson River Day Line.*

In preparing pictorial matter, I was fortunate to have the aid of Robert W. Szembrot, who took a personal interest in getting the maximum obtainable from many a badly faded photograph.

A number of other people assisted in a variety of ways. I have listed them here alphabetically in geographical groups.

In the Kingston area were George N. Betts, whose father chauffeured Captain A. E. Anderson; Herbert H. Cutler at the Senate House Museum; Eugene C. Dauner, who made available his valuable file of old newspapers and correspondence; Dr. Charles A. Galyon, a foremost *Mary Powell* enthusiast; Mrs. Appleton Gregory, who made many a childhood trip on the steamer; Robert R. Haines, photographer and collector; the late Cornelius J. Heitzman; Fred J. Johnston, interested in all things pertaining to old Kingston; the late Cornelius E. Keyser, once a member of the crew of the *Mary Powell;* Alfred P. Marquart, possessor of several *Mary Powell* items; Robert M. Matthews, whose local history collection was a means of preserving some highly pertinent material; the late Louis R. Netter, editor of the *Daily Freeman;* Harry Rigby, Jr., City of Kingston historian; the Misses Cora F. and Pearl E. A. Rightmyer, daughters of Captain Joel Rightmyer (once a *Mary Powell* pilot) and nieces of my old friend, the late George W. Murdock, whose Hudson River steamboat collection is in the New-York Historical Society; and Richard J. Warrington, son of the last master of the *Mary Powell.*

Helpful in the Newburgh area were Homer Ramsdell and Mrs. W. Clement (Mary Powell Ramsdell) Scott, both descendants of Mary Powell; Bernhard Schulze, noted modelmaker; and Walter A. Tuttle, who assisted greatly in research at Newburgh.

In Saugerties, support was rendered by Donald S. Fellows, editor of the Saugerties *Post-Star;* Mrs. Ruth Reynolds Glunt, author of *The Old Lighthouses of the Hudson River;* and the Reverend George D. Wood, another former *Mary Powell* crew member.

In other areas were Richard S. Anderson, Hudson River enthusiast, of New Baltimore, N.Y.; Raymond Beecher of the Greene County Historical Society, Inc.; H. Ernest Bell of Milton, N.Y.; Edward O. Clark, marine historian and photographer of Chalfont, Pa.; Harry Cotterell, Jr., marine historian of Newark, N.J.; Tony Dominski, librarian, of Albany, N.Y.; James R. Dufty, print collector of Albany; Edwin L. Dunbaugh, marine historian of New York City; Richard V. Elliott, author of *Last of the Steamboats;* William H.

Ewen, Jr., marine artist and devoted follower of Hudson River steamboating; the late Arthur D. Fay of the Peabody Museum, Salem, Mass.; David T. Glick, marine historian of Dearborn, Mich.; Kenneth E. Hasbrouck of the Ulster County Historical Society; Douglas L. Haverly, who strongly assisted in research for this project, as he has for previous ones; William F. Helmer, author of *Rip Van Winkle Railroads;* Erik Heyl, marine historian and author of Buffalo, N.Y.; George W. Hilton, author of *The Night Boat* and other marine works; A. Spencer Marsellis, past president of the Steamship Historical Society of America, Inc.; Mrs. Eleanor L. Nowlin, Shelburne Museum, Inc., Shelburne, Vt.; Mrs. Wilhelmina B. Powers, Adriance Memorial Library, Poughkeepsie, N.Y.; Norman S. Rice, director of the Albany Institute of History and Art; F. Van Loon Ryder, modelmaker, of Coxsackie, N.Y.; Jim Shaughnessy, author of *Delaware & Hudson;* W. du Barry Thomas, who helped with the original *Mary Powell* article; William G. Tyrrell, chief, Historic Site Management, New York State Historic Trust; Franklin H. and Emily Welch of Van Wies Point on the Hudson; and Osgood Williams at the Peabody Museum.

Finally, I want to thank particularly the staff of the New York State Library, Albany, for aid and co-operation over a long period of time.

DONALD C. RINGWALD

Albany, New York
January, 1972

In this drawing by William H. Bartlett, an early steamboat makes her way past the Palisades towards New York. Primitive market barges are lashed to either side of the vessel, and a more conventional barge rides alongside the nearer of these. Hudson River sloops are much in evidence. (*—New York State Library*)

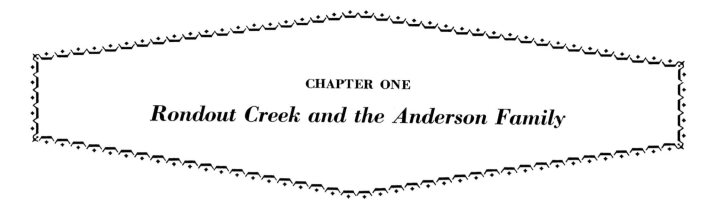

CHAPTER ONE

Rondout Creek and the Anderson Family

"I attend to my own boat and nobody else's."

Captain Absalom Lent Anderson spoke those words, and he did indeed attend religiously to his own steamboat. He cared for her with pride and lavished upon her every sort of attention, for he loved her. Other people's steamboats? They had little to distract him because, as far as he was concerned, his was the finest that ever turned a paddle wheel. She was the *Mary Powell.*

One of the fastest steamboats of her time, she was trim, comfortable and, above all, reliable. Built in 1861 for Captain Anderson's line, she was commanded by him and later by his son for over forty years. That alone is unusual, but the unusual was part of the *Mary Powell.* For more than half a century she ran as a day boat on the Hudson River between New York and Rondout Creek, and many who first traveled on her in their youth were still patrons when they were dignified old ladies and gentlemen. To them and to her other faithful followers the only proper way to journey was aboard the *Mary Powell,* for she was a "family boat" with a homelike atmosphere. Captain Anderson established her as such, and passengers who could not conduct themselves accordingly were not welcomed back. In fact, they ran the risk of being put ashore at the next landing.

To those who lived along her route she brought all the good things in life: pleasant outings, delightful trips to the city, eagerly awaited friends and relations, and excitement of the kind that only a beautifully proportioned steamboat could create. She came to be regarded as a part of the river, but her fame was by no means confined to the Hudson Valley. Her route was such that it was often used by tourists and travelers, both

humble and great, from all over the nation and from abroad as well. They carried away pleasant memories and stories of that paragon of a river steamer so that year by year, by word of mouth and travel memoirs, the name *Mary Powell* spread to many parts of the world. It is said that while Captain Anderson was vacationing in Egypt he embarked on a Nile steamboat and met her captain; he was delighted to learn in the course of their conversation that this officer had heard of only one American steamboat — the *Mary Powell.*

Probably no vessel of her type had more friends. When she was at last retired her passing was noticed by lengthy obituaries in all sorts of publications, from small-town newspapers to international periodicals. Marine chroniclers have often chosen to indicate the high qualities of a particular vessel by saying simply, "She was like the *Mary Powell.*"

To tell the story of the "Queen of the Hudson" we must start with the early days of steamboating on Rondout Creek and the beginnings of Absalom L. Anderson's marine career, which culminated in his building and commanding the *Mary Powell.*

When in 1609 Henry Hudson sailed up the river which now bears his name he passed one of its many tributaries at a point ninety miles from the mouth. This particular stream, flowing in from the west-southwest, has its source high in the Catskill Mountains and is now called Rondout Creek. Hudson was an English navigator employed by the Dutch, and soon after his exploratory voyage Dutchmen established a trading post near the mouth of the creek. In the mid-

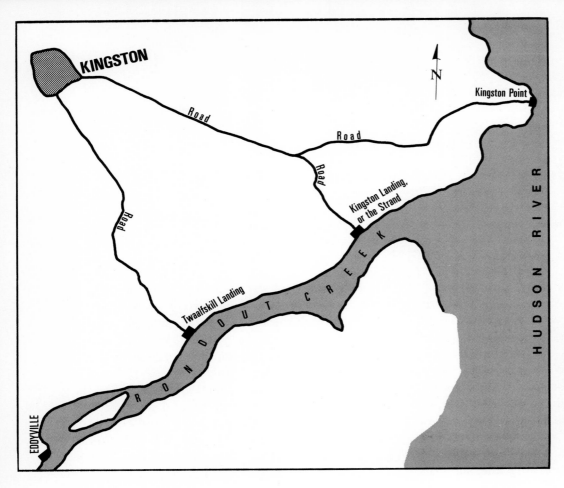

The map contains the following labels: KINGSTON, Road, Road, Road, Road, Kingston Point, N, HUDSON RIVER, Kingston Landing, or the Strand, RONDOUT CREEK, Twaalfskill Landing, EDDYVILLE

At left is a map of Rondout Creek in the early 1800s. A map of the Hudson River showing some of the important steamboat landings is on the opposite page, and is of a much later period.

1600s a permanent settlement was made in the area, although it was far back on a plateau which rose sharply on the north side of the creek, out of sight of both the creek and the river. This village was subsequently granted a charter as Wiltwyck and renamed Kingston some time after the Dutch surrendered the colony of New Netherland to the English. During the Revolutionary War Kingston was for a time the capital of New York State and in 1777 was burned by the British, but not quelled. By 1805 it was sufficiently important to become an incorporated village.

In those days Kingston was not a true river town because of its site on the plateau and because its citizens were not deeply connected with water transportation. For them the river was simply a convenient highway for personal travel and the movement of their goods. In 1820 there were two shipping points for Kingston on the north bank of the Rondout. One of these, called

Kingston Landing or the Strand, was at the foot of a precipitous hill, down which came the road from Kingston, about two miles away. The other, Twaalfskill Landing, was farther up the creek, but the road was shorter by a quarter of a mile and had an easier grade. These landings served the Hudson River sloops, fast sailing craft which were then a highly important means of transportation for passengers and freight.

Steamboating, introduced on the Hudson by Robert Fulton in 1807, was still in its infancy and river steamers were few in number. These few were operated by the line established by Fulton and Robert R. Livingston, protected through a monopoly granted by the State of New York; not until 1824 was this monopoly declared unconstitutional. Steamboat landings were made at Kingston Point, which jutted out into the river above the mouth of the Rondout and was also the terminus of a ferry across the river. The distance from

10

the point to Kingston was about three miles; unfortunately Kingston Point was backed by a marsh and the road was always in deplorable condition. Since the sloops also landed at the point and might block access to its wharf while they were loading brick or waiting for the tide, Rhinebeck landing on the other side of the river was often used in later years as the Kingston steamboat stop, with connections via the ferry.

In 1825 the Delaware & Hudson Canal Company commenced work on a project that was to rouse the placid Rondout from its slumbers. The canal was conceived as a route for anthracite coal shipments from the mines in northeastern Pennsylvania to markets in New York City and other parts of New York State. From Rondout Creek at the head of tidewater, then about three miles from the mouth, the canal would run up the Rondout Valley and over the crest of the Hudson-Delaware watershed to descend to the Delaware River; it would follow the line of that river and its tributary, the Lackawaxen, upward to a terminus 16 miles from the coal mines. The work on this canal transformed the quiet Rondout Valley into a teeming theater of activity, and reportedly in 1826 the first steamboat ever to enter the creek came churning in. This was the *New London,* delivering the hull of an unfinished vessel that was to be laid up temporarily along the south shore of the creek.

On December 5, 1828, the citizens and military of Kingston gathered on a hill along the Rondout to fire cannon and muskets and shout themselves hoarse as a squadron of canalboats, loaded with the first shipment of coal from the mines, came down the creek from the canal entrance at Eddyville to the Delaware & Hudson Canal Company's works at Bolton. On the lead boat the Kingston Band tooted manfully to make itself heard above the din.

The Canal Company employed a side-wheel towing steamer named *Rondout,* built that same year and measuring 71½ feet in statutory length,[1] to haul canalboats back and forth between Eddy-

---

[1]Unless otherwise indicated, the lengths of vessels given in this book are statutory lengths. The statutory length is the official length, arrived at by measuring the vessel in a manner prescribed by law, and is not the same as overall length. See Appendix A.

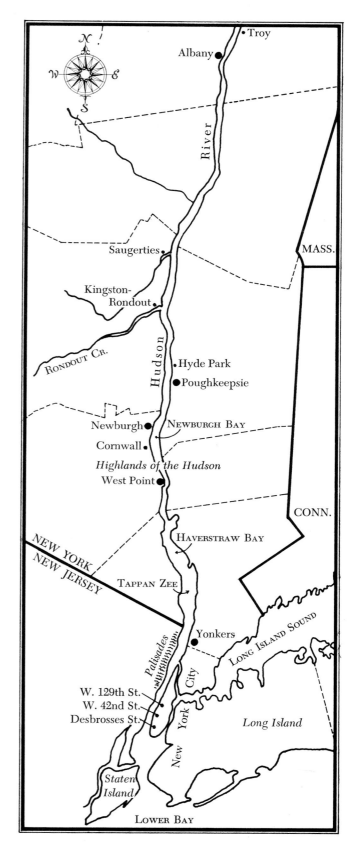

ville and Bolton. Needless to say, she was fitted to burn anthracite coal.

Bolton, immediately above the existing Kingston Landing, was to be the operational base for the Canal Company; here it had laid out storage space for coal and erected a wharf, naming these holdings after its president, John Bolton, with the intention of making that the geographic designation for the area. However, the name was locally regarded as arbitrary and was unpopular. The brothers Maurice and William Wurts, the founders of the company, had frequent differences of opinion with President Bolton, and this seems to have had considerable bearing on the latter's resignation in April of 1831, although Bolton's health was not good. Four days later John Wurts, another brother, was elected as his successor and headed the company until 1858. Allegedly, soon after this occurrence the residents of Bolton met and changed the name of the area, which included old Kingston Landing and the Canal Company's works, to Rondout. One wonders whether the name-changing movement may not have been stimulated by the new president, for the Wurts brothers must certainly have disliked seeing Bolton's name perpetuated in one of the major centers of the Canal Company's activities.

With the flow of people and materials into the Rondout during the construction of the canal, the sloops did a thriving business; now that the canal was completed there should be a steamboat connection between its terminus and New York City. In August of 1828 it was announced that the steamboat *Saratoga* would, upon completion of an overhaul, make her northern terminus the Canal Company's wharf on the Rondout, where she would connect with passenger packets on the canal, making three round trips a week to New York. Built in 1825 for service as a tender, the small *Saratoga* was the last vessel constructed for the old Fulton-Livingston line before it expired in 1826 under the onslaught of competition following the death of the monopoly. Prior to the overhaul she had been plying between New York and Poughkeepsie, on the east bank of the Hudson 15 miles below the mouth of the Rondout, and afterwards, for some reason, her route was not extended northward to the creek. However,

With this newspaper advertisement the *Hudson* appeared on Rondout Creek in competition with the *Congress*. (—Herman F. Boyle collection)

in April of 1829 the 120-foot side-wheeler *Congress* was advertised to leave from Theron Skeel's dock at Twaalfskill, midway between Rondout and Eddyville at the foot of the most convenient road to Kingston. The *Congress* would sail for New York on Wednesdays and Saturdays at 1 p.m. and return on Mondays and Thursdays at 4 p.m. She made way landings and, like other "local" steamboats, not only carried passengers and freight on board, but also hauled market barges which she picked up along the way on southbound trips and returned to the proper landings on the northbound runs. These market barges, generally carrying farm produce and livestock, were fitted with passenger accommodations catering to farmers, who could accompany their goods to market and live aboard while the barge lay at New York in order to take advantage of the best prices. Otherwise, the captain of the barge would handle the marketing. For the trip on the *Congress*, from Twaalfskill to New York with arrival expected "at daylight," one paid 12 shillings (or $1.50), with meals included. For this, of course, the traveler got neither the speed nor the luxury of the through steamers plying between New York and Albany.

Captain C. McEntee, who knew the *Congress* when she ran out of Rondout Creek, described her many years later in what we may hope was a recollection of her at the end of this service. The captain was comparing her to the finer and newer steamboats that followed in her wake when he wrote:

> . . . she was so badly hogged you would be unable to say which way the water would run to get off her deck. She was about the shape of a catfish — all there was of her appeared to be forward — machinery and all. Her narrow hull, running away aft with hardly any guards, and in so many different shapes, she looked as though she was about to part somewhere between her engine and her stern at every turn of her wheels. Her cabin was reached by a slide companionway near her stern post, that at a distance looked like a hen coop unintentionally left on deck.

Nevertheless she ran and ran successfully. She was the first in a long succession of night boats that would ply between New York and Rondout Creek for over a century. She has another niche in history for in July, 1829, the *Congress* sailed from New York with the first two steam locomotives built in England for the Delaware & Hudson Canal Company, intended to haul coal part of the distance between the mines and the western terminus of the canal. One of these was the STOURBRIDGE LION, which in August made the first trip of a locomotive on commercial trackage in North America. However, she was too heavy for the roadbed and was soon laid aside.

In 1832 new competition appeared in Rondout Creek with the entry of the steamer *Hudson*. Built in 1824 and measuring 105¼ feet in length, she was older and smaller than the *Congress*. She sailed from the Rondout wharf on Tuesdays and Fridays, so that the Kingston area now had steamboat service on four days of the week. In the last years trade had increased so much in that general area that both lines could continue without dire results to either.

For the 1834 season the *Congress* passed to the command of Captain John Ketcham, who had in-

vested in the vessel and who was for some time to play an important role in Rondout steam navigation. Since he was a newcomer to the creek, newspaper advertising pointed out, "Captain Ketcham, having by long experience become well acquainted with the New-York markets, will be prepared to receive on board every description of freight, stock and produce, and is in every respect qualified to give general satisfaction." Hudson River steamboat captains of this period, and for many years to come, were primarily business managers. While they were in complete charge of their vessels, they did not need any knowledge of piloting; more important than the ability to avoid a shoal was the proficiency to act as a shipper's agent and dispose of his produce at a satisfactory profit, or to serve as a proper host to the passengers.

With the change in captains the northern terminus of the *Congress* was changed from Theron Skeel's Twaalfskill wharf to Rondout. Skeel had purchased an interest in the vessel and was for a time her captain, but when he sold out, the link with Twaalfskill was severed. The six owners of the vessel, of whom Ketcham was one, decided upon the change in docks, and Rondout had been a way landing for the *Congress*. Through the impetus of the Delaware & Hudson Canal Rondout had become a lusty, fast-growing place where hard drinking alleviated hard toil, in sharp contrast to Kingston with its solid and stolid Dutch background. However, the *Hudson's* operations out of Rondout had demonstrated that the sedate citizens of Kingston were as willing to ship and travel by the steeper road to Rondout as by the easier road to placid Twaalfskill, and it would be advantageous to combine the Kingston and the Rondout business in one terminus. Having read the signs of the times, the owners of the *Congress* moved down the creek.

Captain Joseph P. Dean might be called the father of steamboating between Rondout Creek and New York. He had commanded both the *Congress* and the *Hudson* when they made their first voyages on that route, and in 1834 he was busily engaged in the building of a new steamboat in the creek, which at 155½ feet would be considerably longer than either of her predecessors. The hull was launched on December 11th

13

Though known as an icebreaker, the *Robert L. Stevens* never performed the feat suggested in the painting by James and John Bard. Primitive artists who faithfully delineated American steamboats, the brothers were fond of including strange-looking men on deck, as here. (*—Courtesy of The Mariners Museum, Newport News, Va.*)

as the *Robert L. Stevens* and shortly towed away to New York for completion. But, instead of entering the Rondout-New York trade in 1835, she was placed in service between New York and Albany, allegedly either because her cost had exceeded the estimate, or because of a disagreement between Captain Dean and the other owners.

The last year in which Captain Ketcham commanded the *Congress* out of Rondout was 1837, by which time three night boats were running to New York, providing service six days a week. The *Congress* permanently left the route she had pioneered, but her place was taken by the *Emerald*, built in 1825 and measuring 156.6 feet.[2] In addi-

tion to making the regular trips on the same days as her predecessor, the *Emerald* inaugurated a Sunday round trip from New York, leaving there at 7 a.m. and returning from Rondout at 5 p.m. with "all landings" advertised. Before this time Rondout steamers had never departed from either terminal on the Sabbath.

Captain John Ketcham bought an interest in the *Emerald* and took command of her in 1839. His first Rondout agent was Jansen Hasbrouck, whose father, Abraham, owned valuable waterfront property and other real estate in Rondout, had once operated sloops to New York, had represented his district in Congress and had been on

---

[2]Since all statutory lengths given in this book are taken from official documents, the measurement for the *Emerald* requires an explanation. At the time, the figure was supposed to be expressed in feet and inches. Not until the enactment in 1864 of further legislation, were measurements directed

to be set down in feet and, instead of inches, decimal parts. But, as always, there were exceptions to the legal rules and so the *Emerald* turns up on documents in the 1830s with a length of 156 6/10', or 156.6 feet.

the original board of managers of the Delaware & Hudson Canal Company. Jansen, a graduate of Yale, also operated a store hard by the *Emerald's* landing, selling pork and fish, sugars, flour and salt, orange ale, teas, liquors and merchandise. Likely he was serving in an interim capacity, for in mid-June it was noted in advertising that the agents and storekeepers had become the firm of Anderson & Taylor, composed of Captain Nathan Anderson and James A. Taylor.

Captain Anderson's ancestry was traceable to 1530, when Edmund Anderson of Scottish descent was born in England; he was a judge at the trial of Mary, Queen of Scots, and an author of legal works. But a family tree was of little interest in the booming atmosphere of Rondout in 1839; it was more important that Nathan Anderson had a firm background as a sloop captain and operator. Born on June 25, 1790, in Croton, New York, on the Hudson, he had sailed between there and New York until about 1818, when he moved to Buttermilk Falls in connection with his slooping activities. Attracted by the business opportunities in Rondout, he came there about 1833, although it is said that he had sailed out of Rondout Creek for a time in the early 1820s. He had married

Charlotte Golding in 1810, and the couple had seven children, three daughters and four sons: Absalom Lent, Charles, Nathan, Jr. and David. According to old accounts, Captain Nathan set each of his sons up in the sloop business as an owner and captain in the family partnership.

About the same time that Anderson & Taylor became agents for the *Emerald*, the *Robert L. Stevens* finally arrived in Rondout to begin her previously planned service to New York, running now under the command of Captain D. P. Mapes on his own line. She was the finest of the three vessels then plying this route. That summer she carried a Fourth of July excursion for which several people, including young Absalom Anderson, sold tickets and perhaps had arranged the affair. She was to leave Rondout at 11 a.m. and sail either upriver to the city of Hudson or down to West Point, depending on the will of the majority. The fare was $2.00 for a lady and gentleman; $2.50 for those lucky gentlemen with two ladies; and $1.50 for the unfortunate gentleman who traveled alone. This included a "sumptuous" dinner with music and fireworks on board, but not wine; that had to be called for separately. This outing is the first record, although a minor one, of active

The Rondout waterfront, shown in an Endicott lithograph of about 1844, was a busy terminal. To the left are the coal piles of the Delaware & Hudson Canal Co., while at the wharf to the right is the *Norwich*. (—*Senate House Museum, Kingston, N.Y.*)

participation in steamboating by Absalom L. Anderson. Later he would own this same *Robert L. Stevens.*

In 1841, the agents for Captain Ketcham and the *Emerald* were advertised as Anderson, Taylor & Company, an expansion of the firm to include Absalom as the "Company." Prior to this, reportedly, young Anderson had owned and commanded the sloop *Robert Burns,* considered a model in speed and accommodations, with mahogany staterooms and cabins. Absalom Anderson was born on November 25, 1812, and was thirty years old when, in March of 1843, Anderson, Taylor & Company was dissolved "by mutual consent," and he and his father formed the successor partnership of N. & A. L. Anderson. Just a week earlier he had married Catherine A. L. Eltinge, the daughter of Dr. Richard Eltinge, and her maternal grandfather was Abraham Hasbrouck, the Rondout landowner. Four days before the wedding Catherine had celebrated her 16th birthday. Incidentally, in 1842 one of Absalom's sisters had married Andrew Jackson Ketcham, a relative — likely a nephew — of Captain John Ketcham.

For the 1843 season the Andersons were agents for both the *Emerald* and Captain John Samuels' *Norwich;* although independently owned, these two vessels operated together for that year. The *Norwich,* 160 feet in length and built in 1836, had a long life ahead of her, for when outmoded as a passenger boat she would serve as a towing steamer on the Hudson until 1917. A towing steamer would normally spend most of her time hauling fleets of barges and canalboats up and down the river; this kind of work was an important part of the commerce on the river.

On a Sunday in May, 1844, when the *Emerald* was in the Highlands of the Hudson on one of her round trips, she cracked a shaft about 11 a.m. and, drifting in on a reef near Cold Spring, injured her bottom and began to leak. She was towed in to shore and secured by hawsers, but a fast broke and she fell off into deep water. Her passengers had already been taken off by small boats, and although she carried little or no freight, her safe contained $30,000 in funds and checks for banks in Poughkeepsie and Kingston. Salvage operations recovered the safe and raised the *Emerald,* which was towed to New York for repairs. It is said that before the vessel was raised Ketcham, who may have been trying to get out of an unhealthy situation, sold his interest in the *Emerald* for one dollar to Captain Samuels, who had been removed from his command of the *Norwich* by a change of ownership. That is a story, but it is a fact that an interest in the boat changed hands between the two sometime after the sinking and before the repairs were complete. These included a rebuilding of the upper works and the addition of staterooms to the upper deck. In May of the next year the *Emerald* was dealt a low blow when the New York *Sun* reported that she had been consumed by fire at Rondout. This bit of completely false news, the editor of the *Sun* explained later, had been given to him by a man having the appearance of a boatman — a boatman, no doubt, and probably with a rival line!

The *Victory* was a night boat between Rondout and New York during the 1830s and 1840s.

In a close-up of the lithograph on preceding page 15, the *Norwich* is shown in some detail. Like the *Robert L. Stevens*, she
was known as an icebreaker on the river. Rather than a walking
beam, the *Norwich's* engine was of the crosshead type.

17

The *Telegraph* was painted by James Bard in 1837. James did many paintings without the collaboration of his brother John; after the latter's death he painted alone for decades.

Records indicate that in 1845 the Andersons purchased a piece of the Rondout Landing from the Abraham Hasbrouck estate and advertised the *Emerald* as leaving from Anderson's Dock. They continued as agents for the *Emerald* through 1846 and then became the agents for the New-York, Rondout & Eddyville Steam Freight & Passage Line, run by T. W. Cornell, his nephew Thomas Cornell and three other men. Thomas Cornell, 14 months younger than Absalom Anderson, would in the decades ahead become a great figure in Hudson River transportation, with towing as his special province, and would own the *Mary Powell* for two separate periods. This new line, for which the *Telegraph* was acquired in 1847, was not commenced at a propitious time. With Captain William B. Dodge operating the *Norwich* and the *Mohegan*, Captain Samuels running the *Emerald* and Ezra Fitch trying to revive Twaalfskill — now being called Wilbur — as a steamboat landing with his *Santa Claus*, the Kingston area simply did not have enough business to support five steamboats making as many as fifteen departures a week. The *Telegraph*, as the newcomer, gave up and was placed on a route between Newburgh and Albany and Troy, with the Andersons continuing as her Rondout agents.

Fortunately the Andersons had also become involved in another project that bore sweeter fruit. This was the market barge *Ulster County*, being built on Rondout Creek for a stock company composed of farmers, merchants and mechanics in Ulster County, of which Rondout and Kingston were a part. The Andersons were to be her agents and had an interest in her construction. Decorated with flags and boughs the hull was launched on June 5, 1847, at about the same time that the Andersons acquired additional Hasbrouck property to extend their waterfront holdings. The next month Captain Nathan and another man were seriously injured while inspecting the progress of the construction when the props supporting the hurricane deck gave way and the deck fell on them. Notwithstanding this unfortunate event, the *Ulster County* was soon finished and left on her first trip to New York on August 3rd.

The *Ulster County* measured 126 feet in length on deck. Her accommodations totalled seventy berths in the forward and after cabins — dormitorylike rooms in the hold — and in the ladies' cabin on the main deck aft, plus 14 staterooms on the upper deck. There was room for 6,000 bushels of grain and other freight in the hold, space on the main deck for 140 head of cattle and for many score of sheep on the upper deck. Like other market barges she lay over at New York long enough for the farmers aboard to profit from a possible rise in prices. Barges also appealed to travelers who were still unconvinced that steamboats with their fearful boilers were at all safe, or who were unaccustomed to New York City; by living aboard they could avoid the undue expense and confusion of hotel accommodations and avoid exposure to the "evils of the big city." Of course, to live aboard a barge, with the animal sounds and smells, one must have a bit of farmer in his background to feel completely at home. Apparently the *Ulster County* did well: in Kingston people eventually complained that so much produce was being shipped to New York that local supplies had decreased and prices had gone up.

Regardless of the success of the *Ulster County*, N. & A. L. Anderson had no steamboat departing from their Rondout wharf for New York. Since there was little possibility of a steamboat operator using their facilities, they were impelled to enter the field themselves. Together with William F. Romer, a cashier of the Kingston Bank who resigned his position in February of 1848, they formed, in the following month, Anderson, Romer & Company's Barge & Steamboat Line, which was actually being advertised in the press before the partners were legally joined. Romer retained excellent business connections in Kingston, and the new firm continued the wholesale and retail grocery business, selling such items as pork, fish, flour, and coarse and fine salt. They remained the agents for the *Ulster County*, which they would now tow both to and from New York. Soon the firm bought still more Hasbrouck dock property, to give it an uninterrupted run of 335 feet along the creek. For its most important item in trade, a steamboat, Anderson, Romer & Company came up with a good one, the *Highlander*, built for the Newburgh-New York route and owned at this time by Thomas Powell and Homer Ramsdell.

When the *Santa Claus* was made a towing steamer she was completely rebuilt and enrolled as the *A. B. Valentine*.

19

Above is the youthful *Highlander* in a watercolor by the brothers Bard. To the right is an Anderson, Romer & Company advertisement of 1852 for the *Highlander* and the barge *Ulster County*. In the custom of the times, the cuts are stock items kept on hand by newspaper proprietors and the vessels depicted bear no resemblance to those advertised. The barge *Ulster County*, for example, is shown as a two-stacker with a vertical beam engine. *(Above, Eldredge collection, The Mariners Museum; at right, Herman F. Boyle collection)*

ANDERSON, ROMER & CO.'S
FREIGHT AND PASSAGE LINE,
RONDOUT AND NEW YORK.

THE powerful and splendid steamer HIGHLANDER, Capt. A. L. ANDERSON, leaves Rondout, Anderson, Romer & Co's. dock, every TUESDAY, THURSDAY and SATURDAY, at 4 o'clock, P. M.

Returning will leave New York, (foot of Murray st.,) every MONDAY, WEDNESDAY and FRIDAY at 5 o'-clock, P. M.

THE HIGHLANDER

Is in complete running order, and her reputation as a safe and comfortable boat is unquestioned. Her boilers are new, and her engine has been materially improved. Her saloons and state rooms have been refitted and superbly furnished during the past winter, rendering her not only a safe but pleasant boat for passengers.

The commodious and substantial

BARGE ULSTER COUNTY,

Captain CHAS. BRODHEAD, leaves Rondout, (Anderson, Romer & Co.'s Dock,) every THURSDAY, at 4 o'clock, P. M.

Leaves New York, (foot of Murray st.) every TUESDAY, at 5 o'clock, P. M.

The Barge has ample accommodation for stock, produce, and all other freight, and her arrangements for the comfort of passengers are unsurpassed, having fourteen spacious State Rooms, and seventy roomy berths, always in the neatest order.

N. B.—The Ulster County will not run regularly until July 1. But till then, barge freight will be taken by the Highlander on Thursdays and transferred to and sold from the Ulster County, which will lay at New York city as a market boat.

Freight and Passage on reasonable terms.

☞ Returns paid in current money.

Pork, Fish, Flour, coarse and fine salt, &c., constantly on hand and for sale.

ANDERSON, ROMER & CO.

Rondout, March. 1852.

CHAPTER TWO

The Andersons as Steamboat Owners

In 1848 Thomas Powell was a leading citizen of the village of Newburgh, located on the west bank of the Hudson sixty miles from the mouth of the river. His forebear and namesake had come from Wales and settled on Long Island in the 1600s. He himself was born on February 21, 1769, the son of Henry Powell, who farmed leased land on Shelter Island, at the eastern end of Long Island. Henry Powell was drowned in 1781, and young Thomas and his elder brother Jacob continued to operate the farm until the lease expired; the two brothers moved to Orange County, near Newburgh, and later to New York to embark in the mercantile trade, but a yellow fever epidemic ended their stay. They returned to Newburgh and continued in the same line and in the forwarding business. Before long Thomas Powell took as his bride Mary Ludlow, for whom decades later the *Mary Powell* was to be named. Eventually the Powell brothers were established as private bankers, until Jacob, in his 58th year, died of face cancer in 1823. Soon after this family tragedy Thomas Powell withdrew from the business world until the 1830s.

The firm of T. Powell & Company, composed of Powell and Captains Samuel Johnson and Robert Wardrop, established a steamboat line in 1835. Under Captain Johnson's superintendence the *Highlander* was built for them and entered service in October. She was a fast steamboat, 156 feet long, powered by a vertical beam — or walking beam — engine with a pair of boilers, one on either overhanging guard aft of the paddle boxes. She had little in the way of upper works originally, since the main deck was enclosed only from forward of the paddle wheels to aft of the boilers

and had naught in addition but a cabin at the after end. The pilothouse was forward on the upper deck, and on this deck aft was a promenade for passengers. The white exterior of the *Highlander* was trimmed principally with green. In her schedule for the summer of 1836 the *Highlander* left Newburgh on Mondays at 6 a.m. and Tuesdays and Fridays at 6 p.m.; her New York departures were on Mondays, Thursdays and Saturdays at 5 p.m. The Saturday trip and the early Monday southbound trip from Newburgh were singled out in New York advertising: "This arrangement will enable passengers to spend Sunday in the country and return to the city before the commencement of business on Monday morning." Ah, those long week ends of 1836! The Monday schedule, of course, gave Newburghers a round trip to New York on the same day, with ample time in the big city.

Over the years the *Highlander* plied this route, and then on February 1, 1845, the firm of T. Powell & Company was dissolved. The boat was briefly operated by another organization until August, when Powell, now the sole owner, again engaged her in the passenger and freight business in partnership with his son-in-law, Homer Ramsdell. Ramsdell was born in 1810 and while still in his teens entered the dry-goods trade in New York. When he came of age he formed a partnership to deal in silks, laces and white and fancy goods; in 1835 he married Frances Elizabeth Ludlow Powell, a daughter of Thomas and Mary. Later he moved to Newburgh to engage in business with his father-in-law. He also became a director of the New York & Erie Railroad and would be president of the line in the 1850s.

Thomas Powell. (*—E. M. Ruttenber,*
History of the County of Orange)

In the spring of 1846 Powell and Ramsdell brought out the new *Thomas Powell* for day service between Newburgh and New York. She was a handsome, well-proportioned steamboat, 231′2″ in length, fitted with a walking beam engine and boilers on the guards. In the forward hold was a roomy cabin, with a passageway leading down one side of the engine to the after cabin. Then came a large lower saloon, and a small room aft of it with four berths was for passengers who were ill. On the main deck aft was the ladies' saloon; forward of it the deck over the hull itself was obstructed only by the engine room and the captain's office. A barbershop, baggage room and other facilities were on the sides over the guards. Above the main deck was a spacious promenade deck.

Except on Sundays, the *Thomas Powell* sailed from Newburgh every morning and returned from New York at 4 p.m. On this route she quickly established what was reported as a new speed

record. The *Highlander,* which was re-enrolled[1] to include Ramsdell as an owner along with Powell, continued in service with two sailings from either terminus each week. Her Monday round trips to New York were now superfluous, since they were in the domain of the *Thomas Powell*. In time Powell and Ramsdell decided the *Highlander* herself had become superfluous to their needs.

Even before the firm of Anderson, Romer & Company came into being in 1848, Nathan and Absalom Anderson had entered into negotiations for the vessel, and Powell and Ramsdell agreed to sell a majority interest. Isaac Cocks, engaged in the freight and forwarding business at Eddyville, was also involved, since the original plan was to run the *Highlander* beyond Rondout on up to Eddyville to deliver and load freight. When the change in ownership of the *Highlander* was formalized by re-enrollment she had six men holding shares in her: the Andersons, Romer, Cocks, Powell and Ramsdell. Afterwards the interest of Powell and Ramsdell was acquired; later the Andersons and Romer owned the vessel completely as copartners. Probably a discontinuance of the trips to Eddyville was involved in Cocks' sale of his share.

Although Powell had always kept the *Highlander* in prime condition, she was deficient in night-boat accommodations for the longer run to Rondout, over thirty miles longer than the Newburgh route. A saloon was now added on the upper deck, with a range of staterooms on either side, and berths were installed in the ladies' cabin. Some of the staterooms were double, with folding doors between. As Anderson, Romer & Company put it in their advertising:

[1]To meet legal requirements, vessels plying between United States ports on waters under federal jurisdiction, and above a stated minimum tonnage, have to be enrolled in government records. All information from enrollments, as set forth in this book, comes from document files or from the master abstracts of enrollments carefully preserved in the National Archives, Washington, D.C. Ideally, the first enrollment for each steamboat is equivalent to a birth certificate, giving the name of the shipbuilder, original dimensions, tonnage, and owner or owners, and is supplanted by a new enrollment after such circumstances as a change in ownership or structural alterations resulting in different measurements.

The twelve spacious state rooms and ample saloon attached, and the berths and furniture of the ladies saloon on the main deck of the *Highlander* are new, and equal to the accommodations of the best boats on the Hudson.

The *Highlander* is fast, large and commodious, and one of the best ice boats afloat.

How one reacted to the blurb about equality of accommodations depended on how much he knew about steamboating, for the finest night boats ran between New York and Albany, and the largest of these were over twice the length of the *Highlander* and lavishly appointed. The claim for her abilities as an ice boat must have been comforting reading in the hot, humid days of summer. Captain Absalom Anderson was to command her, and the Rondout *Courier* noted that, along with the personal traits found in a popular master, he had energy, business tact and eight years' experience in river navigation. This last referred to his experience with sloops, for as far as we know this was his first command in steam.

The *Highlander* departed from Rondout on Tuesdays and Fridays at 4 p.m. and from New York on Wednesdays and Saturdays at 5 p.m. In April she added a Sunday departure from Rondout with a Monday return, and on these trips she hauled no barges. In July it was announced that the *Highlander* would make an excursion to the Fishing Banks in connection with her regular service; this simply meant that she would go outside New York harbor for deep-sea fishing during her lay-over period at New York. Although this was a common outing, for those who lived up the Hudson Valley it was in the realm of the extraordinary. She would have a band aboard and, as an added attraction, an experienced shark fisherman to entertain the passengers. From Rondout the total fare was $1.50; breakfast and tea were 25 cents each and dinner 37½ cents (three shillings). The excursion proved to be a pleasant one with smooth seas. Of the 300 who sailed from New York, only about 200 actually fished, for there was some oversight in the arrangements for fishing tackle. Unhappily, the shark fisherman was unable to lure anything befitting a man of his calibre, although he did his best, using suitable bait. The Rondout *Courier* felt the outing would be remembered with pleasure by those who occasionally " 'go down to the sea in ships.' " Late in August this excursion was repeated and again was well received.

Regardless of these happy frolics, in the first months of the 1848 season Anderson, Romer & Company's new line had met with considerable competition; the situation was much the same as it had been the preceding year when the *Telegraph* had entered the field. Then in August Captain William Dodge withdrew from the passenger trade, and his *Norwich* was acquired by T. W. and Thomas Cornell, who had been connected with the abortive Eddyville line of the *Telegraph*. They continued the *Norwich* as a night boat in Rondout-New York service and in 1849, after toying with the idea of adding another steamboat, joined with Anderson, Romer & Company, with schedules rearranged so that between the two organizations there were departures from Rondout and New York daily except Sunday. The proper citizens of Kingston regarded Sunday departures — which the *Highlander* had commenced in the previous season — as an unnecessary breaking of the Sabbath simply so that "get-rich-quickers" — as they put it — could save a night. The cooperative agreement between the Cornells and Anderson, Romer & Company was described at the time as permanent, and indeed it was, for it established the pattern for Rondout night-boat operations which, barring strife in 1850, continued for many years. However, except for the relative placidity in steamboat operations, the year 1849 was to be a bad one.

The act to incorporate Rondout as a village passed in the state legislature in April, but the celebrative air engendered by this momentous event did not last for long. There was fear of the dreaded cholera breaking out, and business slackened in unhappy anticipation. The outbreak came in June. One school of thought believed that cholera resulted from immorality, intemperance in drinking strong spirits or eating such things as unripe fruit and potatoes. On June 22nd the assistant engineer of the *Norwich* fell prey to the fearful disease on the downward journey at 7 p.m. and was dead by dawn the next morning. Since he was a young man of good habits, it was apparent that his character had not killed him. The morbidly curious soon learned that before going to work on the steamboat that day he had eaten a hearty meal of bread, milk and radishes. That did it! In the matter of drinking, the canallers had always been known to partake heavily. Hudson River boatmen drank, too, and Rondout was a wide-open town where the temperate man along the docks would be considered a drunkard up the hill from the waterfront or in Kingston. Spurred on by a universal terror of cholera, it was said, the new Board of Trustees of Rondout decreed that all drinking places must be closed on Sundays. This was indeed a strong step, but for the first time in the memory of the oldest villager the place had the air of the Sabbath on Sunday. People still died; it was generally agreed that one man had sealed his fate by making a meal of clams, topped off by a quart of buttermilk.

Past midsummer, with the epidemic waning, business began to revive, but losses had been heavy. In early fall there came a great resurgence in steamboat travel. One other event of the year bears mentioning. When the new legislation went into effect requiring passenger steamers to carry certain small boats — lifeboats — in keeping with their tonnage, Captain Anderson's *Highlander* was mentioned as complying promptly. There was always a genuine ring to the captain's regard for his passengers.

In 1850 the Andersons became more formidable, as far as the Cornells were concerned, by arranging with the owner of the steamboat *North America* to put that vessel in service out of Rondout with the *Highlander* under the new tag of Anderson, Romer & Company's Freight & Passage Line. A former New York-Albany night boat, the *North America* was considerably larger and finer in passenger appointments than either the *Highlander* or the *Norwich*. She opposed the latter by sailing on the same days, and the best the Cornells could do was to shout with capital letters in their advertising, "Independent Opposition Arrangement," and to point out in finer print that the *Norwich* was now ". . . entirely independent of any other line, has no connection with the *Highlander*."

As the new season was getting under way, the Rondout *Courier* observed:

> The *Highlander* . . . has new boilers, putting her on the score of speed and power far above last season — and then she always made good time. Capt. Anderson everybody knows — and everybody knows too that anybody going on his boat will be well taken care of, politely treated, and made as comfortable as can be by a courteous commander and capital accommodations. The *Highlander* is newly painted, carpeted, &c., and is as neat as a band-box bonnet.

From early May until early August the *North America* was withdrawn from the Rondout route for other service, and during this interval her place was taken by the old *Emerald*, which reportedly had been somewhat renovated. The *Highlander* made two more trips to the Fishing Banks that year, and on the last one, although only 37 passengers were fishing, in three hours they hauled in over 2,100 porgies, bluefish and bass. They were anchored in such a great school of fish that some had been hooked by the tail.

In the fall of 1850 the Cornells arranged for the *Norfolk* to run on their line in connection with the *Norwich*, but the *Norfolk* was an inferior steamer. Since Rondout was probably the most steamboat-minded town on the Hudson between New York and Albany, all of its inhabitants were likely looking ahead to see what the arrangements would be in 1851. They did not have long to wait. Thomas Cornell took over his uncle's interest and now was sole owner of the Cornell line. If Anderson, Romer & Company had any thought of continuing their arrangements with the *North America*, Cornell quickly scotched that by buying the vessel outright. Of course, it may be that the rivals had already agreed to resume the cooperative schedule of 1849, or that the Andersons were unable to find another vessel suitable for their line, but whatever the reason, in 1851 the serenity of two years before was restored by the *North America* and the *Highlander*. The *Norwich*, still owned by Cornell, was placed in the towing business, hauling coal and ice barges and anything else between New York and Rondout.

Ever since Captain Anderson first took command of the *Highlander* his reputation for punc-

The *North America,* in a Bard oil painting, exhibits
changes made between the seasons of 1852 and 1853.
Most notable is her pilothouse, which has been moved
up to the hurricane deck.

tuality and thoughtful attention to his passengers
had been growing steadily. Not even a passenger
who should not have been a passenger was beyond the pale. In the fall of 1849 a stowaway was
found on the northbound run, a bright little boy
of five who could locate his home only as being
on Mott Street in New York. Bother notwithstanding, Captain Anderson treated him kindly, took
him back to New York and managed to restore
him to his parents.

Apparently one of the high spots in the captain's passion for punctuality came in August of
1851, when the celebrated Washington Guards
of New York came up the Hudson on the day
boat *Reindeer* to visit the Harrison Guards of
Rondout. Since the *Reindeer* landed at Kingston
Point, the *North America* was made available to
the host Harrison Guards to carry the military

from the point into Rondout. With her decks alive
with the bright uniforms of the Harrison Guards
and two fire companies participating in the fes-
tivities, as well as with the duller mufti of the
many citizens who turned out for the occasion,
the *North America* left Rondout with flags and
streamers floating in the breeze to the accompaniment of the oompah notes of the local German
band and the boom of a saluting gun from a cliff
along the creek. After the steamboat came back
into the creek there was a parade, then a military
ball, a dinner and a dance until five the next
morning. After a slight pause for rest came target
trials to give some soldierly excuse for the whole
thing and then the awarding of prizes at Clinton
Hall in Rondout. It would seem that anyone who
could hit the target at all, after that long night,
was a likely candidate for a prize. The grand cli-

max might have been the departure of the Washington Guards from Rondout aboard the *Highlander*. But when that fine body of men marched to the landing, there was no *Highlander*; Captain Anderson had sailed on time and the Guards were left behind. The company finally managed to take passage on a small towing steamer to Kingston Point, where they caught a night boat bound for New York from upriver. Perhaps Captain Anderson's prompt departure was motivated not so much by his watch as by consideration of the condition the Washington Guards would be in after two days of revelry. The captain abhorred rowdiness and prided himself on maintaining the homelike atmosphere of the *Highlander*. The comfort of his regular passengers and the safety of his vessel's furniture were guaranteed if he sailed on time. Perhaps he chuckled to himself as the *Highlander* slipped quietly away from the landing.

After the season of 1851 Thomas Cornell withdrew from the passenger business, selling his line and the *North America* to Abraham Sleight, Captain Charles Anderson and Jeremiah A. Houghtaling. Sleight and Anderson each owned nine-twentieths of the vessel, which operated under the firm name of A. Sleight & Company and at first under the trade name of Independent Opposition Freight & Passage Line. Charles Anderson, born in November of 1813, was a year younger than his brother Absalom and like him had married a daughter of Dr. Richard Eltinge; Sleight's wife, his second, was another Eltinge daughter.

With Captain Absalom in command of the *Highlander* and Captain Charles giving the orders on the *North America*, the Anderson family had the Rondout-New York route to themselves. Anyone in Rondout with a personal animosity toward the Andersons had only one alternative if he wanted to travel to New York by steamboat: to go out to Kingston Point and meet one of the steamers from up the river. Still another Anderson brother, Nathan, Jr., was on the local scene in 1852. Born in 1820 he seems to have been connected with a public house on Kingston Point for a time and then in the Gold Rush year of 1849 went to California. Now he was towing vessels in and out of Rondout Creek with the little propeller tug, or "kicker," *M. V. Schuyler*, which had

come to the creek late in the 1840s and is credited with being the first of her type to run at Rondout, which many scores of propeller tugs would later make their home port. The diminutive *M. V. Schuyler*, it was said, could tow anything that sailed — with a little patience. Of course, there was yet a fourth Captain Anderson at Rondout, the father of the family, Nathan, who was busy with the affairs of Anderson, Romer & Company.

The Andersons replaced the aging *Highlander* with the *Rip Van Winkle* in October of 1852, announcing that the business required a larger vessel. The *Rip Van Winkle*, twenty feet longer than the *North America*, was previously in through service on the Hudson and had a Lighthall horizontal half-beam engine rather than the vertical beam engine common to most side-wheelers, but her boilers were on the guards aft of the paddle boxes in standard Hudson River style. She had not been running very long when Captain Absalom Anderson withdrew her temporarily for what, in the words of a newspaper, was a trifling crack in an important part of the machinery. He was applauded for having the defect remedied promptly by "a stitch in time."

Late in December, 1852, the news broke that Nathan and Absalom Anderson had sold, or were about to sell, their interest in Anderson, Romer & Company and in the extensive wharf at Rondout, considered the choicest such property in the village. The buyers, Captain Jacob H. Tremper and Gilbert M. Gillett, now joined with Romer in the new firm of Romer, Tremper & Gillett. Tremper had been a steamboat captain and had also commanded the barge *Ulster County*. The new firm planned to charter out the *Rip Van Winkle* as a New York-Troy night boat for the forthcoming season because she had apparently proven to be a larger and finer boat than was needed on the Rondout route. However, Romer, Tremper & Gillett advertised her as their Rondout-New York steamer for 1853 and added, inconspicuously, "P. S. — The steamer *Highlander* has been fitted up anew, and put in better condition for the accommodation of passengers and freight than she ever was, will take the place of the *Rip Van Winkle* the present season." Actually, the *Highlander* had had new staterooms added and was otherwise improved.

The *North America,* on A. Sleight & Company's line, continued in 1853 under Captain Charles Anderson, who acquired Houghtaling's interest to become the majority owner. At the end of that season Romer, Tremper & Gillett bought out A. Sleight & Company's New York night line, kept the *North America* for their own line and sold the *Highlander* and the Sleight line to Thomas Cornell, who thus re-entered the night-boat business. Cornell ran the *Santa Claus* on his new line and put the superannuated *Highlander* in towing service. Romer, Tremper & Gillett soon became just Romer & Tremper, a firm which would purchase the Cornell freight and passenger line in 1890, and would themselves be absorbed by the new Central-Hudson Steamboat Company in 1899.

After selling his interest in Anderson, Romer & Company, Captain Absalom Anderson invested in the *Robert L. Stevens,* which, it will be remembered, had been launched on Rondout Creek in 1834 and with which he had been involved for the Fourth of July excursion in 1839. For a number of years the vessel had been running between Saugerties, ten miles north of Rondout on the west bank of the Hudson, and New York as a night boat, and in this trade Captain Anderson would continue her. About May of 1853 he changed his residence to Saugerties, to the regret of his Rondout friends. Since there were no Sunday sailings from Rondout Creek to New York, Captain Anderson, now geographically beyond the criticism of Kingston, began calling at Rondout on the Sunday southbound trip of the *Robert L. Stevens.*

The captain plied between Saugerties and New York for three seasons, and by the fall of 1855 he was exploring the possibility of acquiring the *Thomas Powell,* for the *Robert L. Stevens* was over twenty years old and growing outmoded for the passenger trade.

The *Thomas Powell,* after serving on the Newburgh-New York run for which she was built, was sold in 1849 to the New York & Erie Railroad to serve as its connecting boat between New York and Piermont on the Hudson. After a couple of years the Erie auctioned her off for a reported $34,250 to Captain Thomas N. Hulse, who ran her briefly on a daily round trip between Poughkeepsie and New York. Then he sold her for service on the Delaware River for, again reportedly, $45,000, which, if the price is correct, was a shrewd and profitable deal on the part of Captain Hulse. Apparently in the late summer of 1855, after another transfer of ownership, the steamboat

27   The *Thomas Powell* running on the Delaware River. (—*Historical Society of Delaware*)

returned to New York waters and again changed hands.

At this time Hudson River side-wheel passenger vessels could be used temporarily in general towing without structural changes, since it was still the practice to lash the lead boats in the tow alongside the towing steamer and string the others back from the lead boats, rather than to handle the tow on long hawsers off the stern. Of course those timeworn passenger vessels relegated to towing on a permanent basis generally had some of their upper works removed to provide deck space for handling lines and to eliminate maintenance on unneeded superstructure. In the early fall of 1855 the *Thomas Powell* was in service as an opposition towing steamer, at low rates to undercut the regular lines. One of these, the Hudson River Steamboat Company, complained that her captain sent runners ahead to steal the business of those canalboaters who were normally its customers. The New York agent for the Hudson River Steamboat Company wrote to Alfred Van Santvoord, the Albany agent, that the *Thomas Powell's* captain was "more than ugly and gets in front of the Slips that our boats are in and Says he would like to see us get them out. . . ."[2] This operation of the *Thomas Powell,* cast in the role of the hated opposition, was the nadir of her career and fortunately was brief.

Captain Anderson bought the *Thomas Powell* and then spent considerable money to have her overhauled and put in new staterooms, giving her about twice the number carried in the *Robert L. Stevens.* The latter opened the Saugerties route in 1856 and ran briefly until the *Thomas Powell* was ready. When that vessel was advertised to call at Rondout on her Sunday southbound trips, a Kingston newspaper said, "To those who know him [Captain Anderson], the bare announcement that his boat is on hand is all that is requisite to insure the patronage of the travelling public." Obviously there had been some new thinking in Kingston about "get-rich-quickers"!

In 1854 Captain Charles Anderson, whose command of the *North America* had terminated with

²Alfred Van Santvoord letter book, 1855, incoming, Hudson River Day Line collection, New-York Historical Society, New York, N.Y.

her sale to Romer, Tremper & Gillett, began running excursions to the Fishing Banks as master of the small steamer *Laura Knapp.* In this venture he was joined by his father and his brother Absalom, who together bought the vessel; after a year Absalom sold his share to his father. In 1856, with the *Thomas Powell* entered in the Saugerties line, Charles arranged to take over the *Robert L. Stevens* on his excursion route in place of the *Laura Knapp.* The latter, under the command of Nathan, Jr., served as a day boat between Rondout and Albany, going up one day and down the next, except on Sundays.

The *Robert L. Stevens* went out to the Fishing Banks six days a week in 1856, and the format of these excursions was unchanged from those that were the occasional pastime of the *Highlander.* Tackle, bait and all sorts of refreshment were available, and in keeping with the surroundings the latter often tended to be heavily on the liquid side. On Sunday, May 25th, she set out with almost 200 passengers aboard; a few were from the Rondout area, presumably on a family-and-friends outing, including Dr. Eltinge, father-in-law of Captains Charles and Absalom, both of whom were aboard. Of the remainder, some came to escape the city and enjoy the fresh sea air, but the majority came, as always, to try their luck, which on this particular day proved rather bad.

The *Robert L. Stevens* was stopped about three miles off Long Branch on the New Jersey coast, where it was felt the passengers would get their money's worth of fish. All went well until about 2 p.m., when a schooner, the *Francis A. Godwin,* came toiling along bound for New Bern, North Carolina, with a load of bricks, iron and lime. She was bearing straight down on the *Robert L. Stevens* and, to the consternation of those on both vessels, struck the hapless steamboat on the starboard side near the bow. After staving in a hole above the waterline about two feet square, she raked down the side of the steamer. The paddle boxes bore the brunt of the blow, damaging the wheel beams, the pillow blocks supporting the shaft, and some of the arms and buckets of the wheel itself so that it was impossible to operate the engine. Having done all this, the *Francis A. Godwin* cleared herself and took off.

The *America* was one of the few large side-wheelers designed and built for towing on the Hudson. Most of them were converted passenger vessels. (*—James Bard painting*)

There were no casualties aboard the *Robert L. Stevens*, but the peaceful anglers had become a mass of highly agitated individuals. They threw overboard anything that would float and donned life preservers, probably wishing they had stayed at home and gone to church. Captain Charles, no doubt himself alarmed at so much of his equipment going over the side, tried in vain to calm the panic, but the passengers, convinced the steamboat was sinking, would have none of it. Then, inevitably, the wind sprang up suddenly and with violence, and the side-wheeler rolled and pitched helplessly. At Captain Charles' orders the fires in the fireboxes were extinguished, signals of distress were hauled up and the bell was rung.

The captain of the *Francis A. Godwin,* who had been asleep in his cabin at the time of the collision, was thoroughly awakened by the shock. He eventually succeeded in getting his vessel under control and working her back to the *Robert L. Stevens.* Another schooner, the *Margaret Mabee* bound for Keyport, New Jersey, was in

the vicinity and also came to the rescue. Between the two schooners all the paying passengers were taken off the steamboat, except for one man who had apparently gone fishing for alcoholic beverages and been so successful that it was deemed impractical to remove him. The crew and Captain Charles, of course, stayed with the steamboat, and it is likely he took this opportunity to unburden himself of some choice remarks on the subject of navigation to the master of the *Francis A. Godwin.*

After the transfer of passengers, the *Margaret Mabee* set course once more for Keyport, and the *Francis A. Godwin* moved off toward New York, beating into the wind and making but slight forward progress. Suddenly the captain was struck with a brilliant idea, which he set forth to his passengers: the *Francis A. Godwin* would run down to the Delaware Breakwater and put them ashore; from there they could eventually make their way to New York. The captain did not add that he would then be considerably closer to his destination, New Bern, than he was at present.

It was aboard the *Keyport*, shown in a Bard painting, that some of the fishermen from the *Robert L. Stevens* finally got back to New York. (—*Eldredge collection, courtesy of The Mariners Museum*)

Most of the passengers were properly aghast; in their overwrought state they pictured the Delaware Breakwater as being as far from New York as the Spice Islands. When some of them threatened to throw the captain overboard, he agreed that New York was the proper place to go—he couldn't make it that night, but he'd get there.

Meanwhile, on the *Robert L. Stevens*, Captain Charles had sent three of his crew ashore in a small boat to telegraph to New York for a towing steamer. Unfortunately their boat was swamped and they made an undignified landing in the surf. Actually, the steamboat was in no danger, although a pilot boat stood by and rode out the night with her.

On the other hand, conditions aboard the *Francis A. Godwin* were not nearly as comfortable. To begin with, she was crowded: a dozen or so ladies were given berths in the cabin, while over a hundred men took their repose on top of

barrels in the hold and in other likely spots. The captain, not having planned a banquet for the occasion, could only offer the excursionists tea, coffee and bread, but to the many who were seasick this made no particular difference. The collision had started some planking in the bow, so the passengers, four at a time, had to man the pumps.

About 11 p.m. the captain abruptly bellowed, "Fire!" and ordered the crew to turn out. Immediately the rumor flew among the passengers that there was a quantity of gunpowder aboard. For some this latest development was too much for their battered nervous systems to absorb. To be rescued from a vessel they were sure was sinking, by one that had taken to leaking, was bad enough. Now, faced with being blown out of existence, they could only wait quietly for the explosion. The remainder were of a hardier breed and vented themselves with another panic.

Upon investigation the captain and his crew found the source of the current problem: the water leaking into the hull had reached the lime-filled barrels in the hold, causing the contents to slake. The only remedy was to jettison the offending cargo. The activity caused by these diversions, while it lasted, helped to keep the passengers warm. At noon the temperature had been 76 degrees, but it dropped to about 40 during the night; to the passengers, garbed for a Sunday outing, it felt more like zero. They were in a dismal state: cold and sleepy, some were wet, some ravenously hungry and others too seasick to feel any other discomfort.

By dawn the *Francis A. Godwin* was up to the Narrows, where her captain attempted to make Fort Hamilton on the Long Island shore. By now no one was sanguine enough to expect him to reach it. He did not. After three hours he gave up and anchored off Staten Island, where a small boat, later with the help of the side-wheel tugboat *Satellite,* managed to land the excursion party. Only four people fell overboard, and they were quickly rescued.

By comparison, those who had been rescued from the steamboat by the *Margaret Mabee* had an easy time of it. Drenched by the spray, they did not find sailing in the diminutive vessel exactly relaxing, but they had no other difficulties and were put ashore safely at Keyport. On Monday morning they continued to New York by the steamer *Keyport.*

The side-wheel tugboat *Titan* arrived alongside the *Robert L. Stevens* about 6 a.m. Monday and had her back in New York shortly after 1 p.m. Of all those who had set out on the excursion the previous morning, probably no one enjoyed himself more than the solitary customer whose immobility had resulted in his being left aboard the steamer. He had escaped the terror, the cold and the discomfort — everything except possibly a first-rate hangover.

When interviewed by a reporter, Captain Charles Anderson included this practical appeal in his statement, which was carried in the press: "The Captain requests the passengers, who all finally reached their homes in safety, not to be oblivious of the life preservers, but kindly see that they are returned."

More serious than the loss of the life preservers was the disablement of his steamboat; to fill the gap his father discontinued the Rondout-Albany line and sent the *Laura Knapp* to New York. She had not long arrived when, on Wednesday, it was discovered that the captain of the *Francis A. Godwin* was sneaking his vessel out to sea, rather than waiting for the decision as to the liability for the damages to the *Robert L. Stevens.* A United States marshal was summoned and steam was raised on the *Laura Knapp.* They overtook the schooner, and once again the dejected captain of the *Francis A. Godwin* was back in the port he had been trying to put well off his stern since Sunday. However, damage to the steamboat was not more than $1,500, and in June she returned to the excursion business. Captain Nathan Anderson, Sr., ran the *Laura Knapp* as an excursion boat at New York for a time and then sold her. After these harrowing experiences on the *Robert L. Stevens,* Captain Absalom Anderson was probably delighted to get back to the tranquil decks of the *Thomas Powell.*

Both the *Hero* and the *Alida* ran as morning boats to New York, from Poughkeepsie and Rondout respectively, during the mid-1850s. The *Alida's* long and elegant lines easily made her a "floating palace" in the eyes of the Hudson Valley's elite. (—*Above, Bard painting; below, Endicott & Co. lithograph*)

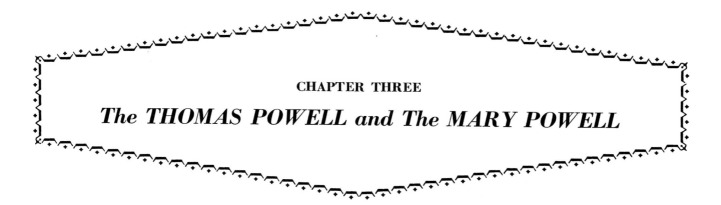

CHAPTER THREE

The THOMAS POWELL and The MARY POWELL

Captain Anderson continued to operate the *Thomas Powell* between Saugerties and New York, but it soon became painfully apparent that she was too much of a steamboat for that run. By the 1855 census, Saugerties had a population of about 3,300, as compared with 4,000 for Kingston and 6,000 for Rondout. Fifteen years earlier Saugerties and Kingston had both stood at about 2,300, with Rondout well in third place at only 1,500. In the fall of 1856 the *Thomas Powell* was taken off the Saugerties-New York route and the *Robert L. Stevens* put back on for the balance of the year. Knowing that in the *Thomas Powell* he had a superior steamboat, Captain Absalom sought an appropriate route on which to employ her with greater profit, finally deciding to operate her as a Poughkeepsie-New York day boat in the 1857 season. The Saugerties line passed to Captain Charles and the *Robert L. Stevens*, which remained on the Hudson to the end of her days.

In the *Thomas Powell's* new service, for which she had been improved by receiving a new set of boilers during the winter, she would leave Poughkeepsie daily, except Sunday, at 6:30 a.m. and return from New York at 4 p.m. On a morning in May there was a minor embarrassment when a defect was discovered in her shaft while the steamboat was warming up her engine, and she was hauled off for repairs. On the whole, however, Captain Anderson's new line was successful.

The concept of a morning day boat to New York was not original. The *Hero* had been on this same route in 1856; the *Thomas Powell* herself was designed to run between Newburgh and New York and for a time she had also run from Poughkeepsie. There had been similar service out of

Rondout Creek in 1853-55 by the fast and fine *Alida*, the "Princess of Steamboats." Built in 1847 as a New York-Albany day boat, the *Alida* had been favorably received in the Rondout Creek-New York trade, but unfortunately she suffered costly accidents and her management was not stable. Finally she was acquired by Alfred Van Santvoord, who returned her to New York-Albany service.

Despite her problems, the *Alida* had established a following on the Rondout route, including Nathaniel Parker Willis, a prominent figure in the Hudson Valley literary set. With George Pope Morris — perhaps best remembered as the author of the poem "Woodman, Spare That Tree"—Willis edited the *Home Journal,* from which the present-day *Town and Country* is directly descended. Due to ill health Willis had retired to Idlewild, his country home in Cornwall, in the shadow of the mountain marking the northern gate to the Highlands of the Hudson. This mountain is today known as Storm King because Willis, in his writings, argued that the earlier name, Butter Hill, was too flaccid. At Idlewild Willis penned his "Letters to the *Home Journal*" and in a collection of them published in 1855 included some comments on the *Alida,* dated from 1854:

> The lady inhabitants of this neighborhood have a summer convenience, which (partly by chance, perhaps) is more fitly arranged for their luxurious enjoyment . . . than would seem to belong to such a shortcomingdom as this our life. Breakfast leisurely over . . . a joyous bell rings across the bay, and the largest, swiftest and most sumptuous of all the day-boats on the river, the steamer

Alida, comes swooping down the mirrored shore-line from Newburgh. You are invited (madam!) to go to town in a floating palace, pass four hours in Broadway, or where you please, and be brought back through the Highlands in the enchantment of sunset. As you *go,* the shadows of the scenery will be thrown with artistic effect towards you, for it is morning. . . . As you *return,* the same accommodating shadows will fall with rosy tints of twilight, the other way. Both ways you will see the river in its utmost beauty. There is an upper and a lower forward-deck, luxuriously provided with seats, where the motion of the boat secures a breeze, though the river be breathless. Or, there is an elegant public saloon and a private one, daintily cushioned and mirrored, where you may read or chat, with the comforts of your own drawing-room at home. On the chance of your wanting all your time in the city, so that it might not be convenient to dine, a hot lunch is served a half-hour before reaching the wharf, and you may start for your shopping or calls with the freshness rather of town-gadders than of country-folks who have come sixty miles down the river. . . . At 4 P.M., you return to your floating-palace, and glide away towards your home again; and, while you pass the first twenty less picturesque miles, perhaps, in lying down upon the cushioned seats of the private saloon, recovering from your fatigues, the ten-mile labyrinth of the Highlands is getting ready to present you with a panorama — a sunset extended through a river-tangle of zig-zag-ing mountains, the splendor of which . . . would make any day memorable. From the class of people whom it mainly accommodates — the occupants of the villas on the Hudson, and the summer visitors at West Point and Cozzen's [sic] — the *Alida* seems rather to be making an excursion of gaiety than a passage of convenience. . . .[1]

This was the type of service that in 1857 the *Thomas Powell* again made available to Willis and to hosts of others from Poughkeepsie down. During the between-seasons lull the citizens of Rondout and Kingston, possibly having had their memories prodded by Captain Anderson, concluded that they had never fully appreciated the

fine service provided by the *Alida* as a New York day boat. The schedules of the through New York-Albany day boats were such that a round trip to New York would take two days, and the railroad in summer was hot, cindery and dirty. Captain Anderson expanded the route of the *Thomas Powell* in 1858 to include Rondout and at about that same time moved back to the Rondout area. He took up residence at Fair View, just below the hamlet of Port Ewen on the river south of Rondout Creek. Fair View had a commanding view of the Hudson and was once occupied by Dr. Eltinge, who turned it over to his daughter Catherine, Absalom's wife, when he decided to locate in Rondout.

Before the new season commenced, the superfluous staterooms of the *Thomas Powell,* a holdover from her service as a night boat, were removed to provide a larger and more commodious saloon befitting her present vocation as a day boat. The season's advance publicity was excellent. The *Kingston Democratic Journal* (issue of April 21st) was elated: "We are really glad to get this day line, and more so, to get a steamer of the *Powell's* class and reputation." In the same item the newspaper said of Captain Anderson, "Of his capacity, we need not speak, for a better officer never trod deck. His courtesy, attention to passengers, and the complete oversight he has of everything about his steamer, have assured him a general popularity and confidence. . . ."

For her first trip on the new route, on Saturday, April 24th, the *Thomas Powell* left Jay Street in New York at 3:53 p.m. and landed her Rondout passengers at 9:28 p.m. The time is not at all remarkable, but since Captain Anderson dallied eight minutes past sailing time it is evident that he was not attempting a speed record. On her regular schedule the *Thomas Powell* left Rondout daily, except Sundays, at 5:30 a.m. and arrived at Jay Street at 11 a.m.; she sailed on the return at 3:45 p.m.

Despite her age the *Thomas Powell* was one of the fastest steamboats on the Hudson; it was only natural, therefore, that a new experimental steamer would want to test her pace with the "Tom." The *Charlotte Vanderbilt,* 205½ feet in length, was designed to try the practicability of

---

[1]Nathaniel Parker Willis, *Out-Doors at Idlewild; or, the Shaping of a Home on the Banks of the Hudson* (New York: Charles Scribner, 1855), pp. 406-408.

The dashing *Thomas Powell,* with statue atop her pilothouse, speeds through the Highlands of the Hudson, whose peaks tower abnormally in this Bard painting.

side propellers on the Hudson. In her case the propellers were four-bladed affairs, 14 feet in diameter. She also had the unusual feature, for that day, of a longitudinal watertight bulkhead together with several transverse bulkheads in the hull and was planned to have first-class accommodations for passengers. Her sponsors confidently expected that she would go through from New York to Albany in five hours and so provide formidable competition for the Hudson River Railroad.

She was ready for trials in May, 1858, and one day went up the river to Yonkers, not far above New York, to await the *Thomas Powell,* northbound on her afternoon trip. Then the *Charlotte Vanderbilt,* with a head of steam so full that her escape pipes were popping, took off up the river, but the *Thomas Powell* serenely passed her and sped away towards Rondout. The *Charlotte Vanderbilt* followed in her wake for a mile or two and then, completely discomfited, turned tail and

splashed back to New York. A failure as a side propeller, she was later stripped for service as a barge, and as such Captain Charles Anderson bought her in 1860. He fitted her with the machinery from the outmoded *Robert L. Stevens,* thereby producing the *William F. Russell,* essentially a new steamboat for his Saugerties run. Perhaps it was high time, for it was said that in her declining years the *Robert L. Stevens* was so overrun with rats that Captain Charles paid the waiters 25 cents, a healthy sum in those days, for each rat caught and killed.

Nathaniel Willis, writing of the *Thomas Powell,* recalled an incident, probably contemporary with the *Charlotte Vanderbilt* race, in which he missed his landing at Cornwall on the northbound run through a rather protracted conversation with a friend. He then observed:

And — talking of the varieties of social intercourse — why should not our friend Captain Anderson advertise his trips up and

35

In an earlier decade, William H. Bartlett's lithograph looks southward across Newburgh Bay toward Cornwall and the northern gateway to the Highlands of the Hudson.

down the river as *matinée* and *soirée?* The *Powell* is certainly a floating drawing-room of great elegance and luxury. She receives on board, daily, a choice company of the best society on the banks of the Hudson — three hours of most agreeable exchange of courtesies, morning and afternoon — and all attended to with the politeness of a well-ordered mansion. . . . Why, just remember what it is — not only the convenience of getting to and from the city and studying the beautiful scenery of the Hudson under the most advantageous aspects — not only this, but *fashionable society at twenty miles an hour!* . . .[2]

[2]N. P. Willis to George Pope Morris, June 12, 1858, published in the *Home Journal,* June 26, 1858.

The serenity of Captain Anderson's "floating drawing-room" was marred on June 30, 1858, by a most unfortunate occurrence. A young Englishman and Oxford graduate, L. V. Wilkins, who was principal of the First Grammar School at Poughkeepsie, had set out with a party of friends in a skiff for a sail up the river. As the northbound *Thomas Powell* left Poughkeepsie, hugging the eastern shore as was her custom there, Wilkins at the sculls either misjudged her speed or her course or both. At any rate, he pulled directly for her. The chief pilot sighted the skiff, signalled to stop the engine and gave the vessel a rank sheer, but Wilkins kept on coming and struck the steamboat in the area of the paddle wheel. The *Thomas Powell* put over two boats and recovered all of the party who had been thrown out of the skiff except Wilkins. Known to be a good swimmer, he had evidently been struck by the paddle wheel and so met his death.

This tragedy was compounded for Captain Anderson when, five days later, while the *Thomas Powell* was southbound near Hyde Park on Monday morning, the linkage connecting the crosshead on the piston rod to the walking beam broke. With the tie gone, the piston dropped down in the cylinder and badly damaged the bottom of it. The consensus was that, during the Wilkins accident, the sudden stopping of the engine from full speed had put a violent strain on the linkage and so weakened it. Now, after the passengers had disembarked, the *Thomas Powell* was towed to Cold Spring for repairs at the foundry there.

The accident happened at the worst possible time, as the heaviest period of annual business, July and August, was just getting under way. All of Captain Anderson's efforts to obtain a replacement somewhat able to make the time and offer the accommodations of the *Thomas Powell* were fruitless. He was finally able to charter the *Rip Van Winkle* for his line, but as a substitute for the *Thomas Powell* she was a poor performer. Just before the *Thomas Powell* had opened the new route to Rondout, the *Democratic Journal* had observed, ". . . both the boat and its captain have

hosts of friends who are not likely to fall out with or forsake the one or the other." Unfortunately, these devotees were not faithful enough to rally around the captain while he was employing the *Rip Van Winkle,* and he suffered through a marked decline in business. Toward the end of July, after repairs reportedly costing $6,000, the *Thomas Powell* was able to resume and the captain looked hopefully toward the future.

To the pleased passengers of the restored "Swan of the Hudson," the epicurean cuisine never tasted so good, and the saloon never looked so beautiful, with its velvet carpets, mirrors, conversation lounges and a grand piano, all topped by a white-and-gold ceiling with chandeliers and ormolu lamps. They studied with renewed interest the many ornaments on the bulkheads. The oil painting of Thomas Powell, who died in May of 1856 at the age of 87, was presented to the vessel by his widow, Mary Powell, in 1857. A Hudson River scene centering about the steamboat itself was thought to be a gift from a group of Newburgh citizens. A painting of the Powell homestead in Newburgh and scenes of the Hudson from the pencil of Charles W. Tice were also displayed in the saloon. With good reason General Winfield Scott, having traveled on many steamboats, considered the *Thomas Powell* to be the most perfect river steamer he had ever boarded.

The *Thomas Powell* was one of the finest boats on the river in 1858, her first season in service from Rondout. As a lure to the safety-conscious, this advertising lithograph shows the words "life boat" clearly on the boat by the pilothouse.

Having begun her career as an experiment, the *Charlotte Vanderbilt* ended it as a conventional Hudson River night boat, shown here in winter quarters. The author's desk chair is from this vessel, salvaged after she was sunk in a collision in 1882.

The *Thomas P. Way* was almost brand-new in June of 1860, when she substituted briefly for the *Thomas Powell* while that vessel was having a defective shaft replaced. This photograph was taken much later in her career. (*—William T. Miller*)

To erase from his mind whatever discouragement remained from the precarious days of July, Captain Anderson was presented with a set of silver. On one of the larger pieces he found engraved, "Presented to Capt. A. L. Anderson, as a mark of respect and regard, from the frequent passengers of the steamboat *Thomas Powell*." Thus fortified, after the close of the season Captain Anderson took his steamboat down to the foundry at Cold Spring for a complete overhaul of the engine. As the opening of the 1859 season drew near, the *Home Journal* expressed hope that there would be "many a trip before the Fall" and promoted Captain Anderson from "steambassador" to Grand Chamberlain of the Storm King. This office, said the paper, he held as much as if elected by a thunderclap on deck — surely the last thing Captain Anderson would want on his tidy decks.

The 1859 season had its low points. The opening trip in April was postponed for three weeks, and then in May it was announced that the steamboat would be withdrawn from service temporarily for some improvements to her chimneys, which is a good way of saying either that business was poor or that she had some more serious problem. In August the captain lost a lawsuit brought by David L. Holley, who the preceding year had been marching up the gangplank in Rondout when the plank had fallen into the creek. According to the defense, he had been advised by a deckhand that the plank was temporarily unsafe because the steamboat was warming up her engine. Finally, in October, there was another tragedy similar to the Wilkins affair of the year before. On a dark and stormy Saturday evening the *Thomas Powell* ran down four men crossing the river in a rowboat in the Highlands, killing

The *Francis Skiddy*, built in 1852 as a New York-Albany day boat, later became a night boat and is so portrayed in the Bard painting below. (—*Eldredge collection, courtesy of The Mariners Museum*)

In 1860 the arrival of the *Daniel Drew* on the Hudson inspired the building of several large steamboats, among them the *Mary Powell*. (—*James Bard painting, courtesy of The Mariners Museum*)

three and badly injuring the fourth. Although his steamer was absolved from all blame, Captain Anderson sent at least two generous donations of cash to the widow of one of the men, William Brown, and later supplied her with a "first-class" sewing machine. Such thoughtfulness as this had gained for him the high regard of those on the Hudson.

The year 1860 is noteworthy in the annals of the Hudson River. There had been a dearth of major steamboat construction since the autumn of 1851, when the river traffic faced competition from the Hudson River Railroad, which was then opened over its entire length along the east shore, from New York to Greenbush, opposite Albany. The last major vessel constructed for the river, the *Francis Skiddy*, entered New York-Albany service in 1852. Having tested the temper of the railroad's opposition, the People's Line, operating the New York-Albany night line, rebuilt two of its vessels on an elaborate scale in the mid-1850s,

but it was not until 1860, after an eight-year interval, that a new steamboat of the larger class sailed on the river. This was the celebrated New York-Albany day boat *Daniel Drew*. In a match race she quickly bested the *Armenia*, which was to be her running mate; this and her general performance in 1860 made her the talk of the river.

Although the *Daniel Drew* was no direct threat to Captain Anderson, who saw the vessel only when she passed by in the opposite direction, she gave him considerable food for thought. He realized that the *Thomas Powell*, fine though she might be, was no longer young and that he would before long have to build a new boat for his own line, the prosperity of which depended largely on the excellent service it offered. He knew that Romer & Tremper had met a similar problem by contracting for a new steamboat for their Rondout-New York night line. Their *North America* was six years older than the *Thomas Powell* and could not be replaced with a suitable secondhand vessel because of the lapse in construction. Now, in August of 1860, Captain Anderson announced that he expected by the following spring to have on his line a new vessel which would outdo every Hudson River steamer, thereby covering the *Daniel Drew*. The new steamboat would be 265 feet in length and 34 feet in breadth of hull, have a vertical beam engine with a cylinder 56 inches in diameter and a stroke of 12 feet, and would cost about $70,000. He made it clear that to meet his requirements the vessel would have to make better time than the *Thomas Powell;* evidently he intended to contract for the vessel with that proviso.

Captain Anderson had hardly unburdened himself of this news when an unexpected salvo gave him pause. Thomas Cornell took time out from multiplying his fleet of towing steamers, looking after his Rondout night line, making money generally and working for the election of Abraham Lincoln. Cornell then gazed into his crystal ball and let it be known that he, too, expected to put a new steamboat on the river that spring. She was to be 260 by 35 feet, with a cylinder 60 inches by 16 feet. Furthermore, she would be equal to any in beauty and inferior to none in speed. That this new boat would leave Rondout in the morning and New York in the evening, almost the same schedule as the *Thomas Powell's,* must have chilled Captain Anderson.

Since neither Cornell nor Anderson took a positive step, the focus of attention became the steamboat actually being built for Romer & Tremper at Allison's shipyard in Jersey City, New Jersey. Into the design of the model Captain Tremper had worked all his knowledge of steamboating, gained through years of experience. Romer & Tremper had apparently planned to call their newcomer *Wiltwyck,* after the early name for Kingston, but a month before the launching James W. Baldwin, a prominent citizen of Kingston, passed away. Since he was the father-in-law of William F. Romer, it seemed fitting to all concerned to perpetuate Baldwin's name. So, when the vessel was ready to slide down the ways in November of 1860, she was christened *James W. Baldwin* with champagne. Besides Michael S. Allison, those involved with her construction had

been Fletcher, Harrison & Company, builders of her vertical beam engine with a cylinder 60 inches in diameter and a stroke of 11 feet; John E. Brown of Hoboken, contractor for her joinerwork; and Hill & Rodgers of New York, the painters. The total cost was said to be about $75,000.

Captain Absalom Anderson was intensely interested in the new steamboat, which was 240 feet 10 inches in length and immediately established herself as a fast traveler. After her first appearance at Rondout in March, 1861, Anderson announced that he and his associates had contracted with Allison for a steamer 11 feet longer overall than previously announced; Fletcher, Harrison & Company would build an engine six inches greater in diameter of cylinder than originally contemplated and equal to or better than any yet built. Michael S. Allison was left to work out the hull proportions, with the understanding that there would be a heavy forfeiture if the vessel failed to better the speed of the *Thomas Powell* by one mile in twelve. She would be finished by September 1st and cost about $80,000. Captain Anderson's partners, it developed, were Captain John Ketcham, for whom the Andersons had once been agents, and John L. Hasbrouck, a cousin of Jansen Hasbrouck who had also been a steamboat agent in Rondout and had prospered in the wholesale grocery and wine business in New York.

It was announced in July that Captain Anderson would name the new steamboat *Mary Powell,* in honor of Thomas Powell's widow. Unbridling civic tongue, the Newburgh *Daily News* observed, "He does well to stick to the [Powell] family, under the prestige of whose name he has won laurels and dollars." This was putting the matter a bit harshly, since the success of the Anderson day line was a combination of the *Thomas Powell's* fine qualities and Captain Absalom's abilities as a steamboat operator and master. But, in truth, *Mary Powell* was a shrewd choice, for the name *Powell,* to a host of satisfied and loyal customers, conjured up a picture of all that was best in rapid and comfortable transportation.

Mary Ludlow Powell had a firm marine background, in addition to being the widow of Thomas Powell. Her eldest brother, Charles, had entered the United States Navy as a midshipman in 1795

was a one-gun row galley that served in the Battle of Lake Champlain on September 11, 1814. The other two, named specifically for Augustus C. Ludlow, were destroyers built for service in the First and Second World Wars; the latter, the "Lucky Lud," received six battle stars and was finally decommissioned in January, 1951.

But the War of 1812 was far in the past and world war was undreamed of in July, 1861, as the time for the launching of the *Mary Powell* drew near. The Civil War was then upon the land, but its only effect upon the *Mary Powell* was to dissuade her possible competitor, Thomas Cornell, for a time from planning his proposed passenger steamer. The launching of the *Mary Powell* was to have been on Monday, July 29th, but that was a black day as far as the new craft was concerned. Mr. Allison and his workmen were unable to get the hull off the stocks. By the super-

Mary Ludlow Powell, from a painting owned by her great-granddaughter, Mrs. W. Clement (Mary Powell Ramsdell) Scott. *(—Photograph by Bernhard Schulze)*

In the yard of Trinity Church lie the remains of Captain James Lawrence and Lieutenant Augustus C. Ludlow. This is the Lawrence monument. *(—Wurts Bros., Inc., N.Y.C.)*

and risen to the rank of captain. The next eldest, Robert, had been assigned to the *Constitution* and was aboard when "Old Ironsides" encountered and captured H.M.S. *Java* in December, 1812. The best-known brother, Augustus C. Ludlow, was James Lawrence's first lieutenant on the *Chesapeake* in the engagement with H.M.S. *Shannon* off Boston on June 1, 1813. It was in this battle that the mortally wounded Lawrence gave the vain command, "Don't give up the ship!" The captured *Chesapeake* was taken to Halifax, where Lawrence was buried; young Ludlow, who had also been wounded, insisted on following the hearse at Lawrence's funeral and passed away from exertion on June 13th at the age of 21. The bodies of Lawrence and Ludlow were brought back to this country and lie together at Trinity Church in New York. The United States Navy has had three vessels named *Ludlow*. The first

The *John L. Hasbrouck*, named for one of Captain Anderson's partners in the construction of the *Mary Powell*, was little more than a market barge with a steam engine and propeller. In this James Bard watercolor of 1864, there is no sign of life aboard as she steams along, her huge name flag flying perilously close to the top of the smokestack. (*—Eldredge collection, courtesy of The Mariners Museum*)

A portrait of Mr. Baldwin graced the centerpiece of the paddle box on the Rondout-New York night boat that bore his name. (*—James Bard painting*)

The U.S.S. *Ludlow*, commissioned in 1941, saw service during World War II, carrying on the valorous tradition of Mary Powell's family. (*—Official U.S. Navy photograph*)

stitions of sailors this is the worst of omens, but the career of the *Mary Powell* should have killed this belief forever.

The launching was postponed until August 1st, when it was successfully completed. In mid-August, as the *Mary Powell* was lying at the foot of Vestry Street in New York while her machinery and joinerwork were being erected, a reporter for the New York *World* seems to have been one of the first to employ the title "Queen of the Hudson," an appellation that stayed with her always.

All went well on a trial trip to test the new vessel's machinery on October 9th, and Captain Anderson wanted to try her out on the route to Rondout before the season ended. However, he needed a good excuse if he were to run the unprepared and incomplete steamboat without offend-

ing his passengers. When the *Thomas Powell* suffered some damage in a collision with a ferryboat the captain decided to withdraw her for repairs after she completed her southbound run on October 12th, and he let it be known for public consumption that his only alternatives were to run the *Mary Powell* on the route or cancel the northbound trip that day. Fortunately he made up his mind sufficiently in advance to have newspapermen on hand for the event. After the *Thomas Powell* arrived in New York, her furniture, dishes and silverware were rushed over to the *Mary Powell;* on board the latter stoves had been hastily set up to combat the autumnal chill. The joiners, painters and glaziers still had considerable work ahead of them, and many of the glassless windows were covered with canvas.

James Bard's oil painting shows the *Mary Powell* as she originally appeared, and across the bottom the artist included the names of those connected with her construction. The painting may have been com- missioned by shipbuilder Michael S. Allison, for his daughter presented it to the museum in 1932. (*—Museum of the City of New York*)

The *Mary Powell* ran from Jay Street in New York to Rondout in about 5¼ hours elapsed time and in the first hour reportedly ticked off 21.6 miles. The editor of the Newburgh *Daily News,* who perhaps had not been invited, thought it unfortunate that the steamboat was carrying passengers while still incomplete. On the other hand, the representative of the *Kingston Argus & Ulster Republican* wrote, ". . . if the *Mary Powell* is like other feminines, we saw the lady under the precise circumstances to judge of her best qualities — for experts say that to find out the true character, temper and trim of a demoiselle you must surprise her at home and in negligee."

After running the *Mary Powell* briefly, Captain Anderson put the *Thomas Powell* back in service through October 30th, when the season ended. Three days later the *Mary Powell* came up from New York without passengers and was greeted lustily by steam vessels as she entered Rondout Creek. Later she was placed in winter quarters with the *Thomas Powell* at Port Ewen. During the winter the latter vessel was sold to the Catskill Steam Transportation Company for use as a night boat between Catskill and New York. Late in March the *Thomas Powell* attempted a passage to New York, but the ice on the river was too much for her and Cornell's towing steamer *Norwich* had to help her back to Port Ewen. The *Norwich* was well suited for operations in the ice and even became known as the "Ice King."

After the river was open in 1862 the *Mary Powell* also went to New York to have her bottom coppered and to receive furniture and such finishing touches as were needed. As might be expected, Captain Anderson's wife helped to select the furnishings. On Saturday, May 3rd, the new steamboat left New York in regular service and was met by turnouts at all her landings; she commenced round trips from Rondout on Monday.

The *Mary Powell* had been enrolled for the first time on April 25th, and the document set

This Endicott & Co. advertising lithograph of 1862 was a little more relaxed than the Bard painting. Also, a lifeboat has been conspicuously included ahead of the paddle box. (—*Eldredge collection, courtesy of The Mariners Museum*)

The *Norwich* makes her way through the ice, with an assortment of boys marching on ahead. Her piston rod and crosshead may be seen in the frame aft of the smokestack.

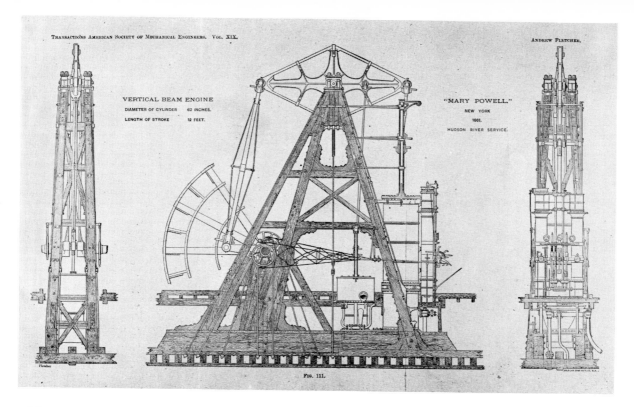

VERTICAL BEAM ENGINE
DIAMETER OF CYLINDER   62 INCHES.
LENGTH OF STROKE   12 FEET.

"MARY POWELL."
NEW YORK
1861.
HUDSON RIVER SERVICE.

FIG. 111.

The middle of these diagrams of the *Mary Powell's* engine shows the cylinder at the right, with the piston rod linked to one end of the walking beam; at the other end a connecting rod runs down to the crank on the paddle-wheel shaft. The view at right shows the engine front; at left, the connecting rod and crank. (*—Courtesy of William King Covell*)

down that Captain Anderson owned half of her and Ketcham and Hasbrouck each owned a quarter. The enrollment also stated that Richard L. Allison had directed construction of the wooden vessel, giving the official measurements as 267 feet in length, 34½ feet in breadth of beam and 9'2″ in depth of hold. By Captain Anderson's figures the overall length was 275 feet and the extreme breadth over the wide, projecting guards was about 64 feet. The vertical beam engine, Fletcher, Harrison & Company's No. 17, had a cylinder 62 inches in diameter with a 12-foot stroke, turning paddle wheels 31'8″ in diameter, and was supplied with steam by two return-flue boilers, one on either guard aft of the wheels. The hull was divided into three watertight compartments and, in the usual manner, was stiffened with hogframes and supported by tie rods running down from her pole masts or spars. The forward spar was ornamented with a large eagle, and the two aft were topped by golden balls. The joinerwork had been done by John E. Brown, who was part of the team that also built the *James W. Baldwin*.

The dining room of the *Mary Powell* was in the hold, as was then the style in Hudson River steamboats, and in the forward hold were a few staterooms which could be engaged by the ill or fatigued; this location ensured reasonable quiet and also kept the staterooms from cluttering the promenade deck. On the main deck aft was the ladies' saloon; the rest of the main deck over the hull itself was largely unobstructed except for the engine and paddle-wheel shafts. The barroom and other necessary rooms occupied the space on the guards along with the boilers. Next above the main deck was the second deck, which in river terminology was also called the promenade deck. Here the main saloon was located, extending from near amidships to a point astern of the after gangway. The comparative smallness of this saloon and the fact that it did not extend far forward were in keeping with Captain Anderson's belief that his passengers should have plenty of open deck space on which to enjoy the scenery and fresh air. For this purpose he considered the forward promenade deck ideal, but for those who

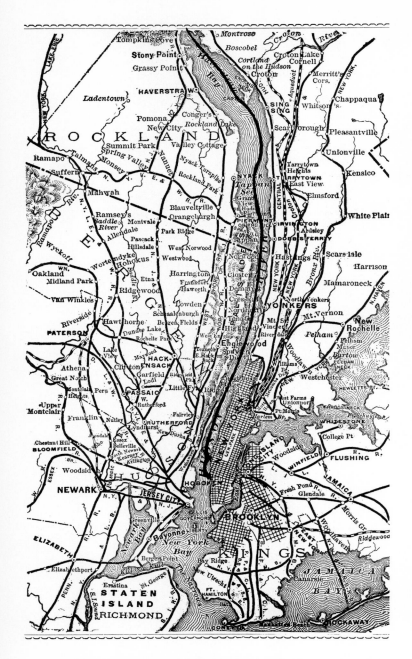

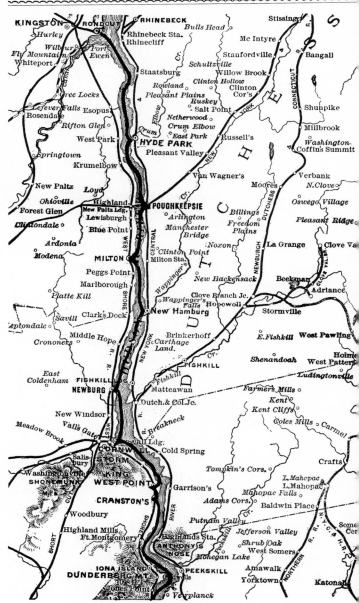

This map of the *Mary Powell's* route between New York and Rondout comes from her guidebook for the year 1899. With minor exceptions this was the same route that she and the *Thomas Powell* plied in the 1860s.

chose not to sit out on deck, either because of bad weather or lack of inclination, the saloon had unusually large windows for a steamboat of the times, cut sufficiently low so that one could look out while seated comfortably within. These windows were fitted with sliding sashes and blinds. Wherever practical throughout the *Mary Powell*, folding doors and doors with glass panes were installed, instead of the usual small, all-wood doors. On the interior, paneling of polished wood was used as much as possible and paintwork kept to a minimum. On the exterior, the popular fan design of the period decorated the paddle boxes, which had paintings on their centerpieces or lunettes; at least one of these depicted the Powell family residence at Newburgh. The finished cost of the *Mary Powell*, as given in the press, was about $80,000.

An unusual feature of the saloon was the glass in the clerestory. Portraits by Mathew B. Brady and other photographers of the day had been transferred to the panes so that they were a gallery of people connected with the Hudson Valley: Thomas and Mary Powell and their son-in-law Homer Ramsdell; Captain Nathan Anderson, Sr., and Dr. Richard Eltinge; Nathaniel Parker Willis and George Pope Morris of the *Home Journal;* and a gamut of others, from such national figures as Washington Irving, General Winfield Scott, Samuel F. B. Morse and John James Audubon to the Rondout agent for the Delaware & Hudson Canal Company, Major L. A. Sykes. Apparently impressed by this novel type of decoration, the artist who portrayed the *Mary Powell* for the first two Endicott & Company advertising lithographs of the steamer included vague portraits on the clerestory windows.

The third or hurricane deck of the *Mary Powell* was not open to passengers since it was simply a light shelter deck. On the forward end was the pilothouse, attached to which were rooms for officers.

Over the new steamboat ruled Captain Absalom Anderson, who, as he had on the *Highlander* and the *Thomas Powell*, constantly kept the comfort and welfare of his passengers uppermost in his mind and always sought new ways to reward their loyalty. For example, he arranged to have a bundle of New York morning newspapers brought to Tarrytown by railroad, where they were transferred to the southbound *Mary Powell* from a rowboat. In this manner his passengers always had the news of the day before they landed in New York. On the *Mary Powell*, as always, "safety first" was the captain's watchword; he believed in speed but never risked either the lives of his passengers or his investment in a steamboat to prove a point. Along with safety and speed, comfort and lines were major ingredients in a vessel acceptable to him; there must be ample and homelike facilities, and the lines should be above criticism.

Once the proper balance of a perfect engine in a perfect hull had been achieved, Captain Anderson felt strongly that nothing should ever be done to disturb it. Excess weight could destroy this balance, and so keeping down the weight of the *Mary Powell* became an absolute fetish with him. To begin with, he eschewed all unnecessary, heavy ornamentation; the panes of glass in the clerestory, for example, weighed no more with or without a portrait, so here ornamentation was acceptable. As he grew older he shuddered to see an extra trunk carried aboard that could be dispensed with, as we shall see. Anyone familiar with this idiosyncrasy could well believe the legend that Captain Anderson detailed a waiter to go around the decks shooing flies so that they would not weigh down the vessel unnecessarily.

Captain Anderson believed that commanding a steamboat was the noblest of callings; he did it better than almost anyone else and thoroughly enjoyed himself. Once on a northbound trip his friend, John Bigelow, going ashore at a way landing, stopped and called out, "Captain, I believe you'll run a steamboat in Heaven." As an observer recalled the incident,

> The captain never responded more promptly, as he seemed to raise himself to his full height, and in that clear, snappy voice of his, rang out, "I don't know why not!" In the next breath, so to speak, and while we were all laughing at the sally, he called out, "Let go that line, Shorty," and pulling the bell [to signal the engine room], and seeing the boat safely started, he took time to say, "Goodbye, John," and join in the laugh.[3]

_____

[3]Kingston *Daily Freeman*, July 15, 1914.

49

After the *Mary Powell* was lengthened, Endicott & Co. similarly altered its advertising lithograph (shown on p. 46). With a minimum of disturbance to passengers on deck or the rowboat in the foreground, the steamboat was turned around, lengthened between the paddle boxes and changed as needed. (—*Einars J. Mengis for the Shelburne Museum, Inc.*)

As far as Captain Anderson was concerned, there wouldn't be much point in going to Heaven if there weren't any steamboats around.

Captain Anderson practiced the worthy belief that his crew should reflect his own regard for the passengers, who were, after all, the only source of income, since the *Mary Powell* carried no freight as such. Any crew member who could not exercise courtesy and thoughtfulness toward the passengers remained on board only as long as did those passengers who forgot that the *Mary Powell* was a family boat. Entering service in 1862, the vessel had as her clerk or second captain Jansen Hasbrouck Anderson, the captain's son, who had been born February 9, 1844, and had received his higher education at Nazareth Hall, a Moravian school in Pennsylvania. The pilot, 31-year-old Guernsey B. Betts, had started his career at the age of 12 on a Hudson River sloop and became in time as much the model of a river pilot as Captain Anderson was of a master. Also in the pilothouse was Daniel Hoffman

Bishop, who served as both assistant pilot and mate; both Betts and Bishop had been with Absalom Anderson on the *Thomas Powell*. The rest of the crew included a first or chief engineer and his second or assistant, four firemen, four deckhands, a baggagemaster and personnel in the steward's department.

Under the heading "On Deck, All Hands!" the Kingston *Argus* (issue of April 30th) announced the advent of the *Mary Powell* for 1862:

> To say that the *Mary* is the Queen of the Hudson, and just *the* prettiest boat in the world, is not overstepping the bounds of truth. Her architect and builder did their best in making this a model boat, and all honor to them for their success. . . . her cabin presents the appearance of a prince's drawing-room. Altogether she is a vessel worth a journey to look at. . . .

On Monday, May 5th, the *Mary Powell* made her first round trip between Rondout and New York as a completed steamboat. Soon after, it was announced that under favorable conditions she had matched the best time of the *Thomas Powell,* and for the benefit of the press Captain Anderson said that the speed of his new steamboat exceeded his expectations. He seems to have been whistling in the dark, because for the rest of the season there was no mention of checkable fast runs, except a vague report in the New York *Times* that in July the vessel had made thirty miles an hour on her southbound run the day before and that her average running time, fully loaded, was 25 miles an hour! There was a story of later years which gained much credence, that the contract with Allison had provided for a forfeiture of $5,000 if the *Mary Powell* did not beat the best time of her predecessor over the New York to Newburgh run by 15 minutes, with a bonus of the same amount if she did. The story alleged that Allison won the bonus when the new steamboat bettered the time of the *Thomas Powell* by twenty minutes, or five minutes over the requirement.

Be that as it may, on October 20th, after the final trip of the season, the *Mary Powell* went to the shipyard to be hauled out and cut in two between the paddle boxes and the boilers. One section was moved away from the other by 21 feet, and then the parts were rejoined with new construction. Lengthening a steamboat to improve the speed was not a new device, for by this means the lines and balance of a vessel, after practical testing, could be changed to remedy deficiencies in the original design. Obviously, the lengthening also guaranteed an increase in the vessel's capacity. The enlarged *Mary Powell,* now 288 feet in length, was relaunched in November.

In the 1863 season the *Mary Powell* turned up the first high-speed run of record on June 11th, going from Jay Street in New York to a point off Rondout Lighthouse in 4½ hours, which included the time lost in making eight landings. The running time from New York to Poughkeepsie was 3 hours 20 minutes to give her an average speed of 22.31 miles per hour over that distance. This run definitely confirmed that the lengthening had achieved the desired result, and Captain Anderson breathed easier.

In 1864 the *Mary Powell* went into service on April 30th but was shortly retired for brief repairs

to one of her boilers. About that same time, Captain Anderson had placed atop the pilothouse a hand-carved figure of the Goddess of Liberty, about six feet tall, which put in many years of sightseeing on the river. Exterior adornments were popular on river steamers, and as far as pilothouse roofs were concerned, Captain Anderson had a weakness for something substantial, provided it didn't weigh too much. Likely it was he who some years before had put atop the pilothouse of the *Thomas Powell* the wooden statue of a man — some say of Powell himself — with his right arm extended dead ahead.

As we have seen, the idea of a morning day boat from upriver landings to New York and return was not even a remotely original concept with Captain Anderson, but over the years, Anderson, the *Powell* and "morning boat to New York" had become synonymous. Many prosperous men of affairs maintained summer homes along the Hudson, and the more fortunate of these adopted the *Mary Powell* as a pleasant means of

The Goddess of Liberty. (—*The Smithsonian Institution*)

The figure atop the pilothouse of the *Thomas Powell* was evident in a Civil War photograph, while the *Mary Powell's* Goddess of Liberty was included in a James Bard painting made after she had been length-ened. The *Mary Powell* is steaming southward down Newburgh Bay. (—*Both, courtesy of The Mariners Museum*)

daily commuting, with between four and five hours in the city and a leisurely passage in which to do their homework. The others regularly went down on Monday morning and returned on Saturday to join their families for the week end. For the upriver businessman who needed to complete a transaction in New York, or for families who wanted a day's outing, combining a sail on the river with shopping and sightseeing in the metropolis, she was ideal.

The delights of traveling on the river, already described for us by Nathaniel Parker Willis aboard the *Alida* and the *Thomas Powell*, were even greater aboard the larger and more modern *Mary Powell*. However, the passengers from Rondout who would partake of these delights naturally had to be aboard long before Willis and his fellow Cornwallers, since the *Mary Powell* left Rondout punctually at 5:30 a.m., although the sailing time was usually set back to 6 a.m. in September as the days grew shorter. The timetable and the landings of the vessel changed over the years, but a general idea of the schedule may be had from Fig. 1.

Figure 1. Schedule of the day boat *Mary Powell*.

Southbound		Northbound	
Leaves		Leaves	
Rondout	5:30 a.m.	New York	3:30 p.m.
Poughkeepsie	6:30	Average time of arrival at	
Milton	6:45	Cozzens'	6:00 p.m.
New Hamburg	7:00	West Point	6:10
Newburgh	7:30	Cornwall	6:30
Cornwall	7:45	Newburgh	6:45
West Point	8:05	New Hamburg	7:15
Cozzens'	8:10	Milton	7:30
Arrives at		Poughkeepsie	7:45
New York	10:45 a.m.	Rondout	8:30 p.m.

All landings were on the west bank of the river except Poughkeepsie, New Hamburg and the New York terminus. Rondout-Kingston, Poughkeepsie and Newburgh were sizable communities; Milton, New Hamburg and Cornwall were smaller; West Point was a military reservation; and Cozzens' was the landing for the near-by Cozzens' Hotel. The majority of the *Mary Powell's* passengers were traveling from the upriver landings to New York, and out of New York back to them. Consequently, the steamboat adhered rigidly to her southbound schedule, so that these passengers could plan their day precisely. Northbound, on the other hand, the

main point was to deliver the passengers to their various destinations as quickly as possible; to set a firm northbound schedule would have meant holding the vessel back when the tide was favorable. Therefore, the landing times on the evening trip were set down as "average time of arrival," and the actual time depended on the tide, which had a noticeable effect on a steamboat. The period of favorable tidal conditions was her "early week," and of adverse tide, her "late week." Those few passengers who might be boarding at the way landings on the northbound trip were expected to be familiar enough with this arrangement either to know or to find out whether it was "early week" or "late week."

In those days, 5:30 in the morning did not seem so early as it does today. Promptly at that time the *Mary Powell* took in her lines and steamed out of Rondout Creek. Passing through the mouth into the Hudson near Rondout Lighthouse, she rounded southward and, with her walking beam moving in steady rhythm, was away on the run to New York. By the time she reached beautiful Newburgh Bay it was almost 7:30, and to those on the *Mary Powell* the day was well advanced. Landing first at Newburgh and then in the lower end of the bay at Cornwall, she entered the northern gateway of the Highlands, those hills which rise abruptly from the Hudson and resolutely confine its waters. West Point and Cozzens', in the Highlands, were only a few minutes apart, after which she was free for more than two hours, with no further landings until New York. On Monday mornings, with many businessmen returning to the city, every effort was made to arrive at New York on or before schedule, and the *Mary Powell* was usually let out over this long stretch. With her paddle wheels thumping and swells rolling off astern, she swept across Haverstraw Bay and Tappan Zee, down along the Palisades and into New York.

By mid-afternoon she was on her way back to Rondout. Captain Anderson liked to point out in advertising that on this return trip the passengers saw "the Hudson Highlands 'at the gloaming,' the finest hour for Mountain and River Scenery." In the youth of the *Mary Powell* one traveler wrote of this trip as follows:

. . . laying at the pier during the hottest part of the day; at 3:30 prompt, she leaves . . . on her return trip. . . .

Leaving the Great Metropolis in our wake, we head due North, and viewing the beautiful panorama behind us, of wharves, shipping and great warehouses, extending for miles on either side towards New York Bay, our steamer rapidly approaches the finest scenery in the world. . . .

[After passing the Palisades, and the] thickly wooded hills, and beautiful greensward of Westchester County . . . [we] are now among the "Highlands of the Hudson." The steamer passes close to the shore, and exposes the rough and rugged sides of these towering peaks, then glides swiftly to the opposite shore, giving a succession of charming views as fast as the eye can take the impression.

Along the east bank of the river, the cars of the Hudson River Railroad pass in quick succession, winding here and there, now out of sight passing through some tunnel, then tearing along at a break-neck speed, leaving a disagreeable dust behind, while we on the steamer quietly drink in the pure and bracing air, free from smoke, cinders, and the din of railroad travel.

We cannot wonder that so many travelers avail themselves of the pleasure of a trip on the *Mary Powell* during the summer months.

For miles after entering the Highlands, the mountain peaks rise abruptly to the height of some 1,500 feet, and we take a winding course, often steaming under the frown of some lofty peak, then passing a rift in the hills, presenting to view such beautiful lights and shades as a trip through the "Highlands" by daylight alone can give, and surpassing even a most glowing description. . . .[4]

For most of the passengers the scenery along the Hudson, in the Highlands or elsewhere, and the activity of the busy river, with passing steamboats, long tows of barges and canalboats and many sailing craft, were in themselves ample entertainment. Others explored the *Mary Powell*, visited with fellow travelers or watched the fascinating movements of the engine. A hearty breakfast or a full-course dinner aboard provided a delicious interlude during the trip. In the 1870s

[4]F. W. Beers, *County Atlas of Ulster, New York* (New York: Walker & Jewett, 1875), p. 51.

the Negro waiters, who hailed from Virginia, often rendered concerts with guitar accompaniment in the dining room after the *Mary Powell* had made her northbound landing at Poughkeepsie and was on the last lap to Rondout. Carried away by their music sometimes, they would sing on far into the night, and many an evening those who lived near the *Powell* dock on Rondout Creek heard the soft, old plantation melodies drifting up from the sleeping steamboat. Soon the "*Mary Powell* Glee Club" became a feature of the vessel.

The *Mary Powell* operated on her route from Monday through Saturday, but not on Sunday. The length of the seasons varied, but in the main they began in the last half of May and extended into October. (The longest of all was the season of 1866, with its first trip on April 23rd and the last on November 5th.) The opening trip in the spring was usually an event along the river, and from Cornwall to Rondout the citizens would turn out in a body on the landings or greet the vessel with bonfires, gunshots and fireworks, and fully lit houses on the banks. At Newburgh Commodore Homer Ramsdell sometimes fired salutes with a cannon raised to the roof of his warehouse along the river. The *Mary Powell's* whistle and bell were seldom silent, and the expenditure of steam was immense.

The only known departure from her schedule in 1862 was on the Fourth of July, when she featured a sail around Staten Island during the time she would normally lay over at New York. Combined with the passage on the Hudson this made a pleasant excursion for upriver passengers and became a regular event each year. In 1863, in deference to the holiday air, the Rondout departure time was set back half an hour on the Fourth. Sometimes, instead of circuiting the island, she went up the East River or to Bay Ridge for overland connection to Coney Island. In 1864 this holiday fell on Monday, making for a long week end with the heaviest traffic on the Saturday northbound trip. According to newspaper reports, which gave no source, the *Mary Powell* left New York with anywhere from 1,950 to 2,100 passengers. A figure in this area, if reasonably correct, would probably represent the maximum capacity of the vessel on a regular trip; at that time there

The *Thomas Collyer*, which briefly ran in opposition to the *Mary Powell*, is shown here when she was a New York excursion boat in the fleet of John H. Starin (notice the Starin houseflag on the after flagpole). After a complete rebuilding she officially became a new steamboat, the *Sam Sloan*. (—Above, from a painting by J. G. Tyler in the Eldredge collection, The Mariners Museum)

GENERAL VIEW OF HARBOR AND RIVER, LOOKING SOUTH, KINGSTON, N. Y.

Many post cards featured the *Mary Powell* at some point along her route. Here she is in the last years of her life, lying at her lay-up wharf on the south side of Rondout Creek. Her flags have been added by the post-card maker to enliven the scene. (—Kingston Souvenir Co.)

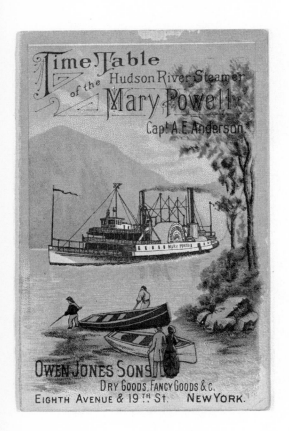

Time Table of the Hudson River Steamer *Mary Powell* Capt. A. E. Anderson

OWEN JONES SONS DRY GOODS, FANCY GOODS & c. EIGHTH AVENUE & 19TH ST. NEW YORK.

CRANSTONS.	WEST POINT.	CORNWALL.	NEWBURGH.	NEW HAMBURGH.	MILTON.	POUGHKEEPSIE.	HYDE PARK.	RONDOUT.	LOCAL RATES OF FARE.
75	75	75	75	75	75	75	1 00	1 00	NEW YORK.
1 00	1 00	1 00	1 00	1 25	1 25	1 25	1 50	1 50	EXC. N.Y.
—	15	15	40	40	40	60	60		CRANSTONS.
		15	15	40	40	40	60	60	WEST POINT.
			15	40	40	40	50	50	CORNWALL.
				25	25	25	50	50	NEWBURGH.
					15	15	40	40	NEW HAMBURGH.
						15	40	40	MILTON.
							25	25	POUGHKEEPSIE.
								25	HYDE PARK.

TIME TABLE OF THE HUDSON RIVER STEAMER MARY POWELL — CAPT. A. E. ANDERSON —

NOT TRANSFERABLE. STEAMER MARY POWELL. COMMUTER'S TICKET. CORNWALL 489 A. E. Anderson G.T.A.

These timetable covers, rate scale and the ticket come from later in the *Mary Powell*'s career, when she was commanded by Captain Anderson's son Eltinge. All are from the author's collection of *Mary Powell* memorabilia.

were no stated or enforced capacity limits, but then too, the hurricane deck was closed to passengers and there would be a great amount of baggage to occupy the space aboard.

Aside from the fact that the *Mary Powell* was overcrowded, the northbound trip on July 2, 1864, was not to be the usual run. Late in June had come competition when the new *Thomas Collyer*, about 200 feet long, was placed in day service, first from New York to Newburgh and then to Poughkeepsie, in opposition to the *Mary Powell*. This *Thomas Collyer* was the third steamboat to be named for the noted shipbuilder and had proved fast enough to be dubbed "Queen of the One-Pipe Steamboats." As the *Mary Powell* pulled away from the pier on that Saturday, the *Thomas Collyer* left her own wharf under a full head of steam and started to race. Not only did the latter strain to the utmost, but she kept so close alongside Captain Anderson's vessel that the guards of the two steamboats touched at times. The captain, with his loaded steamboat, was annoyed, and when, near Yonkers, the *Thomas Collyer* banged into the *Mary Powell* and slightly damaged her paddle box, he ordered his vessel stopped and did not resume until the opposition steamer was well ahead. One account has it that the *Mary Powell* subsequently overcame the *Thomas Collyer's* lead and the two arrived at Newburgh about the same time.

This sort of close-quarters brush was highly dangerous, and it is unusual that Captain Anderson did not stop earlier. Perhaps he was caught off balance by the 1860s hot rodders in charge of the *Thomas Collyer*. Again on July 12th the latter tried unsuccessfully to beat the *Mary Powell*, this time to Poughkeepsie. But later in the month Captain Anderson reduced his fares from Poughkeepsie to New York to 50 cents, a sure sign that the competition was hurting. Soon the *Thomas Collyer* people reduced to 25 cents.

Captain Anderson found it necessary to announce that in no instance had he raced with "another boat on the same route." Any racing had been done by the other boat! An editor added that he knew the captain had been asked by several passengers on one occasion to race, but he had refused. The editor then went on to say that the *Mary Powell* was one of the fastest steamboats in the world, that she could walk away from the opposition boat without effort, and the public could rely on Captain Anderson's abstaining from any token of rivalry. Apparently fare-cutting was not considered to be in this last category. Towards mid-September the *Thomas Collyer* was taken off her route and that ended the competition; later in the year she was chartered by the Government.

In this period the new *Chauncey Vibbard*, which had appeared on the river in June, and the *Daniel Drew* vied for a record run between their termini; both were in service on the New York-Albany Day Line managed by Alfred Van Santvoord. Captain Anderson was sure that his *Mary Powell* was superior to either of these day boats, and it was understood that, with them as his target, he had proposed a post-season sweepstakes in which the *Mary Powell* would run against any combination of vessels, the route to be from New York to either Newburgh or Poughkeepsie. The owners of each competing steamboat would put in the pot an agreed-upon amount, ranging from $1,000 to $5,000, winner-take-all. If only one vessel came forward, then a match race could be arranged. Both lines finished their seasons, but there never was a race. Whether or not Captain Anderson really proposed this sporting contest, the story that he did was widely accepted and was still cited as gospel decades later.

The night boat *Thomas Cornell,* as shown in a James Bard painting, entered Rondout-New York service in 1863. Years later, lying at her landing in Rondout, she displayed the staterooms added on the hurricane deck. *(—Below, Herman F. Boyle collection)*

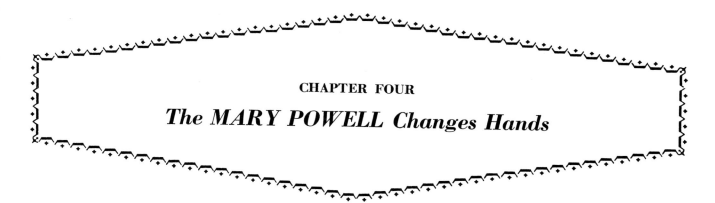

CHAPTER FOUR
The MARY POWELL Changes Hands

In 1863 Thomas Cornell, the Rondout steamboat potentate, finally got around to building a new passenger steamer, the *Thomas Cornell,* but rather than the day boat he had talked of when Captain Anderson was planning the *Mary Powell,* she was a night boat to replace the *Manhattan* on Cornell's Rondout-New York line. Although not quite as long as the enlarged *Mary Powell,* she was the longest night boat ever to be built for service between New York and any terminus along the river other than Albany or Troy. Of course Cornell ran her in line with Romer & Tremper's *James W. Baldwin,* which was lengthened during the winter of 1863-64.

Sometime between April of 1864 and May of the following year Captains Anderson and Ketcham had each sold half of his interest in the *Mary Powell* to John L. Hasbrouck, who was now the major owner with five-eighths of the shares. The *Mary Powell* ended her 1865 season on October 7th amidst rumors that Thomas Cornell was negotiating with Anderson, Ketcham and Hasbrouck for her purchase. The rumors proved to be true, for the bill of sale was executed on October 10th. A newspaper reported the price as $180,000, but it was actually $200,000.

The initial cost of the *Mary Powell,* it will be remembered, was about $80,000, to which must be added the increase in value resulting from the lengthening. Before concluding that Cornell paid an exorbitant price, one must consider that he not only got a steamboat but also the fully developed Rondout-New York day line and the good will of the *Mary Powell's* loyal passengers. Inflation during the Civil War also played its part; the *Chauncey Vibbard,* a comparable day boat but only as long as the *Mary Powell* was originally, had cost about $144,000 when she was completed in the spring of 1864. Perhaps, considering the newspaper report of the price, Cornell figured that he paid $180,000 for the steamboat and $20,000 for the route.

An immediate result of the sale was great speculation as to whether Cornell intended to convert the *Mary Powell* into a night boat to run with the *Thomas Cornell* and so drive Romer & Tremper out of the Rondout-New York trade. Finally, to dispel any such notion, Cornell took up his pen and wrote,

To the Editors of the Po'keepsie *Eagle.*
Rondout, N.Y., Oct. 20 1865

Dear Sirs: — Please allow me to correct an article in your columns of last week:

The Steamer *Mary Powell* will continue on the route she has been running, the coming season, until the New Boat is completed, when it is intended to start the *Mary Powell* from Newburgh at an early hour, touching at the landings below, and arriving at New York about 9½ o'clock, the New Boat taking the through route to Rondout. The New Boat is to be 300 feet long, 40 feet beam, 10 feet hold, 62″ cylinder and 16 feet stroke, intended to be the fastest boat in the world.

Truly Yours,
Thomas Cornell.

Still talking about a new morning boat from Rondout, Cornell had evidently enlarged his plans since he first proposed the project five years before. Doubtless the New Boat would have cut a wide swath in Hudson River annals had she ever appeared. But she never did.

The *James W. Baldwin* was lengthened and later had staterooms added on her hurricane deck. The figures atop her spars were (starting at the bow) an eagle, a ball, a liberty cap and a figure peering through a spyglass. At top, she is steaming out of Rondout Creek; at bottom, lying at her landing in Rondout. (—*Above, Dr. Charles A. Galyon collection*)

As the *James W. Baldwin,* above, sails out of the creek on her way to New York, the piling sticking up directly astern of her marks the dike which, in effect, separated the creek from the river at this point. In the background is Port Ewen. Docked in Rondout, below, she has the *A. B. Valentine* astern. (—Both, Herman F. Boyle collection)

Three days before writing the above letter, Cornell had quietly sold a half interest in the *Mary Powell* to Daniel Drew for $100,000. A long-time steamboat operator and railroad venturer of shady reputation, it was Drew who had revitalized day travel on the Hudson by putting the *Daniel Drew* in service in 1860. Having sold his interest in that vessel, Drew's major activity on the river in 1865 was the People's Line, the night line between New York and Albany. Perhaps his investment in the *Mary Powell* had been planned before Cornell opened negotiations for her, and he had purposely kept in the background until the deal was closed, for Drew would not seem to be the type of man to excite Captain Anderson's admiration. However, by early 1867 Cornell had bought Drew out and was once again the sole owner of the vessel.

This portrait of Thomas Cornell comes from *The Fortieth Congress of the United States* (1867-69), of which he was a member. Defeated for re-election, he later became a member of the 47th Congress. (*—Courtesy of Robert R. Haines*)

The loyal supporters of Captain Anderson, "the prince of captains," were sad that he was retiring from active steamboating on the river, something that may have been part of the agreement at the time of the sale, but they felt he had earned his rest, being almost 53 years old. When the *Mary Powell* entered service in the spring of 1866 she was commanded by Captain Ferdinand Frost, from Nyack on the lower river. Although the passengers naturally missed Captain Anderson, Captain Frost, we are assured, proved to be a "trump"; the traveling public was convulsed by the story that the mornings were now quite cold on the *Mary Powell*, "because there's Frost aboard!" Captain Frost's clerk or purser was William H. Cornell, Thomas Cornell's cousin. Back on board as pilot was Guernsey B. Betts, who had left the vessel by 1864 to work for the New York-Albany Day Line. Since he was a rugged individualist, Betts may have had a difference of some sort with Captain Anderson, who was himself an individualist. Andrew Barrett was the chief engineer, and Daniel Hoffman Bishop continued as assistant pilot and mate.

Late in her first season under Cornell's management, the *Mary Powell* was southbound in the fog above Newburgh and ran on a dilapidated and sunken wharf, badly damaging one of her paddle wheels. The spare boat of the New York-Albany Day Line, the *Armenia*, was secured as a replacement at $200 a day and ran briefly until repairs to the *Mary Powell* could be made. Early in the 1867 season the *Mary Powell* was again fog-bound, this time between Poughkeepsie and Rondout on the northbound trip, and did not arrive at her destination until seven the next morning, more than an hour late for her scheduled sailing for New York, which had to be cancelled that day. Apparently Pilot Betts was taking no more chances in the fog.

Boilers were not as long-lasting in those days as they afterwards became, and between the seasons of 1866 and 1867 the *Mary Powell's* were replaced, the second of six sets she would have in her lifetime. Not long before Cornell's purchase of the *Mary Powell* Captain Anderson had contracted for the new boilers with John Dillon of Rondout. Dillon bought the iron and began the work before Captain Anderson requested that he stop the construction and offered to pay damages. Dillon refused to stop and, when the boilers were completed, sued for the contract price of $21,000; Cornell purchased them, but at a lesser price due to a drop in the cost of iron. When *Dillon v. Anderson* came to court a jury awarded Dillon $5,700 to compensate for the profit he would have made on the original contract plus the decline in the value of the materials which went into the boilers. With the new boilers the *Mary Powell* soon made another of her memorable fast runs when, on June 10, 1867, she steamed from her Desbrosses Street pier to Rondout Lighthouse in four hours running time, at an average speed of 22¼ miles per hour.

On Thanksgiving morning in 1867 the steamboat lost an understandably prejudiced partisan when Mary Ludlow Powell passed away at the age of 82. When her namesake appeared on the river Mrs. Powell was still active enough to take trips to New York on the vessel and whenever possible brought Captain Anderson an old-fashioned bouquet. At the Newburgh landing he would never permit anyone to step on the gangplank before Mrs. Powell.

The strangest trip made by any of the *Mary Powell's* passengers was that of a poor boy, 14 years old, in July of 1868. He needed a job and had heard that there was prosperity in Rondout, but he had no money for the fare. Gazing at the elegant steamboat as she lay at her Desbrosses Street pier in New York, he decided that she was the answer to his problem. He swam out to the port side of the vessel, climbed up the buckets of the paddle wheel and found a spot inside the paddle box with some iron bars to which he could cling. He had not considered that to hang there for hours would be a feat in itself, and he certainly was unaware of the conditions inside a paddle box once the wheels began to turn. After the vessel was under way all of his shouts for help were cut off by the beating of the paddles; it was not until the *Mary Powell* had reached Cozzens' after a steady run of about two and a half hours, that a fireman heard the boy's feeble cries. Going into the paddle box he found him almost drowned, his face and bare feet blue and wrinkled by the continual soaking of the cold water. He was

Thomas and Mary Powell lie buried in St. George's Cemetery, Newburgh. On the monument, the day of Mr. Powell's death was transposed from May 12 to May 21.

scarcely able to retain his hold. After drying out in one of the warm firerooms he was given free passage to Rondout, where a lad of such determination must certainly have found a job.

While he owned her, Thomas Cornell put a few of his own touches into the management of the *Mary Powell*. For the 1867 season he experimented with not serving spiritous liquors at the bar on either the *Mary Powell* or the *Thomas Cornell*. No record survives as to the length or success of this temperance experiment; likely it was short-lived. In the 1868 season the *Mary Powell's* last down trip of the year was on Monday, November 2nd. Since Tuesday was Election Day she would leave New York at 7:30 a.m. and run to Catskill, stopping at way landings on the route, with free passage offered to all who wished to go

The *Oswego*, one of the vessels involved in Cornell's sale of the *Mary Powell*, was built in 1848, the first large side-wheeler constructed exclusively for towing on the Hudson. By a turn of fate, she was also the last to be so employed, in 1918.

home to vote, regardless of political affiliations. Thomas Cornell was running for re-election to the House of Representatives on the Republican ticket and no doubt hoped that all who went up on the *Mary Powell* would keep the free passage in mind when they marked their ballots. This may have helped his cause, but not enough: Cornell lost the election.

In December of 1868 Cornell and Alfred Van Santvoord commenced complicated negotiations revolving around the *Mary Powell*. Van Santvoord, with John McB. Davidson as his principal partner, managed the New York-Albany Day Line, which operated the *Chauncey Vibbard*, the *Daniel Drew* and the *Armenia*. He also controlled a majority of the shares in the Hudson River Steamboat Company, a towing line that had originally been headed by his father; this organization had suffered a sizable loss in 1868 and was now interested in disposing of some or all of its towing steamers. Cornell, on the other hand, was interested in increasing his own towing fleet, for towing was his major activity, more intriguing and profitable for him than his night line or his sortie

into the operation of a day boat. Cornell and Van Santvoord sparred, and to add zest to the contest, it was reliably reported that Captain Anderson stood ready to enter the fray if Van Santvoord backed down.

When the directors of the Hudson River Steamboat Company met on January 14, 1869, they learned from Van Santvoord, their general agent, that Cornell wanted to purchase from them the towing steamers *Oswego*, *Cayuga* and *Anna*. Built in 1848, the *Oswego* had been the first large steamer constructed expressly for towing on the Hudson River at a time when major towing was being handled by outmoded passenger vessels; the *Cayuga*, built the year following, was the second. The directors considered the proposition and a month later, on February 12th, resolved that $80,000 was the lowest figure they would accept for the three steamers.

Six days later Van Santvoord and Davidson bought the *Mary Powell*, paying $180,000 for her in equal shares. As in the previous sale, the selling price included the Rondout route and good will. Then the Hudson River Steamboat Company sold the three towing steamers at their price, $80,000, and in this transaction there was horse-trading between Cornell and Schuyler's Line, another towing company. In the eventual results of the deal, Cornell got the *Oswego* and, from Schuyler's Line, the *New York* and the *Baltic;* Schuyler, in turn, got the *Cayuga* and the *Anna*. Since the *New York* and the *Baltic* were converted passenger steamers and less desirable as towing vessels, at first glance Cornell seems to have come out second best on the trade, but allegedly with the *Baltic* he gained exclusive control of the towing business between Rondout and Albany. At any rate, Cornell likely got what he wanted, and Van Santvoord and Davidson got what they wanted — the *Mary Powell*.

During the course of the negotiations Thomas Cornell had presented traffic summaries for the period 1866-68, which showed the average number of passengers annually carried by the *Mary Powell* as 113,864, with gross earnings of about $100,000 per year. Round-trip passengers were counted twice, of course, once each way. The last two years of the summary ran closely in both passengers carried and earnings, and the statistics reveal the nature of the route as it then was. As we have said, the bulk of the traffic, 83%, was either to or from New York; the remaining 17% represented travel between the upriver landings. About 42% of the passengers were southbound, and 58% were northbound. Of all the passengers arriving at or departing from New York, about 34% had left from or landed at Newburgh, which supplied the heaviest New York commuter traffic; 16.6% were attributable to Cornwall; 16%, Poughkeepsie; and 9.9%, Rondout, which involved the earliest departure and the latest arrival of any landing on the route. On the whole, the figures showed that Cornell had done well with the *Mary Powell* in the three years that he owned her.

The new owners of the *Mary Powell*, Alfred Van Santvoord and John McB. Davidson, immediately ordered the start of such work upon the steamboat as they saw fit. The first job, that of replacing the buckets on the paddle wheels, was begun while she was still in winter quarters at Port Ewen. Most of the work planned for the *Mary Powell* would bring her into line with Van Santvoord and Davidson's New York-Albany day boats, the *Chauncey Vibbard* and the *Daniel Drew,* which had their saloons well forward with a range of windows around the front. Van Santvoord and Davidson felt this was a better place to enjoy the scenery than an open deck, Captain

The smaller *Anna,* another side-wheel towing steamer connected with the sale, was constructed in 1854. Van Santvoord personally owned a fifth of the shares in her.

On this certificate of stock in the Schuyler's Line is pictured the *America*, another of the side-wheelers designed for towing.

Anderson and his theories of balance notwithstanding, and they contracted with the joiners of the *Chauncey Vibbard* to extend the saloon on the *Mary Powell*.

Since this work was far from finished on May 1, 1869, the *Armenia* opened the Rondout route and continued for over a month. Captain Frost, who had been retained as the master of the *Mary Powell*, was advertised as commanding the *Armenia* for this time. Although 76 feet shorter than the *Mary Powell*, the *Armenia* was a fast traveler and added a raucous note to the trip with her steam calliope, a musical marvel once installed on steamboats to lure passengers away from opposition vessels.

Pandemonium reigned on the *Mary Powell* as June 5th, the tentative date for her reappearance on the river, approached and the work was still unfinished. Then on June 2nd the *Armenia* dam-aged one of her paddle wheels on the southbound trip, and the *Mary Powell*, for the second time in her life, was placed on the route in dishabille. When word reached Newburgh that she was coming up, hundreds flocked to the wharf to greet her and every bell within range answered her landing signal. One newspaper observed, "Had it been known that she was coming there is little doubt but a grand reception would have been the result."

The work that had been accomplished on the *Mary Powell* was impressive, and the small remainder could be completed without withdrawing her from service. The forward cabin had been enlarged, and the dining room had been fitted with skylights; a smoking saloon, presumably in the hold, offered a place for tobacco addicts to indulge their compulsion without offending the noses of the female passengers. The stairway lead-

The 14-foot stroke of the *Armenia's* cylinder gave her an unusually high walking beam. *(—Eldredge collection, courtesy of The Mariners Museum)*

ing up to the main saloon was enclosed with glass doors, and that apartment was an opulent place indeed. The saloon now ran about as far forward as the deckhouse on the main deck. Its wainscoting was of solid black walnut, and the black walnut furniture was set off with mottled walnut panels and gilt inlaid stripes; the upholstery was bright blue velvet. The carpeting was "rich and tasteful," and the large mirrors were set in "chaste" frames. The total cost of this work came to about $25,000, a figure that was considerably inflated when it was released to the newspapers. However, all was not perfect in paradise: the editor of the *Kingston Journal* complained about the jarring of the windows in the main saloon and suggested that some kind of rubber fitting might relieve this annoyance.

Only a few days after her reappearance on the river the *Mary Powell* was honored to carry President Ulysses S. Grant, who had always disliked traveling along the Hudson by rail when he could take a steamboat instead. Grant's schedule called for a visit to West Point on June 10th, and although the academy hierarchy had received no word as to the president's anticipated time of arrival, they knew of his preference for steamboats and had been told that Grant had left Washington the night before in a compartment car attached

to the Baltimore & Ohio's through train to New York. Estimating the situation, they decided that he would likely arrive on the northbound trip of the *Chauncey Vibbard* and made every preparation, with provision for a proper gun salute, to receive the president. The *Chauncey Vibbard* arrived; the military strained in anticipation, and the civilians on the landing gawked. There was no sign of the president. Standing at the gangplank, Captain David H. Hitchcock called archly to an army officer to ask if he were looking for President Grant. Upon receiving an affirmative, Captain Hitchcock took out his pocket watch, stared at it for a moment and then announced that the president's train had been many hours late. The *Chauncey Vibbard* steamed on up the river, and the welcoming party returned to the academy.

As the president's train was passing through Annapolis Junction en route to Baltimore it had suffered an unfortunate encounter with a cow. This cow had first been struck by a southbound train and was wandering about in a dazed condition, but even if she was somewhat the worse for wear the cow effectively won the day. After the wreck Grant quietly smoked a cigar, while the wonder grew that so few had been injured in proportion to the amount of damage. Of course Grant

The southbound *Mary Powell*, lying at Poughkeepsie, displays the enlarged saloon extending well forward.

finally did make it to New York, and presumably the West Point reception committee got word of the president's plans this time. He sailed on the afternoon trip of the *Mary Powell,* and after she tied up to the landing the president marched down the gangplank.

Under Van Santvoord's management the *Mary Powell's* operating season had been shortened; in 1869 he reduced round trips by about 10% from the year before, but the number of passengers carried fell by 20%. In 1870, with the *Armenia* replacing the *Mary Powell* in the last two weeks of the season, the total number of trips made by the two vessels was even less than in 1869, although the number of passengers increased slightly. Then, in 1871, with the *Mary Powell* making only 115 round trips, the number of passengers fell off sharply, as it did also on the New York-Albany run, although the average number of passengers per trip was actually higher than in the two previous years. The financial returns were not so disheartening: in the first two years under Van Santvoord the total net earnings of the *Mary Powell* exceeded those of either the *Daniel Drew* or the *Chauncey Vibbard.* Even deducting the entire net loss on the *Armenia,* which took over the Rondout route for a time in 1869 and again in 1870, the remainder of the *Mary Powell's* net earnings amounted to over $40,000, or 27% of the net earnings of Van Santvoord's passenger-boat operations. In 1871 she accounted for anywhere from

20% to 24% of the take, depending on how one figures.

Between the seasons of 1871 and 1872 Van Santvoord planned to have the *Chauncey Vibbard* lengthened to 281 feet. Since the *Mary Powell* was 288 feet long, this would make the two a well-matched pair to run together on the New York-Albany route. The *Chauncey Vibbard's* present running mate, the *Daniel Drew,* had been lengthened after the 1863 season but measured only 260 feet. Although it would be some time before the work of lengthening the *Chauncey Vibbard* commenced, Van Santvoord announced that he was withdrawing her for repairs, and in this way he could replace her with the *Mary Powell* and test the latter on the New York-Albany route against the *Daniel Drew.* Accordingly the *Chauncey Vibbard* made her last southbound trip of the season on October 2nd, and the next day the *Mary Powell* went to Albany. Before the season ended the *Mary Powell* made four round trips in this service.

About her performance on this route, the marine historian, John H. Morrison, observed sourly,

There is one thing to answer satisfactorily, it would seem, for the *Mary Powell* to maintain the claim of the "Queen of the Hudson." In October, 1871, the *Mary Powell* . . . made four round trips on the Albany day line, and during that service was unable to make as good running time as her consort, the *Daniel*

This advertisement for the 1871 season has the *Chauncey Vibbard* and *Daniel Drew* somewhat confused about the return trip from Albany.

Drew, running on opposite days. If she was the "Queen of the Hudson," as claimed, why did she not maintain that reputation while running on the day line?[1]

Since Morrison gives no figures to indicate the difference in running time between the two steamboats, the question is a bit tortuous. The obvious answer is that the enlarged saloon made her heavier forward and destroyed the fine balance created by her lengthening in 1862. Another marine historian, George W. Murdock, who served as a fireman on the *Mary Powell* in 1877-79, when the matter was probably still being discussed, has claimed that shoal waters in the upper river hampered the boat on this run. The Albany *Argus* on October 8, 1871, reported that the river there was unusually low; even though the Hudson is tidal to Troy, the upper navigable reaches were in those days adversely affected by drought. Whatever the

[1]John H. Morrison, *History of American Steam Navigation* (New York: W. F. Sametz & Co., 1903), p. 155.

explanation, this test against the *Daniel Drew* seems to have ended Van Santvoord's interest in the *Mary Powell* and her route.

As a fit closing scene for the Van Santvoord-Davidson ownership, the *Mary Powell* was chartered to participate in the New York reception for the young grand duke Alexis of Russia, son of Czar Alexander II. The Russian frigate *Svetlana,* with Alexis aboard, arrived off Sandy Hook bar about midnight on Saturday, November 18, 1871, and the next day the reception committee issued its elaborate procedural arrangements for Monday. The invited guests and a few members of the press would board the official steamboat, the *Mary Powell,* at the foot of Vestry Street at 10 a.m. The *Mary Powell* would proceed to Lower New York Bay to greet Alexis and then steam back to the city at the head of the combined Russian and American fleets. Off her stern to port would be four United States vessels in column headed by the *Congress;* to starboard would be

RECEPTION OF THE GRAND DUKE ALEXIS—DEPARTURE FROM THE FRIGATE "SVETLANA."

Here the artist has extended the *Mary Powell's* promenade deck to the bow, over 30 years too soon! (—Harper's Weekly, *Dec. 9, 1871, courtesy of The Mariners Museum*)

the Russian flagship *Svetlana,* two other Russian warships and the U.S.S. *Tallapoosa.* Outside each column of warships would sail a column of yachts, and a fleet of yachts would bring up the rear of the naval procession. As the vessels came to anchor off the Battery, Alexis was to be brought by an admiral's barge from the *Svetlana* to the *Mary Powell,* which would then run up the Imperial Russian flag, to the accompaniment of a 21-gun salute from the United States fleet. Finally the *Mary Powell* would land her royal passenger at the Battery for further ceremonies.

Unfortunately, on Monday the rain poured down. The executive committee aboard the *Mary Powell* decided to go down to the Lower Bay, board the *Svetlana* and present His Imperial Highness with the choice of either coming ashore quietly with them and deferring the formal reception or postponing everything until the next day. The Russian minister in full regalia arrived at the Vestry Street pier, and the *Mary Powell's* band struck up the Russian national hymn as he

went aboard. After a hurried conference he disembarked and drove to the Battery; from there he would steam down the bay, with the *Mary Powell* trailing slowly in his wake, and present the committee's proposal to Alexis. The *Mary Powell* got under way, but the minister was detained at the Battery. The steamboat landed and he again came on board to report that the Russian fleet was coming up the bay and nothing could be done until it arrived, which it eventually did. With a strict observance of protocol it was ascertained that Alexis preferred to remain on the *Svetlana* until the following day.

Things went better the next morning. With such notables as Cyrus W. Field, Professor S. F. B. Morse and Peter Cooper on board, the *Mary Powell* left Vestry Street near noon, and eventually the grand duke was transferred from the *Svetlana* to the steamboat, where all on board were presented to him. During this ceremony the *Mary Powell* went for a short sail down the bay, and as she returned Alexis took luncheon in the

RECEPTION OF THE GRAND DUKE ALEXIS ON BOARD THE "MARY POWELL."—[Drawn by C. S Reinhart.]

The young grand duke and his aides are received aboard the *Mary Powell.*
(—Harper's Weekly, *Dec. 9, 1871)*

lower cabin. About 1:30 p.m. she tied up at Pier 1, and His Imperial Highness at last set foot on American soil.

On December 1st the reception committee again chartered the *Mary Powell,* this time to take Alexis and invited guests from New York to West Point and return. Once more the band played the Russian hymn as the grand duke came aboard and quickly ascended to the main saloon. Young Alexis was not one to engender stiffness, and whenever he felt like a cigarette he ducked down onto the main deck. Sometimes to enjoy a better view of the scenery he went up to the hurricane deck, but not for long because the day was cold and the wind strong. As the *Mary Powell*

came off West Point a 21-gun salute rang out, and she made her landing, where most of the passengers went ashore; Alexis remained for a private excursion a bit farther up the river to get a close look at Crows Nest Mountain. Then, back at the Point, he was escorted to the parade grounds. After a review and a whirlwind tour of the military academy he reboarded the steamer. On the return trip dinner was followed by music and dancing; after a long succession of waltzes someone suggested a Virginia reel, and this the grand duke thoroughly enjoyed. It had been a fine day for the *Mary Powell,* and perhaps the only thing she lacked to make it finer was Captain Anderson himself.

If you went to New York on the *Mary Powell* in 1878, you might have sailed on to Coney Island aboard the *Rosedale,* which appears above in as steamboaty a picture as one could want.

The *Ansonia,* the pride of Saugerties, towed the *Mary Powell* down the river for alterations after the end of her 1872 season.

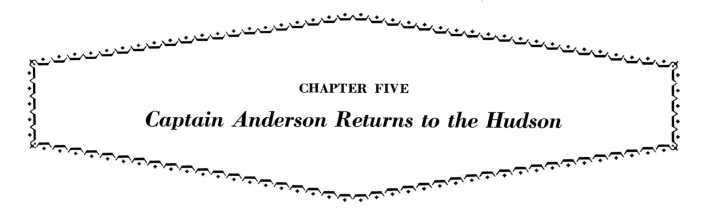

CHAPTER FIVE

Captain Anderson Returns to the Hudson

Early in 1872 Van Santvoord and Davidson disposed of the *Mary Powell,* even though they sustained a loss. Captain Absalom Anderson was still interested in the vessel and bought her as sole owner in mid-January, although his acquisition was reported as a fact well before the sale date. He paid $150,000 for her, or $10,000 less than his best reported offer during the Cornell-Van Santvoord negotiations in 1869; the payment would be made in three installments of $50,000 each, with the last falling due late in June. Since he was not in a position to make any immediate changes in the *Mary Powell,* Captain Anderson would have to run her in 1872 with the enlarged saloon, which must have weighted his heart as much as it did his steamboat.

On April 6th the vessel left New York and deadheaded up to Rondout to be painted. Just eight days earlier, on March 29th, the governor had signed an act, passed by the New York State Legislature, to incorporate the City of Kingston, encompassing the villages of Kingston, Rondout and Wilbur. The downtown section and water front were, and still are, referred to as Rondout, so we shall continue to use Rondout in this book.

The *Mary Powell* made her first regular trip up the river from Vestry Street in New York on May 11th. Captain Anderson, commanding in person, was finally back in business, and at Newburgh a band turned out to serenade him. His predecessor, Captain Frost, was retained by the New York-Albany Day Line and installed as master of the *Daniel Drew.* Captain Anderson was happy to keep his old friend, Mate Bishop, aboard the *Mary Powell* and also continued the services of Guernsey Betts as pilot. Once again the cap-

tain's son, young Jansen, was the purser, and Captain Anderson had such confidence in him that in August he vacationed on Fire Island, leaving Jansen in command. This season the traveling public was convulsed by a joke not unlike the one made at Captain Frost's expense in years before. This time the question was, "Why is the *Mary Powell* preferred by persons in a hurry?" The correct answer ran, "Because her captain is a lander soon." If you weren't particularly sharp, someone was sure to explain, "A lander soon — A. L. Anderson!" Get it?

During the summer, as a way to increase their annual income, Pilot Betts and Mate Bishop arranged with Captain Anderson for what amounted to chartering the *Mary Powell* for a "first class" moonlight sail on August 20th, with music and dancing but without liquor. The affair would tap prospective passengers to the limit, since it combined with the regular northbound trip and actually commenced at West Point on the way up. After completing her scheduled run, the *Mary Powell* would leave Rondout at 9 p.m., go back to West Point and return to Rondout; in this way all moonlight-sail passengers from the landings between West Point and Rondout would get a round trip covering about eighty miles. This method of incorporating a moonlight sail with part of the regular run, although on a more limited basis, was the pattern that churches and social groups would later follow in arranging fund-raising moonlight excursions aboard the *Mary Powell.*

Fortune did not smile too broadly on this first venture of Betts and Bishop. When the steamboat arrived off the narrow mouth of Rondout Creek on the northbound trip she had to wait

In 1869 Van Santvoord had reduced rental cost by moving the landing on Rondout Creek to a wharf near the mouth, in an area known locally as Ponckhockie, and there it remained for many years. The *Mary Powell* then had little problem getting into or out of the creek, but this landing was far from the heart of Rondout. To the right is Rondout Lighthouse. This photograph may have been taken in the spring of 1874. (*—Herman F. Boyle collection*)

for a large tow coming out. Betts and Bishop understandably became impatient and started in before the tow had passed the mouth. Going too far out of the creek channel, they ran the *Mary Powell* aground; twenty minutes were lost in getting her off. Worse still, the weather was threatening, and many of the anticipated Rondout passengers stayed home. A lot of Kingstonians would not attend because the *Mary Powell* could not arrive back in Rondout before 2 a.m. at the earliest, and at that hour they could not be sure of transportation from the wharf to their homes.

It was almost 10 p.m. when the *Mary Powell* finally sailed from Rondout, and fortunately the moon came out then and shone brightly thereafter. As it turned out, it was not until 3:30 a.m. that the moonlight sail came to an end at Rondout. The excursion represented a herculean endeavor on the part of the crew, who now had only two hours in which to clean the vessel and make ready for the scheduled morning run at 5:30 a.m. The affair had been successful to the extent that Betts and Bishop had netted about $200 apiece. The next year they chose September 8th for their "Second Grand Moonlight Excursion," because on the following morning the autumn change in schedule went into effect, and the crew would have an extra half hour to clean up and get some rest.

74

Of the same period is this photograph of the *Mary Powell* northbound towards Cornwall landing, with a sloop off her stern and a schooner on either side. (*—Eldredge collection, The Mariners Museum*)

That Captain Anderson knew his passengers was demonstrated by an incident late in the 1872 season. While the *Mary Powell* was landing southbound at Newburgh on September 18th, the chain block at the top of her rudder broke. Captain Anderson promptly tapped Donald McMillan, a Rondout blockmaker, and requested his services. The captain sent ashore for tools, McMillan doffed his coat and in about an hour the *Mary Powell* was on her way.

When the season ended in 1872, Captain Anderson was ready to have the saloon reduced to its original size and a new set of boilers installed. The *Mary Powell* lay at her Rondout Creek wharf for close to two months, and then almost at the end of November the *Ansonia*, of the Saugerties night line, took her in tow for New York. When it was announced that the saloon would be altered, a newspaper pointed out that Captain Anderson knew what his passengers wanted, an observation for public consumption that no doubt came from the captain himself. He also stated he "wouldn't carry all that stuff if it were covered with pure gold." The contract for the new boilers went to Alexander Cauldwell of Newburgh; the captain was avoiding the boilermakers in Rondout proba-

bly because both John Dillon and the memory of his lawsuit were still alive. In the spring Cauldwell's steel boilers, stronger and lighter than the iron pair they were replacing, were brought down the river and presumably installed at Allison's yard in Jersey City. At the same time the smokestacks were fitted with jets to supplant the blowers; these devices helped to create a draft in the furnaces to permit the desired type of combustion. (Later, in the spring of 1874, the smokestacks would be lengthened and the jets removed in favor of the blowers, because the jets had made the coal burn too fast.) During this overhaul the vessel's name was painted on the paddle box in red letters, and Jansen Anderson took to calling her the "Bloody Mary."

On May 19, 1873, the *Mary Powell* ran from New York to Rondout without passengers in order to test her new equipment. Her paddle wheels had been fitted with feathering-type buckets — the "educated wheels" on which the buckets angled as they entered the water, like feathering an oar — at the expense of the American Paddle Wheel Company. Since these buckets were too heavy for the light arms of the existing wheels, they were removed. Captain Anderson said that he

On June 1, 1874, when a tow grounded on a bar and blocked the *Mary Powell* out of Rondout Creek, the *Sammy Cornell* landed her passengers. For her size, the tugboat sported a giant whistle which gave out a deep, bass tone.

had intended to have the company install entirely new wheels, but had not had time to make the arrangements. Over the years there was further talk of installing feathering paddle wheels on the *Mary Powell*, but the weight they would add to the vessel was always a deterrent.

The regular season opened on June 4th, and soon after, with new boilers and lightened by the curtailing of the saloon, she made another fast run. Her elapsed time came within three minutes of the record she had chalked up in June, 1867, and one newspaper claimed she had lost the equivalent of this through a bad landing at West Point. As always, the accounts of a fast trip were replete with speculations about what might have been if this or that had not happened.

President Grant came up the river to Kingston in July to visit his friend and fellow Civil War veteran, General George H. Sharpe, who was then Surveyor of the Port of New York. On the morning of the 31st the presidential party and General Sharpe at 5 a.m. drove down to the landing of the *Mary Powell*, where the steamboat lay

waiting with all her colors flying. A crowd had gathered to see the president, and as he alighted from the wagon the ladies waved their handkerchiefs and the men raised their hats. Grant responded by tipping his own hat three or four times as he walked to the steamer. Going aboard, the president purchased a local paper, the *Daily Freeman*, and then took a seat up forward with General Sharpe, where he lighted a cigar and proceeded to study the news. In our age of extreme presidential security it is a little difficult to imagine such a thing, but in those days one never knew whom he might run into aboard the *Mary Powell*.

The most important event of 1874 was the arrival of a new officer on the *Mary Powell*; young Absalom Eltinge Anderson, another of the captain's sons, came aboard as steward. He was born in Saugerties in 1856, while Captain Anderson was operating his Saugerties night line, and had received his education at a military institute and at the Eastman National Business College in Poughkeepsie. Eltinge was of course overshadowed by

To show the alterations made to the *Mary Powell* between the seasons of 1874 and 1875, Captain Anderson ordered a new and lively advertising lithograph from Endicott & Co.

his elder brother Jansen, the experienced purser of the *Mary Powell,* but it was Eltinge, rather than Jansen, who many years later would become the captain of the vessel; in fact, Eltinge would hold that position almost twice as long as his renowned father. Eltinge's arrival for duty in that first season was not quite ordinary, for allegedly it gave the captain an opportunity to display his passion for keeping the weight down. One day in the spring, while Captain Anderson was supervising the steamboat's final preparations for service, a porter came up the gangplank with a trunk. Upon asking whose it might be, the captain was told it belonged to "Mr. Eltinge," whereupon the porter was sent to fetch Eltinge. When the boy appeared, his father solemnly told him that if all the officers and crew came aboard with a trunk, then obviously the vessel would be needlessly weighted down. He then ordered Eltinge to take from the trunk only what he could put in a handkerchief and send the rest, including the trunk, back home!

Of course baggage belonging to the passengers was sacrosanct, since it contributed to the vessel's annual income. In those days of voluminous clothing families went away for the summer with several trunks full of apparel, and steamers like the *Mary Powell* handled mountains of baggage piled up on the main deck. Still, it must have been a sad day for Captain Anderson in that same year of 1874 when a party of eight came aboard in New York with no less than forty trunks. Another trunk anecdote that delighted Captain Anderson's admirers concerned a man who had brought his family to Cornwall for the summer; the next day he showed up on the landing as the southbound *Mary Powell* came in. He accosted Captain Anderson and demanded to know why his trunks hadn't arrived. When the captain asked, quite reasonably, if the man had checked them with the baggagemaster, the other realized his mistake and, inwardly furious with himself, became indignant. He vented his annoyance on Captain Anderson and threatened to report him to the owners of the *Mary Powell.* When a bystander curtly told him that the captain was the sole owner, the man became enraged at his latest blunder and lost control, calling the captain unpleasant names and

"FAIR VIEW."

VIEW OF THE HUDSON AND MARY POWELL, WITH RONDOUT, THE CATSKILLS AND RHINEBECK, AS VIEWED FROM CAPTAIN A. L. ANDERSON'S RESIDENCE.

(—*F. W. Beers*, County Atlas of Ulster, New York)

finally saying that, although he had planned to commute on the *Mary Powell* while his family summered in Cornwall, now he would travel some other way. By this time Captain Anderson's own temper was short, and he made one of his rare lapses into profanity as he shot back, "Well, you can travel to hell for all I care, but you can't go there on the *Mary Powell!*"

At any rate, Eltinge was now firmly implanted on the *Mary Powell,* and the 1874 season was about to begin. This time it started on an unusual note, with a preseason charter by the junior class of Vassar College for young ladies at Poughkeepsie. The class had decided to entertain both its own members and the senior class with an evening sail down the river as far as Fort Montgomery in the Highlands and then back to Poughkeepsie. At 5:10 p.m. on May 28th the *Mary*

Powell slipped away from her Rondout landing and went down to Poughkeepsie, where six street-cars loaded with female collegians rumbled down to the waterfront. Eventually the steamer sailed with about 120 students, the faculty and officers of the college and an orchestra. The affair was catered by the Smith Brothers; these well-known Poughkeepsie restaurateurs are better remembered as the "Trade" and "Mark" of their cough-drop boxes. The outing was highly successful, and in the following years preseason excursions aboard the *Mary Powell* became a happy custom. Soon the Eastman National Business College followed Vassar's lead, and over the years the faculty could point to Eltinge and proudly claim him as one of their graduates.

After the *Mary Powell* finished the 1874 season her furnishings were removed, and she went

78

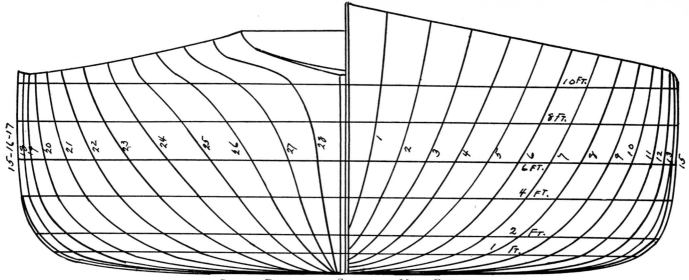

SECTION PLAN OF THE STEAMBOAT MARY POWELL
From The Rudder

This section plan was drawn in 1904. (—*Hudson River Day Line collection, Steamship Historical Society of America, Inc.*)

back down the river on October 8th with invited guests on board. Captain Anderson was taking her to Allison's shipyard, having decided it was time for some extensive structural repairs. The engine was dismantled and parts of it taken to the shop of Fletcher, Harrison & Company. The vessel was placed on a sectional dry dock, and Allison's men set to work rebuilding the hull, while joiners commenced interior alterations and refurbishing. New keelsons, eighty feet long and from four to seven feet thick, were fitted in the hull; the hogframes were extended forward and strengthened aft, and the masts or spars abaft the paddle wheels were rearranged with the addition of a fourth spar. The new spar and the strengthening of the hogframes provided more support for the guards in the area of the boilers. Later, as we shall see, Captain Anderson would find that the rebuilding of the hull was not entirely to his satisfaction. During this overhaul the pilothouse was replaced, the skylights over the dining room removed to afford more space on the main deck, and there was a new entrance to the barroom, which earlier had been relocated in the forward hold. After seven weeks in dry dock she was put back in the water and remained at Allison's throughout the winter.

When the engine was reinstalled, a new cylinder measuring 72 inches in diameter replaced the old one. Fletcher, Harrison & Company consid-

ered this and other improvements to the engine as sufficient reason to change the date on the builder's plate to 1875. The engine bed had been raised so that the machinery now stood higher than before, to decrease the dip of the paddle wheels. When the *Mary Powell* steamed up the river to Rondout on April 29th to be painted, she was anything but eye-pleasing, with newly planked sides, raw timbers and areas of replaced woodwork. Jansen H. Anderson, who knew exactly what his father wanted, had personally supervised all of this work. Captain Anderson had originally estimated that these repairs would cost between $25,000 and $30,000, but afterward the figures were doubled in newspaper accounts.

With a rebuilt hull, a rebuilt engine with a larger cylinder, a refurbished interior and boilers only two years old, the *Mary Powell* entered service in 1875 as a virtually new steamboat. One thing that was not done in the overhaul of 1874-75 was a lengthening of the vessel, but before long the story was abroad that the *Mary Powell* had been lengthened. In 1878 *The Iron Age* attributed to the engine builders, Messrs. Fletcher and Harrison, the information that,

The size of the cylinder was orignally [*sic*] 62 inches, but when the boat was lengthened in 1875, her weight was increased by some 40 tons. As the owners were adverse to

79

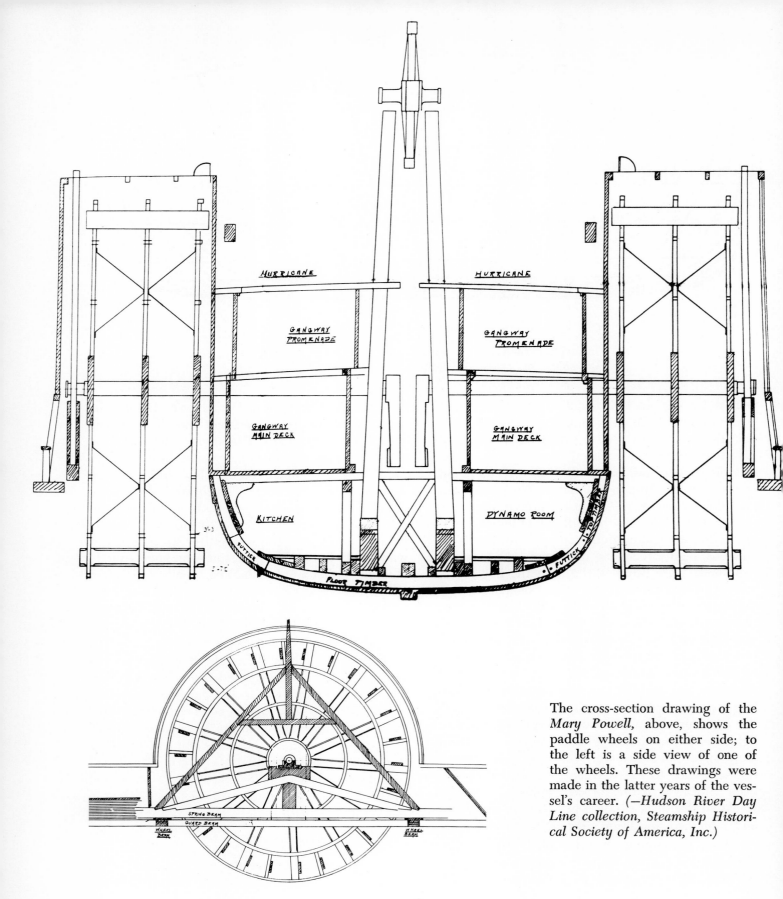

Labels within the drawing: HURRICANE · HURRICANE · GANGWAY PROMENADE · GANGWAY PROMENADE · GANGWAY MAIN DECK · GANGWAY MAIN DECK · KITCHEN · DYNAMO ROOM · FUTTICK · FUTTICK · FLOOR TIMBER · STRING BEAM · GUARD BEAM · WHEEL BEAM · WHEEL BEAM

The cross-section drawing of the *Mary Powell,* above, shows the paddle wheels on either side; to the left is a side view of one of the wheels. These drawings were made in the latter years of the vessel's career. (*—Hudson River Day Line collection, Steamship Historical Society of America, Inc.*)

The photograph at left shows
the center of Rondout, with
South Rondout across the creek
in the background and sailing
craft drying sail along the creek.
Below is a similar view from
a few years later. The piles of
coal have been unloaded from
canalboats onto the D. & H.'s
Island Dock.

The Island Dock with its coal piles was the operational base of the Delaware & Hudson Canal Co., from which the prosperity of Rondout stemmed.

increasing the steam pressure and wished to reduce it somewhat, in spite of the fact that she had new steel boilers, a new cylinder 72 inches in diameter was substituted for the old one. No other change whatever was made in the engine. . . . The boat was lengthened because of her insufficient capacity to accommodate the increase of traffic. The additional displacement is of considerable advantage in passing through shoal water when loaded. . . .[1]

For good reason those associated with the *Mary Powell* made no attempt to correct this tale. It was excellent publicity, for a lengthened steamboat always conveyed the impression of an improved steamboat. Also, as *The Iron Age* stated, a lengthening indicated heavy business on the line and emphasized its popularity. By the 1890s the story was well enshrined in print and has been carried along with considerable consistency ever since.

A few days after the season opened in 1875 Captain Anderson was saddened by the death of his father, Nathan Anderson, Sr., who had staked his future on Rondout so many years before and had been president of the old Rondout village

[1]*The Iron Age,* vol. 21, no. 21 (May 23, 1878).

Board of Trustees. He passed away on June 4th, three weeks short of his 85th birthday. Only four months earlier Captain Charles, once master of the *North America* and the *Robert L. Stevens,* had died in his father's home. Charles had retired from the river to a farm, as good boatmen were supposed to, but in failing health he had moved back to Rondout; he was paralyzed and had not left his room in the four years prior to his death.

On September 11, 1877, the *Mary Powell's* air pump broke when she was above Esopus Island on the northbound run. Chief Engineer Lyman Lawrence and his assistant, Joel N. Hayes, made temporary repairs so that the engine could be operated manually. With the spent steam exhausting loudly into the atmosphere, the steamer literally chuffed over the last few miles to Rondout. With further repairs the vessel left on time the following morning.

Three weeks later, on October 4th, a severe storm broke out before the northbound run and became worse as the day waned. The *Mary Powell* remained at Poughkeepsie until three o'clock in the morning, when the fury of the storm had passed; this was about the same hour that the Rondout night boats, both of which were weather-

The *C. D. Mills* towed the *Mary Powell* to Newburgh for a new hull after the season of 1880. After the work had been done, this same vessel towed her back up to Rondout in the spring for new boilers.

---

bound, also got under way. George W. Murdock, the marine historian, was a fireman on the *Mary Powell* at the time and many years later recalled the incident.

We left New York in a very heavy southeast storm, and coming up the Highlands the wind shifted to the northeast and it was raining and blowing very hard. We neared Poughkeepsie and the blast furnaces near the landing at the foot of Main Street, which usually gave a great deal of light, were almost impossible to see. We nosed in through the storm and got a little above the dock and couldn't see anything. . . . The bow of the *Powell* blew around and she got in the trough of the river. She began to roll and ship water first on her starboard side and then on her port side — all the while drifting down the river. There was danger that she might roll her boilers overboard, but Guernsey finally succeeded in getting her head to the wind

off Blue Point and we returned to Poughkeepsie where we tied up. . . .

The following Wednesday, October 10th, the *Mary Powell* had the lead in a footnote to history when she carried the remains of General George Armstrong Custer from Poughkeepsie to West Point for final interment. The year before, Custer had met his death in the massacre at the Little Big Horn. At Poughkeepsie thousands lined the streets to see the military funeral slowly wend its way to the landing. The casket, draped with the national colors, was placed in the ladies' saloon, and as the *Mary Powell* touched at way landings en route to the Point, passengers coming aboard passed through the ladies' saloon to pay their respects.

At about this time the service offered by the *Mary Powell* was sharpened a bit. It was an-

When the iron-hulled *Albany* appeared in 1880, there was some rivalry between her and the *Mary Powell*. (—*New York State Library*)

After the rebuilding in 1880-81, the *Mary Powell's* forward hurricane deck was open to passengers, as the photograph below shows.

nounced in 1877 that the deckhands would wear uniforms, apparently for the first time, and the officers donned navy caps and blue suits. In March of 1878 the Kingston *Daily Freeman* carried an intriguing item: "A phonograph is to be placed on each deck and in each saloon of the *Mary Powell* to inform 'passengers who have not settled their fare to step up to the purser's office,' and to call out: 'After gangway for Newburgh!' or whichever landing the boat is about to stop at." So far as we know, this experiment was never tried, although it was proposed well over half a century before the use of the loudspeaker on Hudson River day boats. On June 5, 1878, Captain Anderson initiated a new program to lure one-day excursionists from the upriver landings. He had arranged with the operators of the excursion boats *Rosedale* and *Idlewild* to have one of these vessels stop at the *Mary Powell's* Vestry Street landing shortly after she arrived in the morning and take these pleasure seekers on to that mecca of joy, Coney Island, for a couple of hours or more. Tickets for the river passage and the Coney Island jaunt were readily available on the *Mary Powell*.

That year on June 20th Walt Whitman sailed up the Hudson to West Park, almost across the river from Hyde Park, to spend a few days at the home of his friend John Burroughs, the naturalist and author. Wrote Whitman:

> On the *Mary Powell,* enjoy'd everything beyond precedent. The delicious tender summer day, just warm enough — the constantly changing but ever beautiful panorama on both sides of the river — (went up near a hundred miles) — the high straight walls of the stony Palisades — beautiful Yonkers, and beautiful Irvington — the never-ending hills, mostly in rounded lines, swathed with verdure, — the distant turns, like great shoulders in blue veils — the frequent gray and brown of the tall-rising rocks — the river itself, now narrowing, now expanding — the white sails of the many sloops, yachts, &c., some near, some in the distance — the rapid succession of handsome villages and cities, (our boat is a swift traveler, and makes few stops) — the Race — picturesque West Point, and indeed all along — the costly and often turreted mansions forever showing in some cheery

light color, through the woods — make up the scene.[2]

Some time later another literary personage traveled aboard the *Mary Powell*. In August of 1882 Oscar Wilde, on his American lecture tour, took passage on her from New York to Cranston's (formerly Cozzens') hotel landing. The passengers were not at all modest in their determination to get a good look at the young man, then 27 years old, and at one point so many people rushed to one side of the vessel to see him that the *Mary Powell* listed far over. Although we have no record of Captain Anderson's remarks about his unusual passenger, we do have a description by a Kingston hotel proprietor who was aboard that day and, when he heard that Wilde was embarking, stationed himself so that he could get a good look. Said he,

> . . . why I thought it was an Injun squaw coming aboard. He had hair like a horse's mane, way down his back, and his face was the color of [mahogany]. . . .
>
> He had on a fuzzy grey coat with a flannel shirt tied with a green ribbon, . . . and he had on white trousers and smoked a cigarette. . . .
>
> Queer, but dear God you should have seen his mouth. . . . He's the awfullest teeth. I tell you . . . he's a regular man tiger.[3]

Not many days after Walt Whitman's journey on the *Mary Powell*, she was running late in the fog on the southbound trip and got off course in a shoal area near New Hamburg. There was an initial jar, and then her momentum carried her back into deeper water, but the bottom of the hull had been forced up fleetingly, loosening some of the rods from the spars. The incident created a flurry of excitement among the passengers, and after the vessel landed she was inspected for leakage and then continued to New York.

The following year, 1879, at the beginning of September on a northbound run the port paddlewheel shaft was found to be running hot, and an inspection, after the *Mary Powell* landed at Pough-

---

[2] Walt Whitman, *Specimen Days & Collect* (Philadelphia, Pa.: Rees Welsh & Co., 1882-83), p. 114.

[3] Kingston *Daily Freeman*, August 4, 1882.

keepsie, disclosed a crack in the shaft just inside the spring bearing. After a thorough examination it was decided that the vessel could proceed to Rondout. In fact, Chief Engineer Lawrence and Assistant Hayes felt it would be only a slight gamble to finish the season before replacing the shaft, but they were overruled by the captain, who wanted to hear the verdict of Mr. Fletcher, the engine builder, before making a decision. Captain Anderson telegraphed Alfred Van Santvoord to inquire if the New York-Albany Day Line's spare boat, the *Armenia*, were available for chartering. The latter replied that the vessel, then in Albany, was at Captain Anderson's disposal, and the captain sent Mate Bishop and Second Engineer Hayes up to Albany on the next train to bring the steamer down to Rondout. While the *Mary Powell* was fitted with a new shaft at the works of John Roach on the East River, the *Armenia* covered her route, making all the regular landings, for ten days. Her charter cost Captain Anderson $150 a day, or $1,500 in all, proving that the captain's concern for the safety of his vessel and her passengers was a principle he would not lightly abandon.

By the summer of 1880 the *Mary Powell* was ready for her third and final major overhaul during this period of Captain Anderson's ownership. In July he contracted with McEntee & Dillon of Rondout for a new pair of steel boilers; the present set was still in excellent condition but had been designed for use with the 62-inch cylinder, which was replaced in 1875 by one ten inches greater in diameter. The new boilers would be larger and heavier, and to offset this Captain Anderson planned to remove all the oak timbers in the frame of the hull and replace them with lighter butternut. He believed that butternut was stronger and more durable than oak, and it might even produce a vessel lighter than ever.

In September, while he had men searching throughout the country for seasoned butternut, the captain announced that the hull work would be done in Newburgh at the shipyard of Ward, Stanton & Company, which would enlarge its marine railway to accommodate the *Mary Powell*. He felt that a sectional dry dock, such as Allison's, was not the proper place for a vessel undergoing extensive hull work because one of the sections might leak and settle more than the others, throwing the hull out of line. Indeed, Captain Anderson claimed that this had happened while his steamboat was in Allison's dry dock in 1874; the twist in the hull was so slight that only Allison and Captain Anderson were aware of it, but that was enough to worry the captain. Also, once Allison's men had taken the planking off, they had been afraid to remove the timbers that needed replacing and had simply put new ones in alongside. Now all of this useless weight could be eliminated.

After the 1880 season ended, the *Mary Powell* was stripped at Rondout; her furniture, boilers, smokestacks and the buckets on the paddle wheels were removed, and Captain Anderson's stockpile of butternut was loaded on board. Then on November 17th the steamboat was towed to Newburgh. The next day Captain Anderson and Jansen were interviewed aboard the *Mary Powell* by a reporter. The captain said he would spend between $10,000 and $15,000 on replacing timbers in the hull and altering the hogframes, and of course the boilers would cost about $20,000. He would not hesitate to spend a few hundred or a few thousand beyond this to improve the vessel as a family boat, since "it is a matter of pride with me to make this vessel retain her superiority as an airy, comfortable and fast boat. . . ."[4]

Captain Thomas S. Marvel of Ward, Stanton & Company was in charge of hauling out the *Mary Powell* on the marine railway on the morning of November 19th. A crowd gathered to watch, for she was the largest vessel ever to be hauled out at Newburgh. However, the affair was unsuccessful: toward midafternoon a bolt in a pillow block of the railway's gearing broke, loosening the chain attached to the vessel, and the *Mary Powell* slid back into the river, just as side tackle was about to be fastened to her in case such an accident took place. Eight days later Captain Marvel again began hauling her out, this time taking every precaution, and the operation was smoothly completed. There was no need to rush the hull work, for the *Mary Powell* would stay on the marine railway all winter. She was finally put back in the water on April 9th and towed to

---

[4]Newburgh *Daily Journal*, November 18, 1880.

The silhouette of the lady with the bustle on the promenade deck echoes the Goddess of Liberty atop the pilothouse in this photograph taken some time after the *Mary Powell's* 1880-81 overhaul.

Rondout to have the new boilers installed. How much the repairs and alterations cost can only be guessed at from newspaper accounts, which placed the figure at about $50,000.

The external appearance of the vessel had not changed much. The forward hurricane deck had been strengthened and was now open to passengers. Since arch frames had been fitted into the hull with their crowns in the area of the boilers, the hogframes had been shortened and otherwise altered. The guards had been rebuilt, and the arms of the paddle wheels were lengthened to maintain the proper dip of the buckets with the lightened hull. Internally, the dining room and the barroom, both of which were still in the hold, had been rebuilt and floored with yellow pine that had been stained with dragon's blood and shellacked. The single large dining table had been replaced by small tables seating four persons each. The new carpeting in the ladies' saloon was Ax-minster, while in the main saloon there was new English Brussels carpeting; some of Mr. Van Santvoord's black walnut chairs were replaced with long red-plush seats, and the main stairway to the upper saloon was moved aft and rebuilt.

To maintain the trim of a vessel, chain boxes — literally boxes filled with heavy chain — were usually moved from one side of the main deck to the other. During this overhaul Jansen Anderson devised a system of water tanks for ballast, located on the guards and controlled from the pilothouse. In this way the *Mary Powell* reportedly became the first Hudson River steamboat to dispense with the old chain boxes. For safety equipment the *Mary Powell* now carried 1,200 life preservers, three metal lifeboats, six rafts and two inflated pontoons. In addition, the interior doors were arranged so that they could be lifted from their hinges and thrown overboard to serve as life rafts.

87

The *Americus,* in a drawing by James Bard, competed briefly with the *Mary Powell* in 1882. (—*Eldredge collection, courtesy of The Mariners Museum*)

In 1880 the New York-Albany Day Line, which was now corporately known as the Hudson River Line, had placed in service a new steamboat, the *Albany.* Breaking with established Hudson River tradition, she had an iron hull and three boilers athwartships in the hold, although her engine was of the standard vertical beam design. Unlike the *Mary Powell,* which did not hold to a schedule on the northbound trip, the Day Line steamers adhered strictly to a timetable, and so there was no opportunity to demonstrate the *Albany's* speed except on short spurts between landings. After the close of the 1880 season the new steamboat deadheaded from New York to lay up in Albany, and the company took advantage of the opportunity to show her speed, at least as far as Poughkeepsie. As with most fast steamboat runs, the bedrock facts in this case are hard to determine, but it seems that the *Albany,* running with only invited guests aboard, bettered the fastest time that the *Mary Powell* had made over the same distance with passengers on a regular trip. The Hudson Valley had already been polarized into two camps in the feud over whether the *Mary Powell* or the *Albany* was the faster, and this fast run by the latter only added fresh fuel to the fire.

The following season, 1881, the rebuilt *Mary Powell* made two fast runs in June. The newspa-

pers, devoting columns of space to the rivalry, now worked themselves up to the point of almost guaranteeing that there would be a race between the two steamers after the close of their operating seasons. The captain of the *Albany* had no qualms about stating that his vessel could make at least 28 miles per hour, but his chief engineer was reported to have advised betting on the *Mary Powell.* Just like the sweepstakes of 1864, this race was never held, but the publicity had been splendid for both the Hudson River Line and Captain Anderson. Neither of them was about to inhibit all this speculation with a race that would have proven one boat over the other. But if there had been a race, very probably the losing captain could have shown conclusively that he had won.

The 1882 season was not a happy one for Captain Anderson: shortly before it began his eldest son, Jansen, died at the age of 38, leaving a widow and five children. As the purser or second captain of the *Mary Powell,* Jansen had for years been groomed by his father to succeed him. Now Captain Absalom, who reportedly was not in the best of health, would be seventy in November and there was no one to follow in his wake. Soon the rumor grew that someone in Poughkeepsie had approached the captain about buying the *Mary Powell;* Captain Anderson denied it, saying that

88

the public, with Jansen's death fresh in its mind, had reached the erroneous conclusion that he wanted to sell his steamboat. When asked if he had perhaps received an offer from a Rondout steamboat owner, he replied, "Well — I don't care to answer that question. A certain party did make me an offer, but it was low so that I would not entertain it for a moment."[5]

The captain's lot was not made any easier when opposition came to the route of the *Mary Powell* in the late summer of that year. Handbills distributed in Poughkeepsie and Newburgh announced that the steamboat *Americus,* a smart little excursion vessel, would provide service from Poughkeepsie at 5:30 a.m. and from New York at 3:30 p.m., starting September 11th. The most startling feature of the new operation was the fare; under the heading "Anti-Monopoly Columbian Line," the rates were set down as ten cents between any upriver landing and New York, in either direction. Breakfast was served from 7 to 10 a.m. and dinner from 5 to 8 p.m., and the price was thirty cents per meal. (The round-trip fare with meals included was eighty cents, but this did not represent a saving.) Freight would be carried at half of what the monopolies charged. All of these particulars concerning the Columbian Line were signed by "Father Columbia, Manager." The line was supposedly the operation of a secret order then known as the Sons of Columbia, which claimed a national membership of 800,000.

Actually, the *Americus* was chartered by Walter H. Shupe, who was possessed with the compulsion to break what he considered were the great steamboat monopolies on the Hudson River. Apparently he did not think of Captain Anderson as a giant monopolist, for he claimed that his opposition to the *Mary Powell* was only the beginning of an experiment which would be followed by New York-Albany opposition. If sucessful, then in the next year would come a monopoly-breaker from New Orleans to the head of navigation on the Mississippi, and from Buffalo to the upper Great Lakes. The manager of the *Americus,* R. Cornell White, claimed to have no knowledge of Shupe's background; as far as he was concerned, the *Americus* would run only so long as Mr. Shupe

paid for her use on a daily basis. One man in White's organization was more outspoken: he said Shupe was crazy.

Although it was raining hard on September 11th, about sixty passengers were aboard the *Americus* as she departed from Poughkeepsie on her first run. After all, one couldn't go to New York every day for ten cents! Neither could the *Americus,* and on the third day of the opposition she faded from the scene. She was succeeded by another vessel, which kept the opposition warm for only a few days more. Shupe was being hard pressed by his creditors and, as one wag of the day put it, ". . . is not a-meri-cus any longer."

On October 23rd, the last trip of the long 1882 season, the *Mary Powell* was loudly saluted as she steamed up the river. The next day she flew her colors at half-mast to honor an old friend of the captain's who had passed away, but in truth she might have been mourning Captain Anderson himself, for he had made his last trip in command.

At the moment he was contemplating a voyage to Europe for his health, but rumors about the sale of the *Mary Powell* were soon flying again. It was reliably reported that the "certain party" in Rondout and the Poughkeepsian who had approached the captain in June — Thomas Cornell and Captain John H. Brinckerhoff, respectively — were still interested in the vessel and had made offers. To investigate this the Kingston *Daily Freeman* sent a reporter to visit Captain Anderson; the article was published in the November 16th issue.

. . . Captain Anderson's wife said her husband was quite ill with a cold and could not be seen. She said she had heard that a report was being circulated that the *Powell* had been sold, but of course it could not be true or her husband would have told her. But to make sure she retired for a moment to consult with him, and when she returned she said, "I asked Captain Anderson and he said, 'eh?'" She also said her husband had been confined to the house for three days past, being afflicted with a severe cough.

Of course the denial of the rumor by Captain Anderson leaves no doubt of its untruthfulness, but if the boat be not actually sold, we have reasons to believe that Captain Anderson has been made a second offer, which may even yet be under consideration.

[5]Kingston *Daily Freeman*, June 9, 1882.

Endicott & Co.'s last *Mary Powell* lithograph, appeared in 1882.

OLD CHAIN FERRY BOAT, RIVERSIDE, RONDOUT AND PORT EWEN FERRY, KINGSTON, N. Y.

The diminutive *Riverside*, which for decades plied between Rondout and Sleightsburg, bore the nickname "Skillypot." (*—Kingston Souvenir Co.*)

This "denial" caused some discussion, particularly in another newspaper, and the next day the *Freeman* stated that it had made an "absurd error," that the crux of the item should have read, "*I asked Captain Anderson and he said, 'No!'*" Since the other paper said that it had been assured by a most reliable source that Cornell had purchased the *Mary Powell*, the *Freeman* included with this correction the definite denial of the sale by both A. Eltinge Anderson and Thomas Cornell. But in fact it was apparently on this same day, November 17th, that Captain Anderson sold the *Mary Powell* to Cornell for $100,000.

In addition to the death of Jansen and the captain's own advancing years, perhaps he felt impelled to sell before the completion of the New York, West Shore & Buffalo Railway, which would pass through important landings on the west bank of the river: West Point, Cornwall, New-burgh and Kingston. It was later said that the captain feared that this line, opened to Albany in 1883, would have a disastrous effect on the *Mary Powell's* passenger traffic. At any rate, Captain Anderson retired permanently and the next year purchased a home, Stonehedge, near Santa Barbara, California.

Not long after he left the river, a newspaper article said of him,

The captain was a model officer, possessing the courtesy of a finished gentleman, with an energy and alertness that made itself felt in every subordinate, and infused his spirit and personality into the entire management of the craft. His love for the beautiful steamer he commanded was something pathetic and affecting. To him she was a living, sentient thing which held in his heart a place akin to that of a petted child. She seemed almost as much a part of him as he did of her. . . .

Schell and Hogan drew this picture, entitled "The Newburgh Centennial," for the *Harper's Weekly* issue of October 27, 1883. It is rather obvious which vessel most impressed the artists. *(—Courtesy of James R. Dufty)*

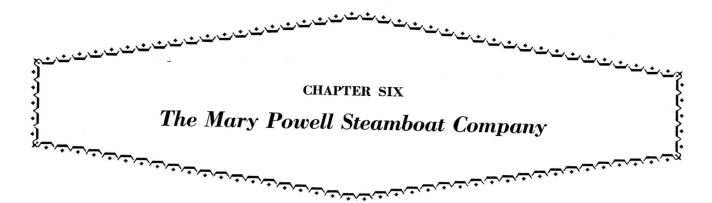

CHAPTER SIX

The Mary Powell Steamboat Company

Soon after Thomas Cornell acquired the *Mary Powell* in 1882, a rumor sprang up that he had bought her primarily to run with his Ulster & Delaware Railroad to the Catskill Mountain resorts, with departures from New York at 1 p.m. So, just as he had done when he first purchased the steamboat in 1865, Cornell wrote the newspapers a letter to set the record straight; in this case the recipient was the Kingston *Daily Freeman*, which prefaced the publication of the letter by saying,

> To-day we received from Hon. Thomas Cornell the following comprehensive communication, which sets aside all idle rumors that are being circulated, and gives the true version of the matter, in the writer's own terse and business like way, and which admits of no comment. . . .

> *Editor Freeman:*

> Dear Sir: — Capt. Wm. H. Cornell has taken charge of the steamer *Mary Powell*. It is expected that the *Mary Powell* will run on the same route and at the same hours from Rondout and New York as last season. . . . Whoever has been circulating the report that the *Mary Powell* would leave New York at 1 o'clock has been meddling with other people's business without authority.

> Truly yours,

> Thomas Cornell

> Rondout, Dec. 4, 1882.

William H. Cornell — "Captain Billy" — was the same man who had been second captain or purser of the *Mary Powell* during the previous Cornell ownership and was Thomas Cornell's cousin, 51 years old and a lifelong bachelor. He had been master of the night boat *Thomas Cornell* in March

of 1882, when she ran aground on Danskammer Point in a fog about five miles above Newburgh. She was so badly damaged in this grounding that she was later dismantled.

Twice in 1882 Captain John H. Brinckerhoff had dickered with Captain Anderson for the *Mary Powell* before he finally lost out to Cornell. Not a man to give up easily, he was soon in contact with Cornell about buying a share of the vessel; the latter offered him three-tenths and afterward agreed to sell 34%, or a third, for $34,000, in keeping with the steamboat's sale price of $100,000. On January 22, 1883, in return for cash and a note Cornell wrote Brinckerhoff a receipt for this share in the ownership, with title to be given "hereafter," and on the following day he prepared a similar receipt for Captain Billy covering payment for 12% of the shares. In both cases, interest on the net cost of the shares was calculated from the original sale date of November 17th. Later in January Cornell had the *Mary Powell* re-enrolled to show the change in ownership resulting from Captain Anderson's sale of the vessel.

After acquiring his 34% Brinckerhoff consulted with Cornell about selling still more of the shares, this time to Captain Isaac C. Wickes. Both Wickes and Brinckerhoff had been involved with the Poughkeepsie Transportation Company, which operated the beam-engined propeller night boats *Daniel S. Miller* and *John L. Hasbrouck*. As captain of the latter — which had been named for one of the original owners of the *Mary Powell* — Wickes had been a stockholder in the organization, and when he sold out, Brinckerhoff had ac-

The *Thomas Cornell* ended her active career when she ran high up on Danskammer Point in a fog. She was floated, dismantled and her hull made into two large barges.

quired his stock; by 1883 Brinckerhoff had become the company's treasurer. Whether or not Cornell did agree with Brinckerhoff to sell Wickes an interest in the *Mary Powell* cannot be determined, but Wickes seems to have bought in at about this time, either from Cornell's or from Brinckerhoff's holdings. Apparently when Cornell first learned of Wickes' intentions, he implied that he might consider selling out entirely, but that step was not for the immediate future.

When the *Mary Powell* went into commission in 1883 without Captain Absalom Anderson, another familiar face that was missing in the crew was that of the celebrated pilot, Guernsey Betts. Either Betts decided he did not want to work for Thomas Cornell, or Cornell would not hire him. The new chief pilot on the *Mary Powell* in 1883 was Hiram G. Briggs, formerly first pilot on Romer & Tremper's *James W. Baldwin;* piloting the latter was Betts. Eltinge Anderson remained aboard the *Mary Powell* as purser, along with Chief Engineer Lawrence, Second Engineer Hayes and Mate Bishop, who continued as assistant pilot. Incidentally, in December of 1881 Eltinge married Fannie V. Elmore, and by November of 1883 they

had a son, called Absalom Lent after his distinguished grandfather.

The *Mary Powell's* first trip with passengers under the new Cornell ownership came on Saturday, May 19, 1883, when she took the Eastman National Business College excursion to New York; the trip included a look at the fine, new Brooklyn Bridge. When the steamer landed at West 22nd Street floral pieces were brought aboard and placed in the main saloon; as a gift from Captain and Mrs. Isaac Wickes Captain William Cornell received a horseshoe of flowers, and Purser Anderson was presented with a basket of roses.

On this excursion Pilot Briggs lost no time in establishing himself aboard the *Mary Powell.* Since this was his first working trip on the steamboat with passengers aboard, one might suppose that he would have wanted to concentrate on familiarizing himself with the handling of the vessel, but an account of the Eastman excursion included the following:

Many of the excursionists availed themselves of the kind invitation of the genial Pilot Briggs to view the handsome scenery

94

from his cosy pilot house, and enroll their names in his new register of distinguished names. This is a favorite resort for young people who desire a secluded spot, supposing that Pilot Briggs being closely engaged on the lookout in front will not notice their affectionate gestures nor hear the soft nothings of cooing couples, forgetting his reflector gave him full view of all.[1]

The happy days when passengers had the run of the pilothouse on Hudson River steamboats were ended the following season by new legislation. On the *Mary Powell*, at least, the passengers were assured that this ruling reflected no complaint on the part of her officers.

Mary Irving Husted's memories of Pilot Briggs are set down in *Hudson River Children*, her recollections of a childhood in the 1880s at a country home below Milton.[2] On the Fourth of July rockets and Roman candles would be placed on the terrace, and the little girls would climb out on the piazza roof to listen for the sound of the *Mary Powell's* paddle wheels as she came up the river. When the vessel passed by, off went the fireworks in a great barrage, and the excited girls would almost fall off the roof as their friend Pilot Briggs responded with three stately blasts on the whistle. All along the stream, showers of pyrotechnic stars and burning red lights marked her northbound holiday passage, and she always acknowledged them with a salute.

The regular 1883 season ran its course, marred only by a breakdown on the October 2nd southbound run: the *Mary Powell's* routine was disturbed when a loud and unfamiliar *click* was heard in the engineering department. The crosshead gib had broken, and the engine was stopped immediately. After an inspection it was decided to proceed slowly to Milton and drop off the passengers, who could continue their journey to New York by rail. The steamboat returned to Rondout for repairs, and service was resumed the next morning. After the regular season closed, the

<hr>

[1]Kingston *Daily Freeman*, May 21, 1883.

[2]Mary Irving Husted, *Hudson River Children* (Boston and New York: Bruce Humphries, Inc., 1943).

Mary Powell carried a Grand Army of the Republic excursion to Newburgh on October 18th for that city's part in the Revolutionary Centennial celebration; Newburgh had been George Washington's headquarters in the last days of the war.

The continuing negotiations between Thomas Cornell and John H. Brinckerhoff culminated in March, 1884, with the sale of Cornell's remaining interest in the *Mary Powell*; Brinckerhoff was joined in the purchase by Isaac Wickes and Eltinge Anderson. In May the owners of the vessel incorporated as the Mary Powell Steamboat Company, capitalized at $150,000, with the officers and their approximate shares in the steamboat as follows: Isaac C. Wickes, one-quarter, president; Captain William H. Cornell, one-eighth, vice-president; A. Eltinge Anderson, one-eighth, secretary; and John H. Brinckerhoff, who with one-half had the largest investment to protect, treasurer.

Before the season started, the *Mary Powell* had been fitted out in April with new smokestacks, and davits were installed for the lifeboats. Her first passengers that year were the Vassarites on an excursion to West Point, and on May 24th she made her first trip in regular service for the Mary Powell Steamboat Company. On August 11th the captain of the steam canalboat *City of Troy*, which had been lying at Hyde Park, decided to get under way just before the *Mary Powell* came in on her northbound trip, even though he had been told that the passenger vessel was due. As the bow of the *City of Troy* was worked out, the ebb tide caught it and pulled the canaller around until she was crossway in the stream. When the pilot of the *Mary Powell* saw her position he put the wheel hard over, but the *City of Troy* struck the steamboat near the after gangway. The canalboat had split a plank in her bow and was beached on the shore before she sank. That night the *Mary Powell* did not land in Rondout until after ten o'clock.

The vessel made a postseason excursion to Albany on October 15th, leaving Newburgh about 8:15 a.m., making way landings and carrying about 810 passengers. She created a minor sensation in Albany, since the *Mary Powell* had not been seen there since she filled in for the *Chauncey Vibbard* on the New York-Albany Day Line

Because of the departure time from Rondout, photographs of the *Mary Powell* bound out the creek are rare. This one was taken in the early 1880s, perhaps 1883. (—*Dr. Charles A. Galyon collection*)

At right, lying together at Poughkeepsie are the night boats *John L. Hasbrouck*, left, and the *Daniel S. Miller*.

Above the *Daniel S. Miller,* running mate of the *John L. Hasbrouck,* poses for her picture with her officers and crew in suitable positions.

The *John L. Hasbrouck,* depicted on p. 43 in her earlier days, became a more orthodox-looking night boat on the Poughkeepsie-New York route. Here she is caught firmly in the ice, and some passengers are amusing themselves on the frozen river.

When the Prohibitionists decorated the *Mary Powell*, in addition to American flags on the main deck forward they also tied one securely to the Goddess of Liberty. (*—Dr. Charles A. Galyon collection*)

in 1871. These Albany excursions would become a regular annual activity of the *Mary Powell.* Two days later she carried the Prohibitionists to a party rally in New York to greet their candidate for president, ex-Governor John P. St. John of Kansas. On this occasion banners reading, "Hurrah for St. John and Daniel" and "More School Houses and No Saloons," were tied to the railings about the upper decks of the vessel.

Between the seasons of 1884 and 1885 Eltinge Anderson devoted considerable time to preparing a pamphlet, *Guide Book of Steamer "Mary Powell" Describing Summer Homes along the Famous Hudson,* which was published for the 1885 season by the Mary Powell Steamboat Company. Designed to promote business, it set forth the attractions of the route and the summering resorts to be reached by the *Mary Powell;* this annual guide was issued for about thirty years.

The 1885 season was Captain William Cornell's last in command of the *Mary Powell,* for at the

end of the year he announced the sale of his share in the vessel to Eltinge Anderson. At the same time it was announced that Anderson had purchased part of Brinckerhoff's holdings and would succeed Captain Cornell as master in 1886. Young Anderson was already one up on his predecessors, since he had gained some sort of fame by having had a steamboat named after him. True, she was not much of a steamboat, measuring only slightly over 42 feet in length, but she carried the name *Eltinge Anderson.* Built in 1882, she was operated by the Haber Steamboat Company, which ran small vessels, or "yachts," in the passenger trade from Rondout up the creek to the head of tidewater at Eddyville or to near-by landings on the Hudson. This company provided a connection with the *Mary Powell,* and at one time or another both Eltinge Anderson and his father had been stockholders in the organization.

Captain Eltinge Anderson's luck temporarily deserted him on Saturday, May 22nd, the first day

The Pennsylvania Railroad's ferryboat *New Brunswick*
and the *Mary Powell* had a very minor collision on
May 21, 1885. Both vessels lived to run another day.
(*—Courtesy of The Mariners Museum*)

of the regular 1886 season. On the up trip near Yonkers Chief Engineer Joel N. Hayes noticed that something was amiss in his department and soon discovered that a pin in the walking beam had worked loose and was running hot. The problem was serious, because if this pin broke, the links to the crosshead on the piston rod would be released and the piston would drop and damage the cylinder. Captain Eltinge had either inherited his father's caution or had it ground into him, particularly in matters where a lack of caution might increase the annual expenditures. The steamer was slowed and lay some time at Cranston's, the first landing, so that she had a late arrival at Rondout. Accounts vary as to what the captain actually did, but apparently he sent for a machinist from the Morgan Iron Works in New York, who examined the pin and pronounced it safe. This verdict evidently did not satisfy Eltinge, for he had the pin removed from the walking beam for a microscopic examination. The pin either passed the test and was reset or failed and

was replaced, but in any event the Monday trip had to be cancelled, and Captain Eltinge Anderson was applauded in the press for maintaining the family tradition of safety and thoughtfulness.

In deference to the growing custom of making Saturday a half holiday, the New York departure time on that day was moved up an hour in June. Then it was announced that on Sunday — yes, Sunday — July 25th, the *Mary Powell* would inaugurate a "series" of Sunday excursions to New York, with Coney Island as an attraction. She would leave Rondout at 6 a.m., landing only at Poughkeepsie, New Hamburg and Newburgh, and arrive back in Rondout about 8:30 p.m. The advertising pointed out that here was an opportunity for everybody to have a fine sail and enjoy the sea breeze, since many laborers and businessmen could not take such an outing on the steamer's weekday passages.

Advertising lures notwithstanding, it appears that these Sunday excursions were frowned upon in some quarters. What was probably only the

The *J. C. Hartt,* named for an officer of the Delaware & Hudson Canal Co., was a large propeller tugboat designed to replace the big side-wheelers in handling tows. Built for the Cornell Steamboat Co. in 1883, she and her proud crew pose in Rondout Creek off the Cornell shops, with Sleightsburg in the background. In the spring of 1884, the *J. C. Hartt* towed the *Mary Powell* back from Brooklyn, where the passenger vessel had gone for dry-docking.

(—*Herman F. Boyle collection*)

At right is the cover from the first of the *Mary Powell's* guidebooks, the one prepared by Eltinge Anderson.

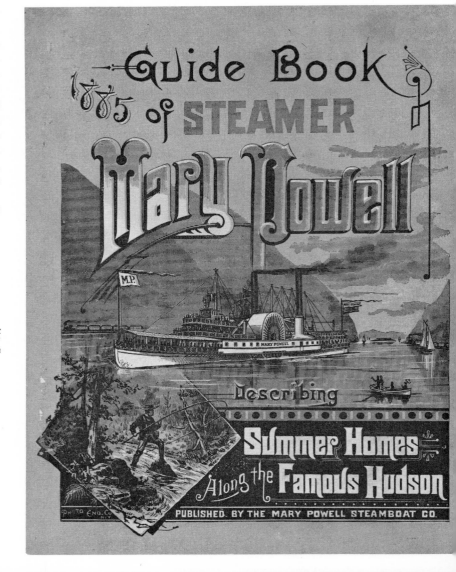

1885 Guide Book of STEAMER Mary Powell

Describing

Summer Homes Along the Famous Hudson

PUBLISHED BY THE MARY POWELL STEAMBOAT CO.

This advertisement is for the 1885 excursion to Albany.

second excursion took place on August 22nd, and that afternoon a report circulated in Kingston that the *Mary Powell* had been sunk in a collision with another steamer near New York and that the loss of life was great. The story rocked Kingston like a dynamite explosion: people ran aimlessly about in search of news, and scores crowded into the newspaper offices. Those who had friends aboard waited with tear-filled eyes. Eventually it became clear that the whole thing was a rumor, and with an enormous sense of relief a great crowd gathered in Rondout to greet the *Mary Powell* and welcome the excursionists, who were completely unaware of the apprehension that had been felt for them. Captain Eltinge Anderson had first heard the disaster report when the *Mary Powell* reached Poughkeepsie and was so agitated that he offered a reward of $100 for the arrest of the person who had started the story. However, the rumor was not sufficiently awe-inspiring to end Sunday excursions entirely, although they were such a minute part of her operations that many later accounts often emphasize that the *Mary Powell* never carried a paying passenger on the Lord's day.

Ten days after the 1886 season ended, on October 28th the *Mary Powell* left Rondout about 7 a.m. to go to the unveiling of the Statue of Liberty. A noble turnout of steamboats was on hand for the great event on this, Bartholdi Day, and many excursions were advertised in the New York papers. In the *Herald* the notice for the *Mary Powell* stood out, for it consisted of only four bold lines:

THE STATUE OF LIBERTY

STEAMER MARY POWELL

LEAVES WEST 22D ST. 1:45 P.M.

FARE, 75 CENTS. MUSIC.

On the other hand, the *Magnolia* devoted ten lines of fine print to assuring the ladies and gentlemen who wished to avoid the crush that she was the steamer on which to go; tickets for her, on sale at such places as the Fifth Avenue Hotel, were said to be strictly limited, and no doubt they were, since they sold for two dollars.

After the unveiling the *Mary Powell* steamed back to Rondout. Captain Eltinge Anderson's first

With the "skyline" of Manhattan behind her, the *Mary Powell* sets forth for Rondout with awnings on her sunny side shielding passengers from overexposure to Sol. For reasons unknown, her flags fly at half-staff.

Below, she has not a flag raised as she speeds by the Palisades for New York. (—*Above, N. L. Stebbins photograph, Society for the Preservation of New England Antiquities*)

The youthful Captain A. Eltinge Anderson displays a necktie of gigantic dimensions and the indispensable watch chain.

season in command had ended on a memorable note, and he had won the respect of his crew, who presented him with an engraved Knights Templar watch charm or badge on the last regular run of the year.

The steamboat spent the winter of 1886-87 at Newburgh, where new paddle boxes were built for her; these were larger than the old ones and gave about 15 inches of additional clearance around the wheels. Since the *Mary Powell* was berthed in the basin of the Pennsylvania Coal Company, Captain Anderson and his crew had to come down in April to rescue her from the clouds of dirt and coal dust that filled the air as the barges were loaded in the spring. She was towed to Rondout for painting and other details of preparation.

On the opening day of the regular season that year fortune did not smile any more brightly than

in 1886. Not long after leaving New Hamburg on the southbound run the *Mary Powell* was proceeding at slow speed in a fog near Low Point, when her pilot heard the whistle of the *M. Martin*, of Romer & Tremper's Newburgh-Albany day line, and signalled to stop the engine. As the two vessels came in sight of each other, the pilot of the *M. Martin* blew two short blasts for a starboard-to-starboard passing, but the pilot of the *Mary Powell*, feeling it was impossible for her to take such a course, blew one blast. At the same time both pilots rang full astern, but a collision was inevitable. The bow of the *M. Martin* tore into the *Mary Powell* forward of the port paddle box, ripping out a portion of the guard and crushing in the side of the barbershop, which was immediately ahead of the paddle box. Luckily the barber stepped out on deck when he heard the cross signal, or he might have become a casualty. The damage to the *M. Martin* was insignificant.

Her captain, Zachariah Roosa, and Captain Anderson politely exchanged offers of assistance, both refusing, and the two steamboats then continued on their respective ways. The *Mary Powell* could have continued to New York, but Captain Anderson was reluctant to have her make her first appearance of the regular season with a big hole in her side. After she landed at Newburgh he checked with the T. S. Marvel & Company shipyard about having the damage repaired at once, and when Captain Marvel and Mr. James H. Case, the joinerwork contractor, decided that this was possible, the passengers were disembarked to proceed by rail if they so desired. Early the next morning the repaired *Mary Powell* left Newburgh for Rondout, arriving there about 3:30 a.m. to begin the southbound run two hours later.

After the 1887 season the *Mary Powell* again wintered at Newburgh, where Captain Anderson planned to have several major changes made in her superstructure, and in the hands of Mr. Case she was indeed transformed.

In 1880 the New York-Albany Day Line's steamers had introduced dining rooms on the main deck aft, which proved to be a popular feature, since this location was cooler on hot days than a dining room in the hold and passengers could eat without missing any of the scenery. Accord-

In government service during the Civil War, the *M. Martin* once carried President Lincoln. Below, the Haber Steamboat Co.'s little *Charles A. Shultz* has been carried by a spring freshet from winter quarters onto the dike near the creek's mouth. (*—Both, Herman F. Boyle collection*)

The diminutive *Eltinge Anderson* had a name too long for her nameboards on the pilothouse but not for the large name flag at the stern. At left, the *Silas O. Pierce*, lying at Rondout, towed the *Mary Powell* up from winter quarters at Newburgh in 1887. (*—Above, Herman F. Boyle collection*)

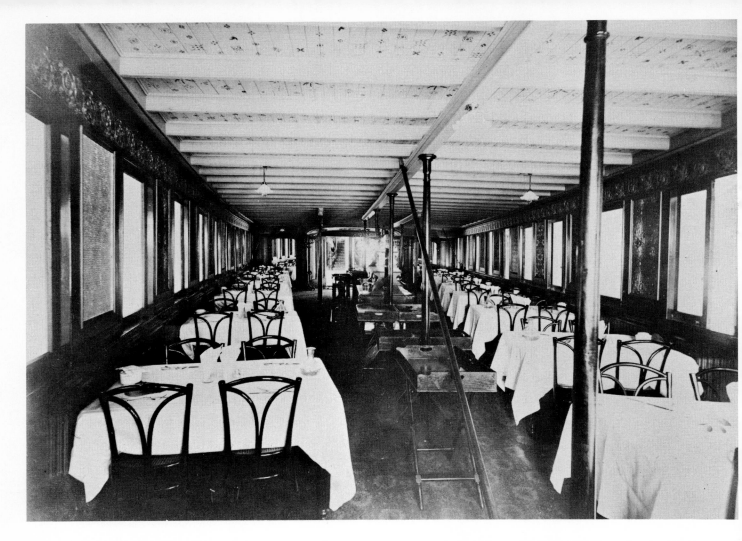

The dining room was moved to the ladies' saloon on the main deck aft. This view looks forward to the grand stairway. Running down diagonally in the foreground is a support tie rod from one of the spars.

ingly the ladies' saloon on the main deck aft on the *Mary Powell* was rebuilt into a dining room, with trimmings of mahogany, olive and whitewood and with a decorated ceiling. The bottoms of the new plate-glass windows were low enough to afford a fine view, and between the windows were panels of hammered brass and silver and various patterns of Lincrusta-Walton. At the forward end of the dining room a doorway seven feet wide opened onto the quarterdeck; large mirrors flanked the door on either side.

To provide more space on the quarterdeck for passengers coming aboard or waiting to disembark, the two baggage rooms in this area were torn out and replaced with a cloak and baggage room in what had been the entrance to the dining room in the hold, and the stairway to the main saloon was moved forward. On the main deck ahead of the paddle boxes, the sides of the deckhouse, which had extended out to the edge of the guards, were partly removed and rebuilt inwards so that there was open deck space on the outside. To compensate for the loss of the ladies' saloon a ladies' lounge was built off the main saloon on the second deck aft of the starboard paddle box, and a ladies' toilet room was added in a similar position on the port side. A private parlor had been constructed ahead of the saloon and was available for rent.

Perhaps the most startling change, considering that an Anderson commanded the vessel, was the extension of the main saloon itself. However, it

106

The main saloon was enlarged in 1887-88. The four square columns enclose the spars, while ahead of the farthest are the windows looking down on the engine.

was not extended nearly as far forward as the old Van Santvoord saloon: the forward bulkhead was about even with the after ends of the paddle boxes, and the forward promenade deck was still open. The trim in the saloon was the same as in the dining room: mahogany, olive and whitewood. The panels which had separated the windows were removed, and the saloon was fitted with closely set drop windows of plate glass. In the clerestory directly above each of these windows was a new pane of cathedral glass, and some of these panes were uniquely decorated; one carried the legend, "When the Swallows Homeward Fly," and depicted a swallow complete with gripsack and umbrella. The after end of the saloon was rounded out and the forward end partially curved; the engine housing in the forward end of the

saloon was fitted with plate-glass windows so that the passengers could watch the operation of the engine without going to the main deck. The after end of the hurricane deck was now open to passengers, but they could not walk the length of this deck because of the intervening clerestory or dome over the saloon.

In addition to all these changes, about a hundred electric lights were installed on the vessel. These alterations were well received by the passengers, who were particularly happy with the relocation of the dining room; so changed was the vessel that for some time after the overhaul she was referred to as the "new" Mary Powell.

She was still the "Queen of the Hudson" and acknowledged as one of the fastest steamboats on the river; even the most partisan supporters of

107

This picture of the *Mary Powell* was probably taken in the spring of 1888 and ordered made to show the newly completed alterations. This landing, used by her from the mid-1880s to mid-1890s, was roughly between the business center of Rondout and the landing near the creek's mouth. (*—Courtesy of Alfred P. Marquart*)

other steamboats paid constant tribute to the prowess of the *Mary Powell* by using her performances to measure the accomplishments of their favorites. Many well-to-do yachtsmen of the 1880s regarded her as the ultimate test and often brought their newest craft to the lower Hudson to lie in wait for her as she started her northbound run in the afternoon. Jay Gould the financier owned the large steam yacht *Atalanta*, built in 1883; during the summer season he would always sail from New York to his estate north of Irvington at about the time the *Mary Powell* was coming up the river, but the passenger steamer always sped by the *Atalanta* without difficulty. A neighbor of Gould's was equally persistent, but no more successful, with his yacht *Stranger*.

Then, on June 10, 1885, the northbound *Mary Powell* found the little propeller-driven steam yacht *Stiletto* waiting for her above the West 22nd Street landing in New York. She was 87.6 feet in length and was anything but conventional; the

New York *Herald* described the *Stiletto* as a "long, low, narrow cigar-shaped craft, with a hump in the middle like a Roman nose and her bow and stern decks tapering down almost to the water's surface." Said the *Sun* in a front-page story on June 11th, "Her general appearance was like that of a lead pencil sharpened at both ends." She had been constructed by those noted yacht designers and builders, the Herreshoffs, at their Bristol, Rhode Island, yard.

There was a crowd of spectators, and many other yachts were in the vicinity to see the start of the unofficial race, since word of the *Stiletto's* intentions had been leaked by her people. The initial excitement was provided by Jay Gould, who reached the foot of West 23rd Street before the *Mary Powell's* departure time and got into a small boat to be taken out to the *Atalanta*. As he was being rowed out to his yacht he was almost run down by a tugboat with a dump barge that was having difficulty navigating in the congestion. The

Jay Gould's *Atalanta*, above, looked like a miniature ocean liner while the *Stiletto*, below in a Stebbins photograph of 1886, was low and sleek. (—*Above, courtesy of The Mariners Museum; below, N. L. Stebbins, The New Navy of the United States*)

The famous *Mary Powell-Stiletto* encounter was dramatized by a contemporary artist, who depicted exulting men on the yacht's deck. After the Navy acquired her the *Stiletto*, below, had a severe appearance. (—*Above, Eldredge collection; both, courtesy of The Mariners Museum*)

It was the incredibly fast *Vamoose*, built for William Randolph Hearst, that sailed a ring around the *Mary Powell* and then raced a train. Also designed by Herreshoff, her lines were similar to the *Stiletto's*. (*—Courtesy of The Mariners Museum*)

crowd was on tenterhooks at the prospect of seeing a man of so much wealth exterminated by such a pedestrian combination as a tug and a dump barge. But there was no collision, and through it all Gould was the calmest man in his small boat.

After the *Mary Powell* sailed from West 22nd Street, the *Stiletto* started upstream. According to the *Herald*, the *Stiletto* was far ahead by 60th Street, and then "a feeling of sadness seized those aboard the demon craft. It seemed a pity that the laurels of victory had been wrested from the beautiful Queen." Gould, steaming up the river in the *Atalanta*, watched the two fast-moving craft approach. He was so elated to see the *Mary Powell* at long last following in the wake of another vessel that he wildly waved his white hat and ordered a cannon fired in salute as the *Stiletto* passed by. The yacht's destination was Sing Sing

— now Ossining — less than thirty miles from the start of the race, and there she turned off and ended the contest. Minutes later the *Mary Powell* passed by, saluting the *Stiletto* with three blasts on her whistle, and continued unruffled up the Hudson. It had scarcely been an old-fashioned steamboat race, since the *Stiletto* was certainly not a commercial vessel, and the *Mary Powell* was carrying over 400 passengers, who disadvantaged her at the outset by rushing to one side of the boat to watch the *Stiletto*.

More than a year passed, and then on Saturday, October 2, 1886, the *Mary Powell* again brushed with the *Stiletto*. The yacht was heading up the river, with John B. Herreshoff aboard, and slowed down off Riverside Park until the passenger steamer came along. In the accounts of what followed there is some discrepancy. According to the people on the *Stiletto*, the *Mary Powell* began

Herreshoff's *Now Then* had a clipper bow and a cruiser stern. (*—Courtesy of The Mariners Museum*)

to pull ahead, but the yacht increased her steam pressure, took the lead and held it for several miles; then the *Stiletto* turned about and the *Mary Powell* went on her way. Since the yacht was headed for Sing Sing it is not clear why she would turn about, unless she wanted to end the race rather than slow down and let the *Mary Powell* pass her. Further, the *Stiletto* people said that they were in no condition to race, since both the bunkers and water tanks were full and there were guests on board. This sounds like strange carping for a winner, because in both contests against the *Stiletto* the *Mary Powell* had been plying her regular route with passengers and certainly was not prepared to race. The *Mary Powell's* version of the story was somewhat different. Pilot Briggs said that at first the *Mary Powell* gained on the *Stiletto*, which dropped back and then suddenly came up again, but try as she would, with trembling and rolling, she couldn't pass the sidewheeler and finally turned back down the river. Captain Eltinge Anderson said the *Stiletto* spurted time and again but to no avail.

The following year the Navy bought the *Stiletto* and converted her into a torpedo boat for training purposes at Newport, Rhode Island.[3] While the *Mary Powell* would not be troubled by the *Stiletto* again, John B. Herreshoff brought the steam yacht *Now Then* to New York in 1889. Measuring 78.4 feet in length, she was almost ten feet shorter than her predecessor. According to one newspaper account, on June 6th the *Now Then* started even with the *Mary Powell* above West 22nd Street and beat her to Irvington by eight minutes. Since the southbound *Albany* was coming along, the *Now Then* turned about, waited for her to come abreast and then beat her to Yonkers; the yacht stopped while the *Albany* made her landing and then beat her once more into New York.

Captain Anderson felt this account was a little unfair. He told a *Herald* reporter that the *Mary Powell* wasn't beaten to Irvington since the *Now*

---

[3]*Dictionary of American Naval Fighting Ships*, vol. 1 (Washington, D.C.: U. S. Government Printing Office, 1959), p. 273.

Then didn't go that far. Instead, she dropped out just south of Hastings when she was only 4½ minutes ahead. Furthermore, the captain said,

> The *Mary Powell* is not a racing machine. . . .
>
> . . . we had no warning whatever that the *Now Then* would tackle us. If these people want to race so badly, why don't they do it in the fall of the year, when passenger traffic is over and we can get into racing trim? . . .
>
> It was the same way when the *Stiletto* "raced" with us. We had several hundred passengers on board and they all got on the side toward the *Stiletto*, giving the *Powell* such a list that one wheel was almost entirely out of the water.[4]

There was good reason for Captain Anderson to be irked. The newspapers played up these encounters, which, after all, were nothing like a match race between the *Mary Powell* and, say, the *Daniel Drew*. The little Herreshoff yachts were designed and built for high speed only, and the fact that they singled out the *Mary Powell* to provide a test was really high credit to the sidewheeler at her age.

In 1891 another yacht came along. This was the 108.7-foot *Vamoose*, the "Herreshoff Flyer,"

[4] New York *Herald*, June 8, 1889.

which had been built that year for publisher William Randolph Hearst. Four years later Samuel Ward Stanton would write of this craft, in his *American Steam Vessels*, "One of the fastest steam vessels ever built, being able to steam as high as 30 miles an hour." On September 11th Hearst and his "cyclonic little wonder" waited for the northbound *Mary Powell* to leave West 22nd Street. Keeping off the port side of the steamboat, the *Vamoose* moved into the lead and then crossed the bow of the *Mary Powell* about an eighth of a mile ahead of her. Near Fort Lee the *Vamoose* turned, ran down one side of the *Mary Powell*, straightened out directly astern and gradually passed the steamboat on the other side, in effect sailing a circle around her. Still holding handily to her lead, the yacht next brushed with a railroad train, a northbound local on the New York Central that was just leaving Riverdale station as the *Vamoose* passed by. Mr. Hearst asked his engineer if he thought the yacht could beat the train to Yonkers, and the engineer quickly demonstrated that she could. Near Hastings the *Vamoose* turned around and raced the southbound *New York*, of the New York-Albany Day Line, but the latter slowed for her Yonkers landing just as the yacht was about to pass her.

On this lithographed post card the *Mary Powell* steams past the gun emplacements at West Point.

This Loeffler photograph of the *Mary Powell* in Haverstraw Bay
is one of the classic pictures of steamboating. It was the basis
for Samuel Ward Stanton's prime drawing of the *Mary Powell*
in his monumental *American Steam Vessels*.

Naturally, passengers did not travel on the *Mary Powell* just because she was sought out by the fast steam yachts. The average traveler was much more interested in the changes made to the vessel between the seasons of 1887 and 1888 than in what the Herreshoffs were up to. And the normal routine of her service was not often disturbed.

In April, 1889, an elaborate celebration was held at New York to mark the 100th anniversary of George Washington's first inauguration as president of the United States. On Monday, April 29th, the day before the centennial itself, the *Mary Powell* participated in a naval parade, holding the position of honor as the lead vessel in the first squadron of the first division of two five-squadron divisions of steamboats, ferryboats, tugboats and other merchant vessels. Captain Anderson later received a letter from his squadron commander complimenting the captain and his officers in the pilothouse on their handling of the *Mary Powell*. The next day she was scheduled to carry the cadets of West Point to New York to march in the military parade, and on May 1st she made another special trip down from Rondout to the civic and industrial parade.

The regular season was under way when an interesting item about Captain Anderson appeared in a Hudson Valley newspaper. It seems that while the steamer was lying at her Vestry Street pier in New York a man came aboard looking for his trunk; he had lost it and was thinking that perhaps it had been left on the steamer. When the captain asked the man's name, he was startled to hear in reply, "A. E. Anderson." That same day

a woman from Philadelphia boarded the *Mary Powell* at Newburgh and went to the office to buy a ticket for Rondout. She said she had always wanted to travel on the *Mary Powell* because that was her name, too. Captain Anderson was completely bowled over, told the lady of his earlier experience and then spent the next half hour with Mary Powell discussing coincidences.

In 1890 the *Mary Powell* lost an old friend when Daniel Hoffman Bishop, the mate and assistant pilot, was forced to retire during the summer because of failing health. Still in his early fifties and a bachelor, he died on Friday night, September 5th, in his home at New Hamburg. On Sunday the *Mary Powell* sailed down from Rondout in the early afternoon with her flags at half-mast and her pilothouse draped in mourning. A great number of Mate Bishop's friends went with her, and at Poughkeepsie many more came aboard. After funeral services at New Hamburg the coffin was escorted aboard by members of the Brotherhood of Pilots and Engineers and the officers and crew of the steamboat he had served so long, while her bell tolled out notes of sorrow. The *Mary Powell* steamed back up to Poughkeepsie, where the final interment would be made. The last of the original officers of the *Mary Powell* to remain active had gone ashore forever.

It was a funeral of which all steamboatmen might dream. Captain Absalom Anderson later wrote from California, in his letter describing Bishop as affable, genial and kindhearted, with a pleasant word for all and fully able to discharge his duties to complete satisfaction. The captain recalled that Mate Bishop had had a host of

In the celebration marking the centennial of George Washington's first inauguration, the *Mary Powell* joined in a naval parade, above, photographed near the Statue of Liberty. (*—Steven Lang collection*)

The *Pontiac,* below, helped the *Mary Powell* when she ran aground in 1890. (*—Courtesy of Franklin H. and Emily Welch*)

"PONCKHOCKIE." ENTRANCE TO RONDOUT HARBOR

The view above overlooks Rondout Creek from Sleightsburg and shows the *Mary Powell* at the landing where she was rammed by the *Transport*. Her earlier landing near the mouth of the creek was close to the building at the extreme right, behind which Kingston Point juts out into the river. (—*Captain William O. Benson collection*)

The ferry *Transport* is shown, center, late in her long career, while at left she is inbound on Rondout Creek, not far from the spot where the ramming took place.

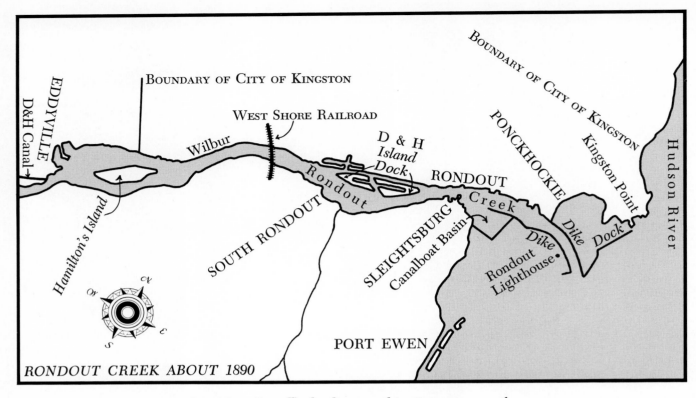

The *Mary Powell's* landing at this time was on the
north side of the Rondout (right above the *k* in "Creek").

friends aboard the vessel, and one among the
many who had handed him a good cigar was
President Grant. Captain Anderson went on,

> The old mate's love for my old pet was
> as strong as my own. He was one of the first
> aboard in the spring to prepare the old
> "Skimmer of the Hudson" for her season's
> work, and the last to leave her in the fall,
> after she had been placed in her winter quar-
> ters. Who can fill his place? He was a duti-
> ful son and kindly brother, good and true.
>
> It was a beautiful tribute . . . for the dear
> old boat he loved so well, to carry all that
> was mortal . . . to his last resting place at
> Poughkeepsie. Peace to his ashes.[1]

None of this was affectation on the part of Captain Absalom, for steamboatmen were sentimental
men, and the love of their lives was their steamboats and the men who manned them.

From a superstitious point of view it would
certainly seem that the passing of Mate Bishop
brought on a spate of bad luck. On September

---

[1]Poughkeepsie *Daily Eagle,* October 7, 1890.

19th, less than two weeks after the funeral, the
southbound *Mary Powell* ran aground in a fog
below Esopus Meadows Lighthouse. She was
hauled off without damage by the tugboats *Sara-
nac* and *Pontiac,* which were in the vicinity. Then,
in the spring of 1891, McEntee & Dillon fitted her
with her fifth pair of boilers. As she lay placidly
at her berth in Rondout Creek on the morning of
May 5th, the work of preparing her for the season
was all but completed: the new boilers had been
inspected and painters were aboard to give the
vessel some finishing touches. Two of the painters
were on the guard on the side away from the
landing, apparently working on the lettering of
the name on the paddle box. All was calm on the
"Queen of the Hudson."

The iron-hulled ferryboat *Transport* was just
starting out of the creek on her 10:10 a.m. trip
to Rhinecliff, across the river, and at the same
time the *M. Martin,* the Newburgh-Albany day
boat that had rammed the *Mary Powell* in 1887,
was coming into the creek for her landing at Rondout. The pilot of the *M. Martin* blew two blasts

The *Mary Powell* is lying at her Rondout landing, photographed probably in 1893. (*—Captain William O. Benson collection*)

The traveling public was not required to keep very far away from the walking beam on the *Mary Powell.* (*—Courtesy of The Mariners Museum*)

Male passengers used their umbrellas as parasols without fear of being considered effeminate. The view above looks aft along the hurricane deck as the *Mary Powell* proceeds northward through the High- lands. Below, the young lady holds on to her hat to thwart the river breezes. (—*Both, courtesy of Robert M. Matthews*)

In the above picture, taken from the top of the starboard paddle box, the big pilot wheel may be seen through the pilothouse's after window. Below, the passengers disembark past piles of trunks on the main deck. (—*Both, courtesy of Robert M. Matthews*)

Private parlors on either side of the promenade deck ahead of the paddle boxes were added between the seasons of 1893 and 1894. The picture was taken from Newburgh, looking across to Fishkill Landing, now part of Beacon. The Mount Beacon incline railway runs up in the right background.

---

on the whistle to indicate that he wanted a starboard-to-starboard passing to keep to the south side of the channel. The pilot of the *Transport* was agreeable, returned the signal and put his wheel over to clear the *M. Martin*. Unfortunately the *Transport* was in an area of shoal water and took a sheer, which the pilot was unable to check.

One of the painters on the *Mary Powell* looked up from his lettering just in time to see the *Transport* bearing down on them. He shouted to his partner, and in the nick of time the two scrambled to safety through the fireroom. The ferryboat struck the *Mary Powell* a massive blow, tore out part of the guard, stove in about fifty feet of joinerwork, knocked the blower for the furnaces on that side out of place and bent the shaft of the blower engine, shifted a spring beam, snapped one of the tie rods from the masts and twisted or bent three or four others.

At that time Captain Eltinge Anderson was standing on the wharf by the steamer. To his utter amazement the side of the vessel suddenly lurched upward, right in front of him, tearing five piles out of the landing and displacing part of the stringpiece. He jumped back for safety, and it was a few minutes before he realized what had happened. The next night the tugboat *Columbia*, of the Cornell Steamboat Company, towed the *Mary Powell* away for dry-docking and repairs, and she did not get back to the creek until May 14th.

But more bad luck was still to come. On Friday, June 26th, in the lower river on the northbound trip, the steamer ran into a severe wind

The *Mary Powell's* crew in the 1890s was photographed with Captain Anderson holding the inevitable newspaper; on his own right is Pilot Briggs, on his left Purser Joseph Reynolds, Jr. The celebrated stewardess, Fannie Anthony, is at the extreme left with the barber, wearing a bow tie, behind her. (*—Senate House Museum, Kingston*)

and rainstorm, accompanied by hail. The initial blast of the elements careened the vessel so that her guard on the lee side dipped beneath the water, and baggage piled up in that area had to be moved by deckhands. The next day, Saturday, with reportedly about 1,100 passengers aboard, the northbound *Mary Powell* again ran into heavy weather. A black cloud bank was sighted ahead, and soon the Hudson was churned into a tumultuous sea in what one old sloop captain on board described as the worst storm he had seen or heard of on the river in almost forty years. The waves were running at abnormal height, and it seems that as the paddle wheels plowed into the tops of these waves they turned up water in such quantities that the bulkheads of the paddle boxes were broken on both sides. The water ran over the

main deck in a cascade, stimulating both crew and passengers to some lively action, except for a few women who promptly fainted. To keep this water to a minimum, speed had to be slackened, and the *Mary Powell* proceeded slowly on up the river. At Cranston's, the first landing, no one deserted the steamer, for the only passengers who went ashore were those actually bound for that destination. Captain Anderson telegraphed ahead to Rondout so that when she landed carpenters and joiners would be ready to start repairs.

Early in the spring of 1892 another of the original band of officers, Pilot Guernsey Betts, expired just past his 61st birthday. Those aboard the *Mary Powell* noted his passing with sorrow, although he had not worked aboard the vessel in some ten years. Then in November of 1892

To the Highlands of the Hudson.

ONE-DAY EXCURSIONS

ON THE

Hudson Steamers,

IN CONNECTION WITH

WEST SHORE RAILROAD

EXCURSION TICKETS

will be sold from NEW YORK to WEST POINT and Return, available by steamer to West Point, returning West Shore Railroad; or by West Shore Railroad, returning by steamer, at following low rates for *Round Trip:*

To West Point and Return.

Steamer MARY POWELL and West Shore R.R.   - $1.00
Steamers of DAY LINE and West Shore R.R.   -   1.50

These Excursions are exceedingly popular during the summer months, and afford the most interesting views of the world-famed HUDSON RIVER.

APPLY AT NEAREST

Ticket Office of WEST SHORE RAILROAD for Excursion Tickets.

An 1894 advertisement.
(*—Courtesy of Jim Shaughnessy*)

Chief Engineer Joel N. Hayes died at 47, after 23 seasons on the steamer. While engaged in laying up the *Mary Powell* for the winter he had developed a chill, which became pneumonia, and he soon succumbed. Oddly enough his predecessor, Lyman Lawrence, who had stepped down because of ill health, was very much alive and, in fact, would live until 1898. Hayes was succeeded by his assistant, A. Van Schaack, who in the twentieth century was followed in turn by Chief Engineers Nathan Purdy and William H. Van Valkenburgh.

Late in the 1880s there had been a growing feeling against the service offered by the *Mary Powell* on her northbound run. Here, it will be remembered, the vessel did not have a set schedule but ran on a "late week" and "early week" basis,

depending on the tide. This arrangement did not seem to work any hardship, except on prospective passengers who took "average time of arrival" literally. Of course it might have inconvenienced friends and relatives who were meeting the steamer and the operators of conveyances for hire, but the latter would certainly be familiar with "late week—early week." However, people were becoming used to being regulated by strict schedules and resented a timetable that required a little thinking. In 1887 one Hudson Valley newspaper reported that the feeling against the "average" method of operation was growing and charged that the *Mary Powell* was not making as good time as usual that summer and that during her "late weeks" was later than ever. Presumably these laments were quieted by the rebuilding that winter which resulted in the "new" *Mary Powell*. In 1892 the subject came up again; the paper gnashed its editorial teeth at the uncertainty of northbound arrival times, pointed out that the New York-Albany Day Line operated on a definite schedule and went on to say, "Just think of a railroad train having a late and an early week. The antiquated craft has seen her best days." That might be, but the "antiquated craft" still had a quarter of a century ahead of her.

The figure of the Goddess of Liberty was removed from the *Mary Powell's* pilothouse after the season of 1892, according to the best available evidence. Large decorations of this sort had become passé aboard steamboats. The story is that the goddess was next secured by a steamboat operator, a friend of Captain Eltinge's, who used it as a decoration in his yard. There it stood for many a year until Mabel Van Alstyne purchased it, and it has since passed to the Smithsonian Institution as part of the Eleanor and Mabel Van Alstyne Folk Art Collection.

The male figure which had graced the pilothouse of the *Thomas Powell* has its own story. When the steamboat was broken up at Port Ewen, Captain William H. Mabie acquired the statue and placed it in the side yard of his Port Ewen home. Those were the days of hobos, and one morning his wife saw a tramp start around the house, bound for the back door and the chance of a handout. Suddenly the vagrant looked up to

In 1895 the *Mary Powell's* landing was changed again, to a choice location at the center of Rondout. The dock had formerly been used by Cornell's propeller night boat *City of Kingston* (successor to the *Thomas Cornell*) and she is shown above at this landing. Be-low, the *City of Kingston* rounds to in busy Rondout Creek prior to landing, a maneuver even more difficult for the *Mary Powell*, longer by over 42 feet. The schooner lies at the tip of the D. & H.'s Island Dock. (*—Both, Dr. Charles A. Galyon collection*)

The nautical canine, Buster, sits at attention as Captain Eltinge Anderson shakes the end of a heaving line at him. The little girl is Elizabeth HasBrouck, later Mrs. Appleton Gregory. (*—Courtesy of Mrs. Appleton Gregory*)

Below, Captain Anderson pretends to read his newspaper while his wife, Fannie, does better with a book. The great Buster also held still long enough to get into the picture. To the left of the lamp are miniatures of Captain Absalom and presumably Mrs. A. L. Anderson. (*—Courtesy of George N. Betts*)

find himself confronted by a formidable-looking man with one arm pointed directly toward him. This was too much for the tramp, who promptly turned and ran.

Between the seasons of 1893 and 1894, the *Mary Powell* got new smokestacks, and two private parlors were constructed on the promenade deck, one on either side ahead of the paddle boxes. These rooms had electric call bells and plate-glass windows, two on the side and one forward, shaded by awnings.

On July 7, 1894, while the *Mary Powell* was southbound, her starboard paddle-wheel shaft cracked, and she had to be withdrawn for repairs until July 17th. Even though the accident occurred during the period of heavy summer traffic, the route was suspended, probably because no suitable vessel could be chartered as a replacement.

The last decade of the nineteenth century was a time of death for the Anderson family. Little Lent, Captain Eltinge's son, had been taken ill the day before Christmas in 1890. Although physicians were summoned, even from New York, the membranous croup did not respond to treatment, and the boy died on December 31st, ending that branch of the family. Captain Absalom Anderson's wife died in May, 1894, and in June of the following year his unmarried daughter, Charlotte Hasbrouck Anderson, passed away. Apparently "Lottie" had lived with him at his estate, Stonehedge, in California, as did his widowed daughter Helen Mary, whose husband Harry had been a son of General Postley. Near by lived another daughter, Nathalie, with her husband, Edwin H. Sawyer.

The captain, now 82, was depressed by Lottie's death, especially since he was still engaged in closing the estates of both his wife and his father, Captain Nathan Anderson, Sr. Under the date of June 13, 1895, he wrote to his son Eltinge,

> We are in the deepest *affliction*, in loosing [*sic*] our *dear Lottie*, poor Girl her *sufferings* are over — and our only consolation is that her *pure Spirit* is now in the *heavenly abode of the God* who gave it — singing her praises — with our other dear *departed ones* — and all the *heavenly Hosts*. — We are all, as well as can be expected.

He then asked Eltinge to thank Mr. Van Santvoord for sending a family pass on the Day Line of Steamers. Even though by his children he was called, "Papa," he closed as he always did, "Affectionately A. L. Anderson," and he added, rather pathetically, "When you feel like it let me know how you are & about the dear 'old Queen' remember me kindly to Briggs, & Engineer & crew."

In handling estate settlements Captain Absalom Anderson was always concerned that everything be done legally so that there would be no "afterclaps." As he worked on the Nathan Anderson estate, he remembered a niece of his, Annie, who was married but poor and might be overlooked. Then he remembered that her father — his brother-in-law, Andrew Jackson Ketcham, now a retired banker — had once borrowed about $400 on a note from Captain Charles Anderson. Captain Charles had never been able to collect it and, when he was "hard up," had sold the note to his brother, Captain Absalom, who had also loaned Ketcham $150 on another note. Now he wrote to his son Eltinge,

> [Ketcham] has promised to pay me although the Notes are *outlawed* — but I don't think he ever will — he is abundantly able — if he were honest enough to do so. . . .
>
> I propose to make Annie a present of the Notes — and write her Father to pay her the amt. of them — with or without interest — as Annie may decide. Unless he does pay her — I may *ventilate* this matter in a way he may not like. . . .

The letter was dated August 26th, when a match for the *America's* Cup, between the *Defender* and the *Valkyrie III*, was in the immediate future. Since Captain Absalom's interest in all things marine never flagged, he added as an afterthought,

> If at any time you see in the papers [anything] interesting about the yacths [*sic*] please send to me. . . . I hope the *Defender* will *beat* the *Englishman*.

Captain Absalom did not know it, but his days were running out. In October he had an accident, which his son-in-law, Edwin Sawyer, not wanting to worry Captain Eltinge, kept quiet about. Finally on October 29, 1895, he sent Eltinge the details:

> Your father had a very narrow escape, over two weeks ago. He was returning from

After the 1896 season the *Mary Powell's* hull was rebuilt at Elizabethport, N.J. At left is the view under her main deck. Below, her colors fly for the photographer while she sits on the marine railway.

Pilot Hiram G. Briggs watches as her starboard boiler is lifted out, probably at Elizabethport. (—*Pictures on this page courtesy of Hudson River Day Line collection, Steamship Historical Society of America, Inc.*)

The *Mary Powell* in winter quarters at Port Ewen.
(*—Photograph by Wallace C. Mabie*)

This landing on the creek, a convenient spot for passengers, was used from 1895 until the end of morning-boat service to New York. F. J. Sedgwick, devoted marine historian and photographer, took the picture in 1902. (*—Sedgwick collection, courtesy of The Mariners Museum*)

The big night boat *Dean Richmond,* which collided with the *Mary Powell* on October 12, 1901, is shown here at Albany. To her right is the *M. Martin,* and beyond is the Day Line's *New York* with the state capitol looming above her.

Santa Barbara, by the beach with "Star", (Lottie's horse) and a small cart; at Booth's Point, (just above where you turn off from the beach) for Montecito, "Star" took fright, and threw him out, down a small embankment. He was fearfully bruised, but no internal injuries. To-day, after ten days, he has not had his clothes on, but is able to get from the back parlor, to the front and sit in the bay window.

I think he is doing as well as could be expected considering his age, but the first few days, we were terribly anxious. Of course he is nervous, and restless. . . . I think it will be a long time before he fully, if he ever does entirely recover from the shock. He feels older and more infirm, since the accident than ever before.

While I think there will be no serious, immediate results, it certainly would be an immense relief to his mind, if you could possibly come on (if only for a short stay, to talk over business matters with him).

On November 18, 1895, one of the most famous steamboatmen ever to ply the Hudson passed on; we hope he could run a steamboat in Heaven as he so confidently expected he would. Sawyer and Captain Eltinge were executors of his estate, and they would be engaged in this matter for many years to come, since Absalom Anderson had sizable investments in California real estate. It seems that for his own fortunes Captain Eltinge preferred New Smyrna, Florida, over California, for he wintered there and bought property.

No one has ever hinted that the *Mary Powell* had any relation to Noah's ark, but there are indications that she had proclivities in that direction. Back in 1879 it was reported that a swallow had a nest under the guard and rode contentedly up and down the river with the steamboat. Later there was a lame gray cat which one year had been taken with its family on a summer holiday in the Catskills. Allegedly, each year thereafter,

Always dapper in the fashion of his day, Captain A. Eltinge Anderson poses by the port after gangway. Over his head, also in the fashion of the day, is the name of the vessel painted on the after end of the boiler cover. (—*Senate House Museum, Kingston*)

A metal coat and baggage check from the *Mary Powell* is shown full size.

at the start of the boarding-house season, the lone cat would come aboard at New York, slip into the ladies' saloon and sail up to Rondout; where it went from there Heaven only knows.

To dogs the *Mary Powell* was particularly attuned. Mary Irving Husted in *Hudson River Children* recalls a collie named Eric who always stood on a bluff below Milton about seven o'clock to bark a "good morning" as the steamboat went down the river and get an answering salute from Pilot Briggs. The passengers would look all along the shore to see who was being saluted and never guessed that it was the bushy yellow dog running excitedly back and forth. Little Lent, the captain's only son, had a dog that remained an integral part of the Anderson family after the lad died. This dog could recognize the whistle of the *Mary Powell* and upon hearing it would run to the Rondout landing as a four-footed welcoming committee. At midnight the dog would go from the Anderson home to the steamer to make sure that all was well and to help the watchman eat his nocturnal meal. Apparently this dog never traveled with the vessel, although he may be the one depicted on board in the *Mary Powell* guidebook as "The 'Mascot.'"

However, the greatest of all the *Mary Powell* dogs, and a far better-known mascot than his predecessor, was the storied Buster, Captain Eltinge's brindle bull terrier. Buster was born in 1897 and grew up under the tutelage of the captain and the rest of the crew as an accomplished sailor. Unlike some sailors, he loved to swim and when Captain Anderson gave the word would leap overboard; he could amuse himself in the water for an hour or more without tiring. Since Buster could not climb the straight side of a wharf, the procedure for getting him back on board was a little complicated. One of the deckhands would get on a float and throw Buster a stick, which he would hold tightly in his mouth. Then he would swim to the deckhand, who would grasp the stick and pull the attached Buster out onto the float. Another deckhand aboard the steamer would throw a line down to the man on the float; after this line had been fastened around the dog, Buster would dive back into the water to be hauled aboard. Once, while the *Mary Powell* was being

painted in the spring, one of the painters fell overboard, and Buster immediately went over the side to grab him by the collar. Since the painter was a good swimmer and needed no assistance, Buster then paddled off and retrieved his hat.

Buster was also a religious dog. At Captain Anderson's command he would jump into a chair, place his front paws on the back of it and bow his furry head. He would remain in that position until the captain intoned, "Amen," then Buster would jump down and become once more a happy brindle bull terrier. As befitted a dog who was the alter ego of the *Mary Powell's* master, during the day Buster was an amiable gentleman and tolerant of children, but at night he was a changed dog, a man-eating watchman ready to make any prowler about the Anderson premises unhappy. This steamboating prince of dogdom was much publicized and even received a pass on a Kingston trolley line.

In the fall of 1896 the *Mary Powell* went to the yard of the New Jersey Dry Dock & Transportation Company at Elizabethport, New Jersey, to be hauled out on the marine railway for another rebuilding of the hull. Part of the white-oak keel had to be removed because of the way the floor timbers were mortised into it. Captain Eltinge used the removed keel by having small souvenirs made from pieces of it. When she was refloated in the latter half of December, the steamboat was taken to Hoboken and then to New York, where the interior was refurbished. In 1897 the *Mary Powell* went into commission rather early, for on April 27th she was chartered by the government to carry the West Point cadets to the dedication of the tomb of one of her old passengers, Ulysses S. Grant.

The *Mary Powell* added a seven-piece orchestra as a regular feature in 1899; this was over a decade after the New York-Albany Day Line inaugurated concerts aboard their steamboats. The orchestra of Emanuel Ellis of Rondout began its summer engagement aboard the *Mary Powell* on June 14th, and to earn something extra they played at Kingston Point in the evening after the steamboat had finished her day's work. In 1896 the point had replaced Rhinecliff on the east bank of the river as the landing for the New York-

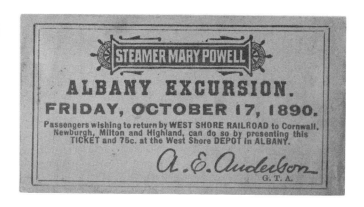

These season passes and tickets for special events reflect the service that the *Mary Powell* made available in the Gay Nineties. (*—Author's collection*)

TIME TABLE
Steamer
Mary Powell
Captain
A. E. ANDERSON

HUDSON RIVER BY DAYLIGHT.

FREEMAN PRINT, RONDOUT, N. Y.

The cover and inside of the *Mary Powell's* timetable folder, above and
below respectively, come from about the year 1890. Convenient railroad connections allowed her to advertise a wider service than merely
to cities along the Hudson. (*—Author's collection*)

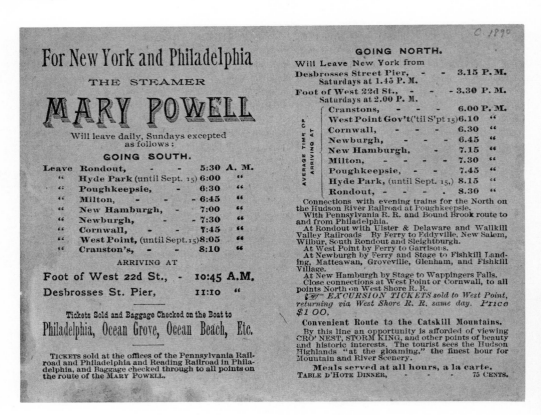

For New York and Philadelphia

THE STEAMER

MARY POWELL

Will leave daily, Sundays excepted
as follows:

GOING SOUTH.

Leave	Rondout,	-	5:30 A. M.
"	Hyde Park (until Sept. 15)	6:00 "
"	Poughkeepsie,	-	6:30 "
"	Milton,	-	6:45 "
"	New Hamburgh,	-	7:00 "
"	Newburgh,	-	7:30 "
"	Cornwall,	-	7:45 "
"	West Point, (until Sept. 15)	8:05 "
"	Cranston's,	-	8:10 "

ARRIVING AT

Foot of West 22d St., - 10:45 A.M.

Desbrosses St. Pier, 11:10 "

Tickets Sold and Baggage Checked on the Boat to

Philadelphia, Ocean Grove, Ocean Beach, Etc.

TICKETS sold at the offices of the Pennsylvania Railroad and Philadelphia and Reading Railroad in Philadelphia, and Baggage checked through to all points on
the route of the MARY POWELL.

C. 1890

GOING NORTH.

Will Leave New York from

Desbrosses Street Pier,	-	3.15 P. M.
Saturdays at 1.45 P. M.		
Foot of West 22d St.,	-	3.30 P. M.
Saturdays at 2.00 P. M.		

AVERAGE TIME OF ARRIVING AT

Cranstons,	-	6.00 P. M.
West Point Gov't ('til S'pt 15)	6.10 "
Cornwall,	-	6.30 "
Newburgh,	-	6.45 "
New Hamburgh,	-	7.15 "
Milton,	-	7.30 "
Poughkeepsie,	-	7.45 "
Hyde Park, (until Sept. 15,)	8.15 "
Rondout,	-	8.30 "

Connections with evening trains for the North on
the Hudson River Railroad at Poughkeepsie.

With Pennsylvania R. R. and Bound Brook route to
and from Philadelphia.

At Rondout with Ulster & Delaware and Wallkill
Valley Railroads By Ferry to Eddyville, New Salem,
Wilbur, South Rondout and Sleightsburgh.

At West Point by Ferry to Garrisons.

At Newburgh by Ferry and Stage to Fishkill Landing, Matteawan, Groveville, Glenham, and Fishkill
Village.

At New Hamburgh by Stage to Wappingers Falls.

Close connections at West Point or Cornwall, to all
points North on West Shore R. R.

EXCURSION TICKETS sold to West Point,
returning via West Shore R. R. same day. Price
$1 00.

Convenient Route to the Catskill Mountains.

By this line an opportunity is afforded of viewing
CRO' NEST, STORM KING, and other points of beauty
and historic interests. The tourist sees the Hudson
Highlands "at the gloaming," the finest hour for
Mountain and River Scenery.

Meals served at all hours, a la carte.

TABLE D'HOTE DINNER, - - - 75 CENTS.

134

The *Mary Powell's* orchestra, with leader Isaac Collins, Jr., holding the violin, poses at Albany on October 12, 1901. Earlier that day this post-season excursion almost met disaster when the *Dean Richmond* rammed the northbound *Mary Powell* on the port side in a fog. (—*Herman F. Boyle collection*)

Albany Day Line's boats, and Kingston Point Park had become a thriving amusement center in the summertime.

Initially the *Mary Powell* concerts were presented in three parts; the program for the first full week of concerts, ending June 24th, opened southbound with the march from *Carmen* and closed northbound with "Phonograph" by Burton. In between were such numbers as Ellis' own "Nutmeg Dance," a Sousa march, a Brahms Hungarian dance, selections from Victor Herbert's *The Fortune Teller*, "Hearts and Flowers," and waltzes, ragtime, a gavotte and a polonaise. Almost immediately Mr. Ellis turned up in an advertisement for a new song, "When Dewey Comes Sailing Home." The advertisement included, "E. Ellis, leader of Ellis's Band, steamer *Mary Powell*: 'We have played it but once, and our passengers applauded it; we consider it fine.'"

Almost simultaneously with the introduction of these concerts the *Mary Powell* had her best-remembered bout with the elements. On the northbound trip on June 20th she had just come out of Haverstraw Bay and was at the southern gateway to the Highlands when the fury of nature struck. Great banks of clouds had been piling up to the southwest and to the north, accompanied by an electrical display. As these two storms met, a funnel-shaped cloud of dust formed on the west

bank of the river and moved out across the water to the *Mary Powell*. The steamboat seemed to be sucked up and then released, rolling to starboard at the same time. The starboard stack was blown down and fell toward the bow, smashing into the paddle box ahead of it; then the port stack blew down across the hurricane deck. Showers of sparks scattered over the steamboat, but the two stacks were held aboard by their iron braces, which had bent like straws. With the storm came the blackness of night, and the buffeting by the howling wind and the torrential rain lasted for a quarter of an hour. A sliding door was blown in; the lifeboats were raised from their supports and shifted far enough to pull the davits out of shape; many campstools went overboard, and some of the stanchions supporting the hurricane deck were loosened. Although there were 200 passengers on the vessel, no one, luckily, was injured.

Captain Anderson, who had been sailing the Hudson for 25 years, considered it the worst storm he had ever seen. Fortunately it had not struck a little farther down in the broad reaches of Haverstraw Bay, the widest part of the river. After it was over, the blowers were set to work, and with her smokestacks in their strange positions the *Mary Powell* continued on her way, making the usual landings. After she arrived in Rondout repairs went on through the night so that she might cover the regular trip the next morning.

The *New York,* in a picture that may have been taken on her maiden voyage to Albany in 1887, was then 301 feet long, as compared to the *Mary Powell's* 288 feet. The *Mary Powell* is here making a northbound landing at W. 129th Street in August, 1903. (—*Above, William H. Ewen collection; below, Sedgwick collection, courtesy of The Mariners Museum)*

CHAPTER EIGHT
The Hudson River Day Line Buys In

Captain John H. Brinckerhoff, who owned 715 of the 1,500 shares of the Mary Powell Steamboat Company, died in December of 1901 as a result of a fractured skull sustained in a runaway accident. He was not long buried when the Central-Hudson Steamboat Company approached Captain Anderson and Isaac Wickes about buying their shares in the company, which together represented a controlling interest in the *Mary Powell* and her route. Rumors flew that if the Central-Hudson acquired the *Mary Powell*, it would run her as usual until the Hudson River Day Line built a new steamboat, which was also rumored; then the Central-Hudson would purchase the *New York* from the Day Line and dispose of the *Mary Powell*. (Hudson River Day Line was the new corporate name of the New York-Albany Day Line and was adopted in 1899 to supersede the name "Hudson River Line." The company still had in service as its only vessels the *Albany* of 1880 and the *New York* of 1887.) Why the rumor-mongers thought the Day Line would sell the *New York* rather than the older *Albany* is a moot point. Both Captain Anderson and Wickes supplied the Central-Hudson with a figure for their shares, but nothing came of it; probably they wanted to sell at the par value of $100 per share.

The Central-Hudson Steamboat Company had been formed in 1899 as a consolidation of the night lines from Rondout, Poughkeepsie and Newburgh to New York, and the day line between Newburgh and Albany. Both the latter line and the Rondout-New York night line had been operated by Romer & Tremper. At this time the Central-Hudson's fleet consisted of six night boats, two day boats and a spare boat, all of which

handled both freight and passengers. Other New York night lines originating at landings north of Rondout were the Saugerties & New York Steamboat Company; the Catskill Evening Line from the Catskill-Hudson-Coxsackie area; the People's Line, the major night line on the river, from Albany; and the Citizens' Line from Troy. In 1902 the Maine-born speculator and promotor, Charles Wyman Morse, acquired control of the Albany and Troy night lines, and the operators of these other steamboat companies suddenly became uneasy about the future, for they had heard and believed the rumor that Morse's goal was a monopoly of Hudson River steamboating.

The prosperous Hudson River Day Line was headed at this time by the dynamic Eben Erskine Olcott, who had become president after the death of his father-in-law, Alfred Van Santvoord. The only steamboat which could be seriously considered to provide direct opposition to the Day Line was the *Mary Powell*. Although she was over forty years old and smaller than the *New York* or the *Albany*, both of which had been lengthened, she had been kept in peak condition and could be a gadfly to the Day Line if Morse chose to buy her and operate her at slashed fares between New York and Albany, or in daily round-trip service between New York and Poughkeepsie, a popular outing for New Yorkers. And it was known that Wickes and Captain Anderson would sell control of the *Mary Powell*, since they had offered the Central-Hudson a fair price for their holdings.

The 1902 season had its minor embarrassments for the *Mary Powell*. Due to the coal strikes, like other Hudson River steamers she was forced to

Above is the *Mary Powell's* unshipped walking beam, probably during the 1903-04 overhaul at Shooters Island. Below, the steamboat displays some of the Day Line's changes made during this overhaul. (—Above, *Hudson River Day Line collection, Steamship Historical Society of America, Inc.; below, courtesy of H. Ernest Bell*)

During only one season, 1903, did the *Mary Powell* look like this, with promenade deck extended to the bow, black stacks and windows in the outer joiner work on the main deck. She is here leaving Poughkeepsie, southbound. (—*Bernhard Schulze collection*)

burn bituminous or soft coal for part of the summer. Since Hudson River engineers and firemen were not familiar with this fuel, they at first had some difficulty in keeping up the steam pressure. Then in September there was a vigorous freight-train wreck along the banks of the river in the Highlands. Dynamite was used to blast away the tangled cars, and a charge was stupidly set off just as the *Mary Powell* came along. Flying debris broke eight panes of window glass aboard the steamer, and it was not until ten months later that the Mary Powell Steamboat Company received $18 in payment from the railroad.

The *Mary Powell* made her last regular trip of the 1902 season on October 2nd and on Saturday, the 4th, made a postseason excursion to Albany. During the year the steamer had carried more passengers than in 1901, with the average

for the two years at about 103,000; this was less than 2% under the average for the five years 1866-70, but now the average number of passengers per trip was far above that of the earlier period, reflecting the shorter operating season and the changing pattern of transportation. Over all, the total number of passengers going to or leaving New York had risen from 83% in 1867-68 to 91% in 1901-02; consequently, traffic between the up-river landings had dropped from 17% to 9%. The distribution of passengers among the upriver landings had also changed: the traffic to and from New York through Rondout was 19.7% of the total passengers carried in 1901-02, as compared with 9.9% in the 1867-68 period; Poughkeepsie, 22.4% compared with 16%; Newburgh, 26.1% compared with 34%; and Cornwall, 12.4% compared with 16.6%. The decline in New York traffic

The *General Slocum* carries spectators at a yacht race. (—*Photograph by N. L. Stebbins, Society for the Preservation of New England Antiquities*)

through Newburgh and Cornwall probably reflected the decline in commuter traffic more than anything else.

But, even before the *Mary Powell* carried her last passenger in 1902, a national magazine ran an article stating that Charles W. Morse was planning to start a day line between New York and Albany, and for that purpose he was having designed two new steamboats that would far surpass the Day Line steamers in speed.

This, then, was the over-all situation on the Hudson when on October 6, 1902, the Hudson River Day Line acquired 419 of Captain Anderson's 420 shares in the Mary Powell Steamboat Company, 359 of Isaac Wickes' 360 shares and four of the five shares that had been transferred from Wickes to Joseph W. Hatch in the preceding year so that Hatch could be elected treasurer to succeed the deceased Brinckerhoff. The Day Line's purchase of over 52% of the Mary Powell Steamboat Company was accomplished with an air of secrecy. Many days passed before newspapers carried the stale word that Wickes and Captain Anderson had given an option on their

stock to a "corporation," and it was almost a month before the facts of the transaction were announced. A secretive air was appropriate if Eben Olcott had indeed decided to buy the *Mary Powell* to keep Morse from doing the same, as was rumored at the time by many boatmen. On the other hand, Olcott may only have wanted to add another day boat — the only suitable vessel that was available for purchase — to his fleet, as the late Alfred Van Santvoord had done in 1869. Certainly Olcott's purchase of the steamer spiked the rumor that the Day Line would be consolidated with other Hudson River lines, for it indicated that the Day Line would strongly oppose any attempt by C. W. Morse to start a rival line.

Olcott later said of the *Mary Powell* that she had once belonged to the Day Line, "and for the purpose of effecting certain desirable changes in our business we decided to get control of her again." Years later, in a letter to his brother-in-law, he wrote that he considered

. . . the purchase of this steamer a fine stroke of business for it got the best man on the

140

The *General Slocum* is shown above, heavily loaded. In June of 1904 she burned in the East River with the loss of over a thousand lives; the sunken remains are at left. This tragedy prompted a re-examination of all steamboats.

This striking view of the *Mary Powell* southbound off the Palisades was copyrighted in 1906 by the Detroit Publishing Co., manufacturers of superlative post cards. (*—Library of Congress*)

The *Mary Powell,* below, lies head up at her landing on Rondout Creek while the tugboat *John D. Schoonmaker* picks up two coal barges. (*—Herman F. Boyle collection*)

In this photograph, copyrighted 1906, a stylish group of surreys meet the *Mary Powell* at Cornwall. (*—Barton & Spooner*)

river [Captain Anderson] working for us instead of against us. Governor Odell [of the Central-Hudson Line] was very much put out that he did not succeed in getting it when he sent Major Weston to Captain Anderson. Weston came up to $60,000. for control. We paid $75,000. I think. . . . Besides the large amount that this boat has helped us to pay in salaries, rents, etc., we got the advantage of her fame. . . .

Later in the fall of 1902 Eben E. Olcott acquired Joseph Hatch's remaining share, and an Olcott relative obtained the solitary share still held by Isaac Wickes. This left outstanding only Captain Anderson's one share and the 715 shares in the estate of John H. Brinckerhoff. The latter were acquired by Benjamin B. Odell, Jr., former governor of New York State, at auction in 1903 for a reported price of $35 per share. Odell became a director of the Mary Powell Steamboat

Company, and in 1906 he sold out at $25,000 (which at $35 per share would have been his investment) to the Hudson River Day Line. The Day Line thereafter computed the cost of acquiring the Mary Powell Steamboat Company at $103,500; this was the total for the Brinckerhoff stock plus the 785 shares of the Anderson-Wickes stock at par and odd shares held by individuals.

The sequence of ownership in the history of the *Mary Powell* was somewhat unusual, even in the tight society of steamboat operators on the Hudson. First, Captain Absalom L. Anderson had built the vessel, selling her eventually to Thomas Cornell, who in turn sold her to Alfred Van Santvoord, operator of the New York-Albany Day Line. Then Captain A. L. Anderson purchased the steamboat to start the second round, sold her again to Thomas Cornell and retired. Cornell soon disposed of his interest, and the new owners,

143

Not long after entering service in 1906 and still unfinished, the *Hendrick Hudson* nears the landing at Poughkeepsie. Below, Chief Engineer Warren Welch mans the controls of her inclined engine, which was then completely new on the river. (*—Below, courtesy of Franklin H. and Emily Welch*)

Above, the southbound *Mary Powell* arrives at the Day Line's landing at Newburgh. At left, among these happy young men in front of the pilothouse is Fred Davis (second from right), the author's uncle and briefly a *Mary Powell* fireman. Below is the *Robert Fulton* in the days of her youth. (—*Above and below, Hudson River Day Line collection, Steamship Historical Society of America, Inc.*)

In these 1908 photographs are some of the *Mary Powell's* crew. Deckhand Arthur A. Warrington, the future captain, sits to left of the life ring above, with First Pilot William B. Maines in white vest and Mate Philip Maines second from right. Below, Warrington stands to right of the firehose with First Porter Seymour Darling, who called out the landings, to his own left. (—*Both, courtesy of Richard J. Warrington*)

Covering the Day Line run from Albany to New York on October 1, 1909, the *Mary Powell* drags her guard in the water off Newburgh as her passengers crowd the port side to see some of the marine activity depicted at the top of page 149.

including Eltinge Anderson, formed the Mary Powell Steamboat Company, which was now controlled by the Day Line.

The first news of the sale of the *Mary Powell* to the Day Line after the close of the 1902 season caused immediate consternation. As the New York *Evening Sun* pointed out to its readers, New Yorkers could not possibly imagine the effect that a change in the *Mary Powell's* service would have on the people living between West Point and Rondout. Between those two landings and for miles inland, said the *Sun*, there was hardly a person who had not made a trip on the *Mary Powell*. "She is a part, so to speak, of the town life, and is woven in the warp and woof of every person's life experience." There were rumors that the *Mary Powell* would carry freight, or that she would be withdrawn from Rondout service and made an auxiliary to the *Albany* and the *New York*, and each rumor had its believers and perpetuators. Of course, seeing the statistical breakdown on passenger totals for the 1901-02 period, the Day Line had no intention of abolishing the *Mary Powell's* regular Rondout run.

Eben E. Olcott's initial move on acquiring the *Mary Powell* was to extend the promenade deck to the bow to make her in that respect just like the *Albany* and *New York*. This alteration has an historic ring, echoing Alfred Van Santvoord's extension of the saloon in 1869. However, if Captain Absalom had been alive in 1902, he probably would have approved of the increased deck space available to the passengers, although he would have worried about the effect on the vessel's balance. Obviously, the change increased her capacity. The cost of this work broke down into such charming vignettes of the times as: two deckhands, 60 days and board, $74; board for two carpenters at a Rondout hotel, 180 meals at 22½ cents each; and two painters, two days, $4.50.

At the annual meeting of the Mary Powell Steamboat Company on December 31, 1902, there was no move towards a dissolution of the organization, which continued as a corporate entity throughout the rest of the *Mary Powell's* active life and for many years afterward. Mr. Olcott was elected to head the company; Captain Eltinge Anderson ceased to be secretary but became general manager in lieu of general passenger agent and continued as captain of the vessel. The company officers then reduced their salaries: Mr. Olcott as president paid himself $2,000 instead of the $4,000 his predecessor, Isaac Wickes, had received; Captain Anderson's salary dropped from $6,500 to $2,500; and William Y. Hawley, in the combined office of secretary-treasurer, received $1,800 instead of the $2,500 previously paid to the treasurer alone.

Before opening her regular Rondout run in 1903 the *Mary Powell* spent nine days in May

The *Chrystenah* helped the *Mary Powell* handle passengers and baggage on occasions. At right is her unusual staircase, while the photograph below looks forward in her main saloon. (—*Above, Sedgwick collection, courtesy of The Mariners Museum; right and below, Thomas H. Franklin collection, Steamship Historical Society of America, Inc.*)

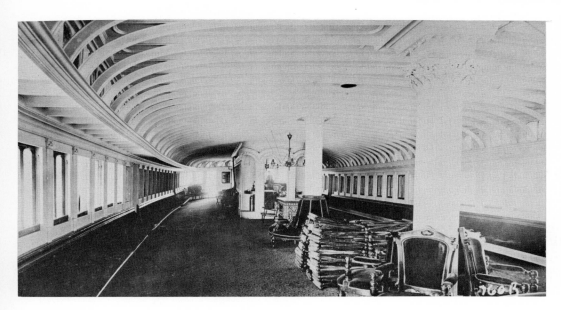

The 1909 Hudson-Fulton Celebration featured a naval parade from New York to Newburgh on October 1. In the photograph above, the *Clermont*, a replica of Fulton's first Hudson River steamboat, is anchored in Newburgh Bay with the *Puritan* of the Fall River Line in the background. Below, the *Norwich* participated in the celebration. (—*Above, photograph by H. Ernest Bell*)

When the *Mary Powell* cracked her crosshead in 1910, the *Emeline* took off her passengers. The *Chrystenah* then ran in the *Mary Powell's* place, aided by the Central-Hudson Line's *William F. Romer,* a vessel originally built for Chesapeake Bay service. (—*Immediately above, Roger W. Mabie collection)*

The Central-Hudson Line brought out the *Benjamin B. Odell,* a single-screw night boat, in 1911. She replaced the *Central-Hudson.*

Formerly the *James W. Baldwin,* the *Central-Hudson* as a night boat was the *Mary Powell's* counterpart in Rondout-New York service. The photograph, taken about 1906, is from the Detroit Publishing Co. (—*Library of Congress*)

on the Poughkeepsie route, steaming north from New York in the morning and returning in the afternoon, until the regular New York-Albany route opened. After the close of the season in October she went to Shooters Island, off the north shore of Staten Island, to the yard of the Townsend-Downey Shipbuilding Company (whose corporate name had a way of getting mixed up into "Townsend & Downey Shipbuilding & Repair Company" and "Townsend, Downey & Company"). Here extensive repairs and other work were planned, including new stacks, the reduction of the diameter of the paddle wheels, engine work and the installation of her sixth, and final, set of boilers. When Alexander Rodie, who was in charge of the boiler shop there, heard that Townsend-Downey had been selected for the job, he wrote to Captain Anderson, promising to do his utmost to build as good a set of boilers as the present pair his "dear old father" had made. It was said that a member of the Rodie family had worked on three of the five sets of boilers that the *Mary Powell* had had into 1903, and Alexander's pair would make it four out of six.

After this rebuilding in 1903-04 the general appearance of the *Mary Powell* had changed in several ways. In the main deckhouse, from ahead of the paddle boxes to the after end of the boilers, the rectangular windows were removed and a number of portholes installed. This step, it was felt, would modernize the vessel's features and was mentioned in the press as a "great improvement." Her new stacks were painted the same near-yellow color used by the Hudson River Day Line on its other vessels; the gallows frame was repainted to match, and the walking beam was brightened with a coat of aluminum paint. Since the *Mary Powell* had had black stacks all her life, a touch of color here certainly gave her a new look.

In 1904 the schedule of the *Mary Powell* in her Rondout service got a new look too. The southbound departure was set back from 5:30 to 6 a.m. in deference to the changing times. Americans were becoming sluggards! Also, before long the old arrangement of "average time of arrival" at the northbound landings gave way to an unqualified "due."

151

The *Mary Powell* arrives at Albany with an excursion. In the background, beyond the bridge, is the night boat *Adirondack*. (—Tracey I. Brooks collection, Steamship Historical Society of America, Inc.)

On June 15th the New York excursion boat *General Slocum* burned in the East River with the loss of over a thousand lives. In terms of mortality it was one of the worst disasters in United States steamboating, and the fire spotlighted flaws in the current method of inspecting passenger vessels. On Sunday, July 10, while the *Mary Powell* was having her guard repaired following a clash with a tugboat, inspectors from Louisville, Kentucky, spent eleven hours going over her as part of a government program to re-examine all steamboats in the wake of the tragic fire. One of these inspectors stated that she was in better condition than any vessel he had ever examined. In this connection it is interesting to note that at the time of the regular annual inspection in May, 1904, an entry was made in the books of the Mary Powell Steamboat Company to record the names of the inspectors and an expenditure of $10. Coupled with this entry was a notation to show that the $10 was for cigars!

In 1906 a New York newspaper sent a reporter to investigate the health of the *Mary Powell* under Day Line control. In the old regime, tickets at New York were probably sold aboard the vessel by the purser, but after the Day Line took over it had its own ticket sellers handle the business. According to the reporter, they ran into a problem at first because some passengers would walk up to the window, put down their money and say nothing. Upon being asked the important question, where were they bound, these passengers would start and apologize, "Oh, I forgot" — forgot that they were no longer being waited on by a *Mary Powell* employee, who knew them and their destination at a glance. The reporter also mentioned that many *Mary Powell* passengers would say to Captain Anderson in the spring, "Well, captain, I am so glad the *Powell's* running again. I haven't been to New York all winter." For them, there was no acceptable way of going to New York but on the *Mary Powell*. Except on crowded

With a good crowd aboard and all flags flying,
the *Mary Powell* comes into New Hamburg.

days, such as Saturday, the passengers were like guests at a large family party, one presided over by a genial host, Captain Anderson. It has been said that one of the participants in these *Mary Powell* "parties" was Franklin Delano Roosevelt, who lived at Hyde Park, and that he and Captain Anderson became firm friends.

For the Hudson River Day Line the major event of 1906 was the commissioning in August of the new *Hendrick Hudson,* which at 379.1 feet was the largest day steamer built for the river up to that time. The Day Line employed her during the summer season on the New York-Albany route, running with the *New York,* while in 1907 the *Albany* offered a new one-day round trip from New York to Poughkeepsie. Of course, a passenger could go to Poughkeepsie on the regular northbound boat and return aboard her running mate as she came down from Albany, but he would have almost no time ashore since the two vessels passed just above Poughkeepsie. The *Albany* was sched-

uled to leave New York an hour after the northbound steamer and would lie at Poughkeepsie for an hour and a half before starting downriver at 4:10 p.m. This schedule afforded ample time ashore for passengers to visit Poughkeepsie, Newburgh or West Point.

To mesh the *Mary Powell* into this new service, the Saturday departure time from New York, which from 1890 through 1906 was 1:45 p.m., was made the regular sailing time throughout the week. The Day Line was then able to offer New Yorkers an afternoon-and-evening round trip on the river, because the *Mary Powell* reached West Point before the southbound *Albany,* to which these passengers could transfer. However, this early afternoon departure cut the available time in New York for the *Mary Powell's* upriver passengers. Those who went ashore at the Desbrosses Street pier in downtown New York had only two hours for shopping and business instead of close to three and a half (which itself was a reduction

153

At 400.5 feet the *Washington Irving* was the largest day boat on the river. Her arrival in May, 1913, signaled some changes in the Day Line's service. Here the steamboat is off West Point about 1923.

from over four hours as a result of the change in Rondout departure time from 5:30 to 6 a.m. in 1904), but by leaving the steamer at one of the uptown landings a passenger could gain an extra hour or so in the city. With the increasing tempo of the times it is unlikely that many businessmen utilized the *Mary Powell*. Her route had essentially become an excursion service for those who wanted to enjoy the relaxation of a trip on the river with ample time in the city for shopping, sightseeing or a visit to Coney Island, and this sharp reduction of layover in New York naturally lessened the *Mary Powell's* attraction for these people.

Those who lived in the section of the river that the *Mary Powell* had served so long and so well remained fanatically loyal and confidently expected that she would go on forever; to them she still was and always would be the "Queen of the Hudson." But in the broad picture her glory was fading; newer, larger and more luxurious boats were taking over the river. After the *Hendrick Hudson* of 1906 came another new day

boat, the *Robert Fulton*, built in 1909. She was smaller than the *Hendrick Hudson* only because she had been built in a hurry to replace the *New York*, which was destroyed by fire at a shipyard in the autumn of 1908.

The early autumn of 1909 was to bring the Hudson-Fulton Celebration, marking the 300th anniversary of Henry Hudson's exploration of the river in 1609 and the 1907 centennial of Robert Fulton's introduction of steam navigation on the Hudson River. Said the Day Line in its literature,

> No such celebration has ever been seen in America before, and the thousands of visitors will be amply entertained and greatly edified. The Day Line, with its great new steamers *Robert Fulton* and *Hendrick Hudson*, will care for its patrons as never before. The famous steamers *Albany* and *Mary Powell* will also be kept in commission to do their share in this gracious task.

While the *Mary Powell* did her share, she was carefully kept out of the limelight. Twenty years before she would have been a star, as she was at

154

Steamer "Albany"

FOR a number of years the Day Line Steamer "Albany" has enjoyed an unusual popularity among travelers and excursionists. She is noted for the unusual grace and beauty of her lines and also commands attention for her great deck room forward.

Length over all 325 feet, width over all 75 feet. Her licensed capacity is 3000 but on charters she will be limited to 2500.

For Charter—Season of 1913

THE ADDITION to the Day Line Fleet of the great, new Steamer "Washington Irving" makes it possible to offer for charter for special parties the Steamer "Mary Powell" during July and August, and in the Spring and Fall the Steamer "Albany." Ideal outings may be planned for parties at reasonable rates, from New York, Albany and points along the Hudson River.

All Day Line Piers are conveniently situated and up-to-date and the luxury and comfort of the "Albany" and "Mary Powell" may now be enjoyed by private charter parties, especially church societies, patriotic orders, conventions, etc. No bars, and no liquors sold or allowed on either steamer.

For further particulars, terms, etc., address:

Hudson River Day Line

DESBROSSES STREET PIER, NEW YORK

Steamer "Mary Powell"

THE Steamer "Mary Powell" for a long time held the title of "The Queen of the Hudson," both for speed and beauty. She was thoroughly overhauled in 1910 and it would be difficult to find a piece of wood or metal which lent strength or grace to her when launched. In rebuilding, care was taken to preserve her original lines. She is 300 feet long, 64 feet broad over guards and draws 6 feet.

Licensed capacity 1800; on charters she will be limited to 1500.

A Day Line advertisement for 1913,
or, the handwriting on the wall.

the Washington Centennial. But now, with two new steamers that were the finest of their type, the Day Line had no intention of emphasizing in public display a vessel that was almost fifty years old and in appearance an antique. Of course, compared to the towing steamer *Norwich* the *Mary Powell* was a mere child, and the *Norwich* was a prime attraction during the celebration, flaunting her age with "Built 1836" painted on her paddle boxes.

The situation with the *Mary Powell* was different. She had closed the Rondout route two days before and on Saturday, September 25th, when the Hudson-Fulton Celebration opened with a monster naval parade in New York, the *Mary Powell* was bound for Albany on the regular Day Line schedule. On Monday she made the southbound trip from Albany to Kingston Point, where the *Robert Fulton*, which had deadheaded to Kingston, took over the run. On October 1st both the *Hendrick Hudson* and the *Robert Fulton* participated in the naval parade from New York to Newburgh, while the *Mary Powell* made a round trip in the New York-Albany service, going up on September 30th and coming down on the first.

The following year, 1910, the *Mary Powell* suffered a serious accident while northbound on Friday, August 5th. The crosshead on the piston rod cracked when she was a short distance south of the first landing, Highland Falls. The engine was stopped, and after he had ascertained the extent of the fracture Captain Anderson decided to anchor. The passengers were taken off by the *Emeline*, a small day boat for freight and passengers that plied between Haverstraw and Newburgh, and landed at Highland Falls. Here the *Albany*, on her southbound run from Poughkeepsie, picked up the one-day round-trip passengers from New York; the rest continued upriver by railroad.

Arrangements were promptly made to have the *Mary Powell* towed to Hoboken to the shops of W. & A. Fletcher Company for repairs. To run as a replacement on the Rondout route the Day Line chartered the *Chrystenah*, a fast and nicely furnished day steamer, 196.5 feet in length, known as the "Queen of the Lower Hudson." Because of the *Chrystenah's* limited capacity the *William F.*

Romer, of the Central-Hudson Steamboat Company, was employed to help with the usually heavy Saturday traffic out of New York. Repairs to the *Mary Powell* were completed in time for her to deadhead up to Rondout for her Monday morning departure on August 8th.

The Central-Hudson Steamboat Company in 1911 added a new single-screw night boat to its fleet. This was the *Benjamin B. Odell,* 263.6 feet in length, built to replace the *Central-Hudson*, formerly the *James W. Baldwin*, which in 1861 had influenced Captain Absalom Anderson's decision to build the *Mary Powell*. Some observations by marine historian Samuel Ward Stanton are worth repeating in connection with the *James W. Baldwin:*

> Both this vessel and the *Mary Powell* have been companion boats, although operated by different companies, and running on different lines, one being an exclusive day passenger boat and the other a night boat carrying freight as well as passengers. It is doubtful whether at any other place in the world will be found a similar case to this: Two steamboats built at the same time — and that 48 years ago — operating between the same points throughout their entire careers. As no one's education is complete without taking a sail on the *Mary Powell* so it ought not to be finished without a trip on the *Central-Hudson*, once the *James W. Baldwin.*[1]

As the proprietor of a fleet of aging steamboats, the Central-Hudson Steamboat Company was extremely proud of the *Benjamin B. Odell,* the first vessel to be constructed for the company; the people of Newburgh, where the Central-Hudson Line had its headquarters, felt this pride as well.

The *Mary Powell* made a postseason excursion to New York on October 3, 1911, and she sailed for Rondout rather late in the afternoon, landing at West 129th Street to take on some homeward-bound excursionists. After she had departed, the northbound *Benjamin B. Odell* landed at the pier; sailing at 4:47 p.m., or about 17 minutes behind the *Mary Powell*, she began a stern chase that lasted for 36 miles. The officers of the Central-Hudson Line steamer were nettled by a news-

---

[1] *The Master, Mate and Pilot,* vol. 2, no. 5 (October, 1909).

With the coming of the *Washington Irving*, the *Albany*, seen here at New York, was demoted to sharing the Rondout route with the *Mary Powell*.

Here the mate of the *Mary Powell*, Philip Maines, poses with Robert F. Stenson, second mate, directly behind him. Clockwise from Stenson are the deckhands: Elmer Durr, Cornelius E. Keyser, Frank M. Sass, Algot J. Benson and Ed Bridge. The last survivor, Mr. Keyser, spoke of them as "a fine crew"; he passed away in August, 1971. (—*Captain William O. Benson collection*)

157

The *Mary Powell*, still trim despite
her years, lies at the Sunflower Dock.

paper report that the *Mary Powell* had recently passed them, and they had decided that here was an excellent opportunity to display their vessel's capabilities. If the *Benjamin B. Odell* could not catch and pass the side-wheeler, then no one else would be the wiser.

Many of the *Mary Powell's* passengers were from Newburgh, and as the *Benjamin B. Odell* drew closer, with her Central-Hudson Line house flag waving on high, they cheered and exulted. In return they became the target for cold and annoyed stares from the loyal crew of the *Mary Powell*. Off Iona Island the night boat finally drew alongside, and the enthusiasm of the Newburghers on both vessels knew no bounds. Up through the Highlands the steamboats sailed, briefly side by side, until the *Benjamin B. Odell* moved into the lead. Afterward Captain Anderson denied that there had been a race; the *Mary Powell* was too old for racing, and he wouldn't have permitted it in any event. As a final touch, allegedly the captain never spoke to the chief engineer of the *Benjamin B. Odell* again.

After the close of the 1910 season a rumor had circulated that the *Mary Powell* would not run in 1911; the following year the rumor was heard again in the spring that the 1911 season would be the vessel's last. Captain Anderson thought it expedient to brand the report as absolutely false and wrote a newspaper letter promising, "The *Mary Powell* will ply the Hudson river for many years to come." However, 1912 was to be the last year in which the *Mary Powell* would put in a full season on her old route. In the early fall of 1912 the *Albany* made a round trip to Rondout to determine what changes in berthing and coaling arrangements might be necessary to accommodate her, for the Hudson River Day Line was planning some operational changes. Of course, the appearance of the *Albany* in Rondout Creek revitalized the old rumor, but once again it was premature.

The largest of all Hudson River day boats, the new *Washington Irving*, 400.5 feet, entered service in May of 1913, almost simultaneously with the commissioning of the New York-Albany night boat *Berkshire*, which at 422.4 feet was the larg-

The *Mary Powell* and the *Albany* in winter quarters on the creek at the Sunflower Dock. (*—Courtesy of Richard J. Warrington*)

est Hudson River steamer ever built. The Hudson River Day Line planned to run the *Washington Irving* and the *Hendrick Hudson* on the New York-Albany route during the busy summer season; the *Robert Fulton* would replace the *Albany* on the New York-Poughkeepsie round-trip service, and the *Albany* would share the Rondout route with the *Mary Powell*. Since the *Albany* was 26 feet longer than the *Mary Powell* and licensed to carry two-thirds more passengers, she would handle the route during the busiest months of July and August, while the *Mary Powell* would be available for chartering. At other times the *Mary Powell* would run on her old route, freeing the *Albany* for charter service. With this arrangement the Day Line made its first serious entry into the charter business, whereby a church, fraternal society or some other organization might rent a vessel for a single outing, providing entertainment for its members and perhaps generating additional funds for its treasury. In the years to come charters developed as an important item in the Day Line's income.

Since the *Mary Powell* and the *Albany* would in a sense become partners, the Day Line rented an isolated wharf on the south side of Rondout Creek near the mouth as winter quarters for both vessels and for use by one as a lay-up berth during the operating season when both steamboats were in the creek at the same time. This wharf had been used by the Cornell Steamboat Company and was known as the Rat Dock; even though the Day Line so carried it in the account books, Captain Anderson shuddered to think of connecting the *Mary Powell* with such an odious name as Rat Dock. He suggested to the vessel's master carpenter, Albert Benson, who lived near by, that he plant sunflower seeds on the wharf. When these flowers waxed and blossomed, the more acceptable and certainly more pleasant-sounding name Sunflower Dock was introduced. (Incidentally, one of Mr. Benson's sons, Algot J. Benson, served as a deckhand aboard the *Mary Powell*, beginning a career that led to officership on other steamboats. Another son, Captain William Odell Benson, is a leading collector of all

159

In charter service, the *Mary Powell* has landed at Bear Mountain Park, on the west bank of the river. (—*Roger W. Mabie collection*)

Above, puffs of steam drift away as the *Mary Powell* blows her whistle in New York. The McAllister Steamboat Co.'s *Highlander*, right, ran with her in excursion service in 1915. (—*Right, Captain Edmund F. Gray collection, Steamship Historical Society of America, Inc.*)

The *Mary Powell* arrives at Bear Mountain on a rainy day while the *Highlander* lies at the pier there.

that pertains to Hudson River steamboats, particularly with respect to the *Mary Powell.*)

The *Mary Powell* plied her regular route in 1913 through the fifth of July, and then on Monday, July 7th, the *Albany* replaced her. On that first trip under the new system the master of the *Albany*, Captain William Van Woert, was in command, but Captain Anderson was also on board to keep an eye on the transition. Said a newspaper on July 8th,

> Clocks stopped all the way down the Hudson River yesterday from Rondout . . . to New York. Persons living on the shores couldn't tell what was the matter. Something seemed strangely missing. Everything seemed to be out of sorts. There was a reason. For fifty-one years during the summer season the waters of the Hudson have been accustomed to bear the *Mary Powell.* . . . Yesterday for the first time she was superseded. The *Albany* took her place. . . .

Said the company in its *Hudson River Day Line Souvenir Magazine:*

> Residents of the Hudson Valley to whom the graceful lines of the Day Line steamers are almost as familiar as the river banks themselves, are missing the daily passing of the Steamer *Mary Powell* these days. Because of increased traffic her run is now being performed by the larger *Albany* and the *Powell* is at present on the reserve list. It should not be imagined, however, that the latter has outgrown her usefulness, as frequent overhaulings have kept her in excellent trim. . . . It is very probable that a lessening of traffic later in the season will see the *Powell* back on her old Kingston route.

In her new role as a charter steamer the *Mary Powell* carried a Sunday-school excursion from Rondout to Bear Mountain Park on July 9th and two days later had a moonlight sail under the auspices of a Poughkeepsie church club. After handling a number of other special trips in July and August she resumed her Rondout route in the middle of September and finished the season. In this first year of the joint *Mary Powell-Albany* operations, the number of passengers carried on the regular route totalled 107,000, or somewhat more than in 1902, the last season prior to Day Line control. In part this reflected a change in the route's schedule which provided for the northbound half of an afternoon excursion to West Point. Northbound passengers to that place were almost 12,000 more than all the passengers both arriving and leaving there in 1902.

161

Captain Anderson was an early automobilist. At the wheel is George N. Betts, Sr., who became the family chauffeur in 1909. Steamboating was still a reasonably healthy business before World War I, as this picture of Captain and Mrs. Anderson, below, indicates. (—Both, courtesy of George N. Betts)

The Anderson family plot is in Montrepose Cemetery, Kingston, where many an ancient Rondout steamboatman sleeps quietly.

162

In that September of 1913 Eben E. Olcott commented on still another article which "chronicled an obituary" of the *Mary Powell*:

If you had had the opportunity and pleasure of seeing the *Mary Powell* hauled out this week on the Tietjen & Lang's Dry Dock at Hoboken you would have been able to refute the statement that the *Mary Powell* is going to the "scrap heap." Capt. McCann of the drydock said that she has not changed her shape a particle since the last time she was hauled out some three years ago. She was searched over to see if there were any open seams, and scarcely anything could be found to do on her. She was lying there on the drydock with fourteen inches of water in her, which had been run into her through hose, and there was not even any sweat coming out. Her bottom copper was dry as a bone....

... There was not a piece of soft timber found in her at the recent examination. She is too small for the numbers that have been coming to us this summer, and it is better to have the larger boat, *Albany*, in place of the *Mary Powell* on the old *Mary Powell* run because she is larger and has more spare power. . . . The *Mary Powell* will continue for years to give pleasure and satisfaction to all who travel on her. . . .

When the *Albany* was placed on the Rondout route in 1913 it was announced that Captain Eltinge Anderson would probably continue to command the *Mary Powell* whenever she was employed on her old run. However, it is understandable that Captain Anderson would not want to stay on as full-time master of the steamboat, because in a sense he had a two-boat fleet to look after. So it was that in May, 1914, the consolidated enrollment and license of the *Mary Powell* was endorsed to show a change in master from A. Eltinge Anderson to William Albertson, who had been a pilot for a number of years.

Captain Anderson's luster had increased without pause as the years went by and was not tarnished in the least by the story that he once left his wife behind. The wife-leaving story has been told about more than one captain, who is always cast in the role of the courageous man who sailed on schedule, with his hurrying but tardy wife still on the wharf. Such tales are popular probably because many a husband dreams of doing something

similar and gets a vicarious thrill out of retelling this sort of "gospel truth." The most widespread version of Captain Anderson's story was that Mrs. Anderson rushed onto the landing at Rondout just as the *Mary Powell* started to move away. And the steamboat continued to move as Captain Anderson called back, "Take the train to Newburgh and catch us there!" In another version, Mrs. Anderson had gone shopping in New York and was left behind when the *Mary Powell* sailed for Rondout. The actual incident, according to George N. Betts, whose father was the family chauffeur and who called Mrs. Anderson "Aunt Fannie," was that one morning Mrs. Anderson planned to go to New York, and the captain was well aware of her plans. But earlier they had had some disagreement, and he went down to the steamboat first. Mrs. Anderson was delayed in her preparations, and when Mr. Betts finally drove her down to the Rondout landing the *Mary Powell* had departed. But Mrs. Anderson did catch the steamer farther down the river.

The pattern of the *Mary Powell's* service in 1914 was similar to that of the previous year. On Friday, July 10th, the Trinity Methodist Episcopal Church of Poughkeepsie chartered her for a moonlight sail and Captain Anderson was in command. Among the scheduled stops was Marlborough, which was not a regular landing for the steamboat. The wharf was maintained by the Central-Hudson Line, and there was a misunderstanding in the arrangements for a landing fee, which the church committee had been assured would not be levied in this case. However, the Marlborough agent warned the *Mary Powell* off and demanded $10, and Captain Anderson could do nothing but proceed, while the would-be Marlborough passengers vented their feelings. Despite this embarrassment the moonlight sail was a success, and during the evening Captain Anderson, who appeared to be in fine health and spirits, waxed autobiographical with newspaper reporters about his forty years on the river. It was to be his last trip.

That year he and Mrs. Anderson were summering at Greenkill Park Inn, a resort near Kingston, and on Sunday evening, July 12th, he heartily joined in the familiar old hymns at a song service. The following morning, singularly enough at

The *Mary Powell* lies at Bear Mountain while the *Hendrick Hudson* steams down off Anthony's Nose. (*—Hudson River Day Line collection, Steamship Historical Society of America, Inc.*)

The *Albany* was damaged in a fog while southbound between Rondout and New York in September, 1915. The *Homer Ramsdell*, below, rendered assistance and the *Asbury Park* made part of the northbound trip until the *Mary Powell* relieved her. (*—R. Loren Graham*)

With her stacks removed, the *Mary Powell* lies in the creek for the fitting of new steam chimneys between the seasons of 1915 and 1916. Below, the Sandy Hook Route's *Asbury Park* briefly filled in for the *Albany* in September, 1915. (*—Above, photograph by Edward Hungerford, courtesy of The Mariners Museum; below, J. O. Osgood collection, Steamship Historical Society of America, Inc.*)

UNITED STATES OF AMERICA

DEPARTMENT OF COMMERCE

STEAMBOAT-INSPECTION SERVICE

TEMPORARY CERTIFICATE OF INSPECTION

(SECTION 4421, REVISED STATUTES)

NAME OF VESSEL: ....M A R Y P O W E L L..................

The undersigned, Local Inspectors for the District of ...Albany..

in the State of ....New York............., hereby CERTIFY that the..... Passenger ....
(Passenger, freight, etc.)

..............Steam.................vessel, named.. MARY POWELL ....
(Steam or motor.)

of........983.........gross tons, of.............Rondout.................................., in the State of

.......New York........................., whereof... The Mary Powell Steamboat Co..............

....is....owner and..William Albertson..................

is master, was regularly inspected on the.......3rd.....day of....May..........................., 1915 ,
by inspectors of the Steamboat-Inspection Service, and found to conform in all things to the requirements
of the laws governing the Steamboat-Inspection Service and the Rules and Regulations Prescribed by the
Board of Supervising Inspectors.

This Temporary Certificate of Inspection is issued under the provisions of Section 4421, Revised Statutes
of the United States, ~~as amended by an act of Congress approved June 11, 1906,~~ in lieu of the regular
certificate of inspection, and shall be in force only until the receipt on board said vessel of the certified copies
of the original certificate of inspection ~~filed with the Chief Officer of Customs at~~ ....
this certificate in no case to be valid after one year from the date of inspection.

The said vessel is permitted to navigate the waters of the.. Hudson River..........................

...., between...

and.., a distance of about................miles, and to
touch at intermediate ports.

This temporary certificate must be framed under glass; and, during the period of its validity, must
be conspicuously placed on the vessel where it will be most likely to be observed by passengers and others.

Number of Life Preservers 1,600

PERSONS ALLOWED TO BE CARRIED.

Officers and crew	20
Passengers (regular)	1,550
Passengers (excursion)	
Total number allowed	1,589

Robert B. Kelly
Inspector of Hulls.

Andrew Saul
Inspector of Boilers.

This form of Certificate of Inspection was adopted by the Board of Supervising Inspectors, Steamboat-
Inspection Service, on February 7, 1911, and approved by the Secretary of Commerce on March 8, 1911.

11—3346

166

After her annual inspection in 1915, the *Mary Powell* had this temporary certificate until a regular certificate of inspection could be issued.

Captain Warrington and
Second Mate Stenson are
at the stern, above left;
at right Captain Warrington
signals to the engine room.
(—Both, courtesy of
Richard J. Warrington)

The *Benjamin B. Odell* slips
past the *Albany* and the
Mary Powell on her way
out of the creek. (—Courtesy
of The Mariners Museum)

New Saturday Service

Beginning Saturday, July 1st, 1916, and continuing through Saturday, September 1st, the Day Line will run an afternoon boat to Albany, (Saturdays only), leaving

Desbrosses Street at 12:30 noon.
West 42nd Street " 1:00 p. m.
West 129th Street " 1:20 p. m.
Yonkers - - - " 1:45 p. m.

The first stop will be Kingston Point at 6:15 p. m.; Malden, 7:00 p. m.; Catskill, 7:30 p. m.; (connecting with trains of the Catskill Mountain Railways), Hudson, 8:00 p. m., connecting boat to Athens, and arriving at Albany about 10:45 p. m.

This afternoon service will be operated by the fast steamer "Mary Powell" and will permit of full advantage of the half holiday for week end trips.

HUDSON RIVER DAY LINE

Desbrosses Street Pier   Telephone, 4141 Spring

To utilize the *Mary Powell* in 1916, the Hudson River Day Line inaugurated the Saturday Specials.

In her later years the *Mary Powell* could still attract a good crowd, as the picture below shows.

(—Photograph by Arthur Finley)

168

This view, taken from out in the river, shows the *Mary Powell* in the mouth of the Desbrosses Street ferry slips at New York. (—*Photograph by Dr. T. C. Miller, Peabody Museum of Salem*)

5:30 a.m., the sailing time of the *Mary Powell* for so many years, he was stricken with apoplexy in his bedroom at the inn and died a few hours later. The funeral was held at 3 p.m. on July 15th, and while it was in progress memorial services were held on both the *Mary Powell* and the *Albany*. The *Mary Powell* was on a Lutheran church excursion to New York, and off Fort Washington Point the engine was stopped. As the bell tolled somberly, the passengers and crew assembled in the saloon, and an expanded choir sang "Nearer My God to Thee." Then the pastor offered a short prayer and spoke briefly of Captain Anderson.

At their annual meeting that year the directors of the Mary Powell Steamboat Company spread upon the record a tribute to Captain Anderson which read in part:

> . . . We hold in pride and regard his wonderful record for ability and straightforward manliness. We have affectionate memory for his consistent life and his kindly, courteous acts. The burden of responsibility for human life in his care he conscientiously assumed and carefully executed. Captain Anderson was to the manner born and the responsibilities and stewardship of the properties and position which came by inheritance to him, he administered with the true spirit of noble manhood. He was positive, without obstinacy; just, without harshness; and commanding with quiet dignity. . . .

Rodney Wood, the Day Line's pier superintendent at Poughkeepsie, put it in more common terms: "He was the commander always, firm but courteous. He would stick to his men through thick and thin, and for that reason they all loved him. He was one of the best captains that ever sailed the river."[2]

In 1915 the *Mary Powell* opened the Rondout service under a new schedule, with the departure time pushed back from 6 to 7 a.m., which cut the scheduled layover at Desbrosses Street in New York to only one hour. In July and August of that year she reached her lowest point, running

---

[2]Poughkeepsie *Evening Star*, July 13, 1914.

169

Billy Sunday was a popular attraction in 1917. A professional baseball player of the 1880s, he was ordained in 1903 and became an evangelist.

Nearing the end of a run down from Rondout, the *Mary Powell* steams along with the New Jersey shore in the background. (— *Eldredge collection, courtesy of The Mariners Museum)*

In the upper Hudson the *Mary Powell* has set up a great roller in the shallow water. *(—Captain William O. Benson collection)*

as a New York excursion boat to Bear Mountain. She operated in conjunction with the McAllister Steamboat Company's *Highlander,* a modern incline-engined side-wheeler that was a far cry from the *Highlander* Captain Absalom Anderson had commanded so long ago. Since the heaviest traffic in the excursion business was on Sunday, when the *Mary Powell* did not run, the propeller *Newburgh* of the Central-Hudson Line filled in for her on that day.

Shortly before the *Mary Powell* entered service in 1916, the announcement was made that Arthur Anderson Warrington had been appointed to command her. In his late twenties, Captain Warrington succeeded the retired Captain Albertson and, according to a press release, had joined the steamboat 15 years before as a deckhand and served for six years as pilot. Actually, the new captain first worked aboard the *Mary Powell* as a bootblack. The fact that Warrington's middle name was Anderson was only a coincidence; he was no relation to the line of steamboating Andersons that had ended with Captain Eltinge. The *Mary Powell* made her first trip with passengers under Captain Warrington's command on May 25th; she received the usual salutes, which perhaps were a little heartier than normal to greet her new captain.

That year the Day Line ran the *Mary Powell* on a special Saturday-afternoon trip to Albany, scheduled to leave Desbrosses Street at 12:30 p.m., touch at West 42nd and West 129th streets and make a landing at Yonkers. Since the New York-Rondout run of the *Albany* would cover the regular landings, the next stop on the Saturday Special would be at Kingston Point, followed by Malden, Catskill and Hudson, with the *Mary Powell* due in Albany at 10:45 p.m. Then she ran light back down the river to the Sunflower Dock to lay in. On the opening trip of this new service the *Mary Powell* had about 300 passengers out of New York and Yonkers and landed approximately 50 at Albany, where she did not arrive until 11:40 p.m. In 1916 between July 1st and September 2nd she made ten trips on the Saturday Special.

In all, the *Mary Powell* made only 52 revenue-producing trips that year, figured by the Day Line's system of counting each northbound and southbound trip separately. A Sunday-school excursion to Bear Mountain would be two trips, as would a round trip over the Rondout route, of which she made the equivalent of 14 that year. These, the Saturday Specials, a moonlight sail, and charters and excursions filled out the 1916 total. The handwriting on the wall was becoming clear.

171

MORNING PROGRAM—Part I.

ISAAC COLLINS, Leader.

1. March—"The Fairest of the Fair" .... Sousa
2. Overture—"Mirella" .... Gounod
3. Waltzes—"Southern Roses" .... Strauss
4. Song—
   a. "Nosie Rosie Posie" .... Edwards
   b. "Climb a Tree With Me" .... Harris
5. Marche—"Tannhauser" .... Wagner
6. Gems—From "Mikado" .... Sullivan

PART II.

7. Two Step—"The Grizzly—Turkey Trot" .... Roberts
8. Morceau—"Awakening of Spring" .... Bach
9. Selection—From "Il Trovatore" .... Verdi
10. Serenade—"Cunning Cupid" .... Aletter
11. Suite—From "The South" .... Nicode
12. Finale—"Your Daddy Did the Same Thing Fifty Years Ago" .... Piantadose

AFTERNOON PROGRAM—Part I.

1. March—"The Venture" .... Franko
2. Overture—"Orpheus" .... Offenbach
3. Songs—
   a. "Good-bye Rose" .... Ingraham
   b. "I'm Afraid, Pretty Maid, I'm Afraid" .... Berlin
4. Waltzes—"The Kiss Waltz" .... Ziehrer
5. Novelette—"Little Kinkies" .... Williams
6. Medley Overture—"Jerome and Schwartz, No. 1" .... Schwartz

PART II.

7. Two Step—"The Hayseed and the Coon" .... Rosey
8. Italian Serenade— .... Ozibulka
9. Selection——From "The Siren" .... Fall
10. Intermezzo D'Amour—"Dream Kisses" .... Wilson
11. An Island Idyl—"Avalon" .... Moret
12. Finale—"Waiting For the Robert E. Lee" .... Muir

The Hotel Chelsea, at West Twenty-third Street and Seventh Avenue is an ideal stopping place for transients. It is a brick and steel structure, absolutely fire-proof. The hotel is conducted on the European plan—Restaurant both a la Carte and Table d'Hote. Rooms spacious and handsomely furnished—Telephone service in all rooms. The hotel is situated in the shopping district and convenient to all railroads, car lines and ferries.

In leaving the Powell at Forty-second Street pier, take West Thirty-fourth Street car and transfer at Seventh Avenue, going down to Twenty-third Street. For fuller descriptive booklet and Map of the City of New York, ask the Purser on the Mary Powell.

This is a sample of concert selections presented on either the *Mary Powell* or the *Albany* — whichever might be covering the route — in the closing years of the Rondout service. To anyone steamboat minded, the finale for the afternoon program on the northbound trip is particularly interesting.

PROGRAM OF CONCERTS

MARY POWELL AND ALBANY

W. Y. HAWLEY Secy. & Treas.

E. E. OLCOTT Pres.

HUDSON RIVER BY DAYLIGHT.

DAILY EXCURSIONS TO BEAR MOUNTAIN OR WEST POINT

CHAPTER NINE
The Final Years of the MARY POWELL

One prelude to the 1917 season reflected the unsettled times immediately preceding the entry of the United States into World War I. Under the date of March 27th Purser Joseph Reynolds, Jr., who served as the official overseer of all matters pertaining to the *Mary Powell*, wrote of his problems to Alfred V. S. Olcott, the son of Eben E. Olcott and later head of the Day Line. Captain Warrington wanted to hire the deckhands to start scrubbing and painting in preparation for the season, but these men asked for $15 a month board while they lived at home before the vessel went into service; previously the rate was $12 a month for board. The mate, with years of service behind him, was pressing for an increase in salary from $50 to $60 per month, plus $15 for board at home. It was said that shipyards on Rondout Creek were offering him $3 per day, and that an unsuccessful request for a raise in salary had been entered with Eben E. Olcott the year before. Captain Warrington also wanted to hire a new second pilot and had one in mind at $100 per month on a five-month basis, which was the salary paid to the second pilot in 1916. These problems were of course resolved, and the *Mary Powell* was made ready for what was to be her last season.

Her operations were further curtailed in 1917, although the Saturday Specials were continued. On Labor Day afternoon the *Mary Powell* left Poughkeepsie for New York on a special trip to help handle the holiday traffic. Then she deadheaded to Rondout, made a regular round trip on her old route on Tuesday, and on Wednesday, September 5th, she again sailed from Rondout, right on time, at 7 a.m. It was to be the last trip with

passengers that she would ever make. That afternoon the *Albany* took the northbound run to Rondout while the *Mary Powell* stayed in New York. According to her chief engineer, Burt R. Greenison, she remained there until Saturday, when she served as a baggage boat to assist the through boat to Albany. Such a vessel would carry baggage for another steamer when heavy traffic was anticipated, and over the years the Day Line had occasionally chartered a steamboat for this work. This may not have been the only time that the *Mary Powell* was employed as a baggage boat in her twilight period, although nothing is recollected on the subject. Actually, there was no need for her to assist the regular boat that day, since passenger movement was light, but the Day Line had decided to use her anyway, as she had to go to the Sunflower Dock to lay up. Chief Greenison recalled that after unloading the last of her baggage cargo at Catskill she sailed back down the river to Rondout Creek. Although no one knew it, the *Mary Powell's* active career was over.

In 1917 she had made 41 revenue-producing trips, the last of which was on September 5th. Since the Day Line entered only revenue-producing trips in its official records, that September 5th southbound, and not the trip as a baggage boat, was set down in company records as the final trip of the *Mary Powell*, and in the years that followed when answering inquiries on the subject the Day Line always supplied that date. The final run on the Rondout route was made by the *Albany* on September 15th, marking the close of a line that had been served by the *Thomas Powell* and the *Mary Powell* for sixty years.

173

Rondout Creek in 1918 looked liked a home for aged steamboats. At left is the *M. Martin* with the *Oswego*, which made her final trip that year, beyond her. In the distance is the *Norwich* and on the other side of the creek, at the Sunflower Dock, is the *Mary Powell* herself. In the foreground is the cross-creek chain ferry *Riverside.* (*—Courtesy of Captain Francis M. Don*)

The following spring the Day Line announced that the Rondout route would not open until July 6th and would close on August 31st. The work of preparing the *Mary Powell* for service went on as usual; in May she was inspected and her license renewed for another year. At this point the Day Line explained that the reason for the late start on the Rondout line was the government's request that the company practice coal conservation because of the war. On Thursday, May 23rd, a tugboat towed the *Mary Powell* from the Sunflower Dock to the Rondout coal pocket, where she coaled up; then she was towed back to the dock. On the next day the regular Day Line service to Albany opened, and not long after that the company made what, for it, was a radical announcement: beginning June 16th its steamers would operate on Sundays. Only a family-controlled line could have abstained for so long from reaping the great additional profits available on Sundays.

This change in policy meant that four steamers instead of three would be needed to cover the Albany route and the round-trip Poughkeepsie service, as each vessel required about one free day a week to give the crew a rest and to perform any necessary maintenance. As a relief steamer for this purpose, the *Albany* would be taken off the Rondout run; accordingly, if that line were to continue, the *Mary Powell* would have to cover it the greater portion of each week. However, the Rondout service was only a minor part of the Day Line's business, and putting the *Mary Powell* back on full-time duty was impractical, considering that she was 57 years old and obsolete by the company's standards. So the Day Line announced that there would be no service on the Rondout line in 1918 in order to hold down coal consumption; emphasizing the coal shortage in connection with the closing spiked the possibility of civic remonstrances. Soon the rumor grew that the *Mary*

The *Mary Powell* spent the 1919 season lying at the Sunflower Dock. (—*Photograph by Edward Hungerford, courtesy of The Mariners Museum*)

Powell would be chartered by the government for use in New York harbor, but she was not. Finally, during the great influenza epidemic that autumn her last master, Captain Arthur Warrington, died on October 12th at the age of 31.

In 1919, with the war over, it became apparent even to the wishful thinkers that the Day Line had no intention of resuming the Rondout service. The *Mary Powell* was not inspected or licensed and remained quietly laid up at the Sunflower Dock. Her decks were uncommonly still: no hubbub of passengers, no bells from the engine room, no cheerful call for the next landing. Gone for years were the men who had run her in the days when, with a rainbow of spray on her bow and a white wake tumbling astern, she had sailed between the Hudson's green hills, through the Highlands at the gloaming; the Andersons, Betts and Bishop, Lawrence and Hayes, Thomas Cornell and a host of others — she had survived them all.

The Day Line was in a quandary. The next logical step would be to sell the *Mary Powell* for scrap, but this would create a furor that the company would prefer to avoid. Finally the inevitable decision was made, and the Mary Powell Steamboat Company announced that it would receive bids for the purchase of the vessel up to 10 a.m. on Monday, November 17, 1919; if the company decided to make an award, it would do so in two days. The company published the terms and conditions of the sale in part as follows:

The purchaser shall execute a contract with bond for the faithful performance of the following obligations and guarantees:

That the vessel shall be removed from its present berth before any work of demolition or the quartering of any personnel on board shall be done.

The vessel shall not be used in passenger or freight service on the Hudson River again.

The vessel is not to be made the subject of any fire or destruction for the production of moving picture films or destroyed in any such manner as shall be deemed by present owners, prejudicial to the public estimate of the safety of steam navigation.

William H. Ewen, widely known marine historian, both writes and lectures about Hudson River steamboats. Here he poses with the whistle from the *Mary Powell,* one of the gems in his extensive collection of marine relics.

The last clause was said to have been inserted because the film industry was extremely interested in acquiring the vessel for a production that would be climaxed by a marine disaster, which obviously would be bad advertising for the steamboat operators. A story current at the time had it that Eben E. Olcott had refused an offer of $100,000 from a movie company.

The deadline for receiving bids came and went, and on November 19th one was accepted. This had been tendered by Israel Levinson and Ruby Cohen, who with William E. Friedman later gave bond in the amount of $5,000 according to the terms of the sale. Levinson operated the Newburgh Iron & Metal Company, and Cohen was in charge of its Poughkeepsie branch. Throughout

the Hudson Valley and particularly in Kingston there was a "curious interest" about the sale of the *Mary Powell.* It was reported in the press that the steamboat had brought $40,000, a figure which Levinson stated was too high. That it was, for he and Cohen had bid $3,250. As a wooden-hulled steamboat with a wood superstructure, the *Mary Powell* had little in the way of scrap metal except her machinery, the boilers and the copper sheeting on the hull. At the time of the sale she was carried on the Mary Powell Steamboat Company's books for $5,000, so her sale brought a paper loss of $1,750.

Prior to the transaction the Day Line had removed such furnishings as it might wish to use on its other vessels. The big landing bell, cast by the famed Meneely's of West Troy, was placed in a tower at Bear Mountain and then moved to Indian Point when the Day Line opened its own park; it rang as a warning before steamers departed. Eventually the bell was presented to the New-York Historical Society. The *Mary Powell's* whistle was installed on the *Robert Fulton;* when that vessel was sold in 1956 for use as a floating community center in the Bahamas, William H. Ewen, a prominent marine historian, writer and lecturer, acquired the whistle for his extensive collection relating to Hudson River steamboats.

Not unexpectedly, the announcement of the sale of the *Mary Powell* unleashed the irate, the sentimentalists — most of whom considered themselves poets — and the souvenir hunters. Certainly in the highest rank of the last category, Elwin M. Eldredge was the first to contact the Hudson River Day Line. Then only 26, he was already amassing his monumental collection of pictorial matter, data and relics pertaining to American steam navigation which is now in the Mariners Museum at Newport News, Virginia. Mr. Eldredge's instant action in this case indicates why his collection grew as it did; he was not a man to put something off until tomorrow and then find that someone else had acquired what he wanted. Under the date of November 24th, 1919, he wrote to Eben E. Olcott to inquire about a painting of the vessel that hung on board and also about the possibility of buying a chair from the saloon. Mr. Olcott replied that he was considering having the paint-

The *Albany* lasted a long time. In 1934 she was sold and renamed *Potomac*, running on the Potomac River through the 1948 season. She retained the name when her iron hull was stripped and converted into a barge, afterwards renamed *Ware River*. In 1968 she became a bulkhead at Chesapeake, Va., and these pictures are from the following year. (—*Both photographs by John L. Lochhead*)

ing restored and hung in the Day Line office, but he would be glad to sell a chair and would have one brought down in the spring, after the company steamers entered service. Mr. Eldredge, on tenterhooks, immediately offered to pay express charges if the chair could be shipped in the near future, but there was no reply from Olcott until June, when he reported the arrival of the chair. What Mr. Eldredge paid for the chair we do not know, but the ledger of the Mary Powell Steamboat Company has a 1923 entry of $15 for a chair sold at the 42nd Street pier. Whether or not it was Eldredge's chair belatedly entered, the selling price was close to one-half of one percent of the going price for the entire steamboat. As far as *Mary Powell* relics are concerned, this transaction was typical.

Another who came on stage right behind Mr. Eldredge in the dual role of irate citizen and souvenir hunter was Wallace Peck, who was connected with the Hudson's Bay Company agency in New York. On November 29th he wrote,

> I notice the good old *Mary Powell* has been sold for scrap, and being an *old* Hud-

son River boy I would like to purchase some good memento of her, for the sake of *lang syne*. I would greatly appreciate the name and address of the buyer.

> You, of course, know your business best, but it does seem to me that "the *Mary*" was good for several years more, and that from the time she passed into the hands of your line she was seemingly snubbed and treated "contemptuously," if I may so describe the passing out of a grand old River boat!

To this Alfred V. S. Olcott replied with a masterpiece of diplomacy:

> It is needless to say that we share the regret and a sense of personal loss in the fact that the *Mary Powell* has carried her last passenger.

> As you know the *Mary Powell* was nearly sixty years old, and we hesitated about taking any action toward operating her in which there might be the slightest risk to the passengers or injuring the pleasant memories that so many have of her. We have found during the last few years that she was operated that a [*sic*] number of people that felt about it the way you did was not as numerous as those who, to use your own words,

On a cold winter's day in 1920 the *Mary Powell* lies at the Sunflower Dock, quietly awaiting her fate while the scrap dealers negotiate.

178

The gallant vessel sails again, surrounded by other notables from the Hudson's history, in a mural by John Pike in the Kingston Savings Bank.

"snubbed her and treated her contemptuously," in comparison with the newer boats. Largely on account of sentiment she was kept in commission for years after increasing cost of repairs necessary for safe operation made her unprofitable.

But Mr. Peck was not as biting, nor as poetic, as J. H. Deane, who wrote to a newspaper,

> What are the heads of the steamboat company thinking of? Have they no vision, no imagination that they resign her to such an ignominious fate? Must Shylock have his pound of flesh in these late days? Is there no Portia to save her from the junkmen's hammer? Far better that she go in the blaze of glory in the movies there to be seen the last time by the entire civilized world than to be just scrapped for the sake of the old metal, etc., that is in her. . . .

It is enough to move one to verse.[1]

> O death, where is thy stingaling?
> O bell, where is thy ringaling?
> *Mary,* though thou art no more.
> We wilt remember thee as of yore,
> Though thou canst no more our Queen be,
> Thy name wilt go down in history!

Ah, Mr. Editor, "it is to weep."

---

[1]For the efforts of others who were moved to verse, see Appendix D.

179

The *Rob,* which towed the *Mary Powell* to the
end of the trail, breaks ice in Rondout Creek.

Another letter writer called for a new vessel. "A boat similar to the *Albany* would do. But her name should be *Kingston* and the great booming whistle and the sweet-toned bell of the *Mary Powell* would sound fine on her."

In this period, too, there was the matter of the mirrors. Professor Myron J. Michael, superintendent of schools in Kingston, understood that the mirrors from the *Mary Powell* were then in storage on the *Albany,* and he wanted two of them for installation in "the girl's gymnasium" at the new Kingston High School. He contacted the Day Line's traveling passenger agent in Kingston, who contacted Alfred V. S. Olcott early in 1920, and Mr. Olcott turned the matter over to his superintendent, C. G. Whiton. On February 2nd the mate of the *Albany* advised Mr. Whiton that Dr. Michael had been aboard and picked out the two mirrors that had flanked the doorway inside the dining room of the *Mary Powell;* someone had come up with an estimate that they were worth $63. At this point F. B. Hibbard, the general passenger agent of the Day Line and a resident of Kingston, learned of the matter and wrote to Mr. Whiton,

I would most urgently advise that the [mirrors] be offered to the High School as a gift without any strings attached. . . .

. . . the High School will have plates made reading

"From the *Mary Powell*
"Presented by the Hudson River
Day Line"

or anything you care to suggest. The High School gymnasium is attended by 800 students annually and the advertisement would be perpetual. The Day Line officials have no idea of the deep attachment in which the *Powell* is held by the people of this section and it would seem almost criminal to throw away this splendid opportunity of keeping her memory before the public for years to come. It would be a graceful act and much appreciated. I think Mr. Alfred [Olcott] after careful consideration will agree with me on this. . . .

Mr. Olcott did. Soon a Kingston newspaper announced that the mirrors had been installed, but they were in the girls' dressing or locker room, which isn't quite the same as the gymnasium!

The *Mary Powell* was not owned for long by Messrs. Levinson and Cohen. Later it was said

A view of the *Mary Powell*, taken from the hurricane deck of the *Albany*, which was laid up ahead of her, in March of 1920. (—*Captain William O. Benson collection*)

that they had a prospective purchaser who would continue her in service in the South, but that deal fell through. In any event, by January of 1920 Cohen was in negotiation with John A. Fischer, a Yankee trader of the old school who, among other things, operated a hotel along Rondout Creek. The preceding November he had submitted a bid of $2,600 to the Mary Powell Steamboat Company, but of course this was rejected. On April 15, 1920, Fischer announced that he and his brother expected to buy the vessel within a few days, and so they did, on April 17th. In a newspaper interview many years later he said that Levinson and Cohen had sold her for the same amount they had paid, $3,250; he also told this writer that she had cost him $3,200. On April 20th he had the tugboat *Rob*, of the Cornell Steamboat Company, tow the *Mary Powell* up the creek to a wharf at the upper end of Connelly — formerly South Rondout — about two miles from the mouth of the creek on the south bank across from his hotel. Fischer planned to sell the vessel and even advertised her for sale, in condition to run and with boilers in good order. However, either he had no response, or his efforts were

thwarted by the conditions laid down by the Mary Powell Steamboat Company in the original sale contract, and he was left with little alternative but to scrap the steamboat.

In any case, the *Mary Powell* did not change hands again, so it may be of interest to note the date on which she was removed from documentation. To marine historians this date has a holy quality, for it is the final entry in the hallowed records of government, beyond contradiction; it is the burial. But the *Mary Powell*, since her license expired in May of 1919, had been officially in limbo — neither licensed for service nor removed from documentation. This oversight was corrected between the Day Line and the deputy collector of customs at Albany, and the *Mary Powell* was officially abandoned on March 31, 1920, about three weeks before she was towed away for eventual scrapping.

Her obituaries were many and prolonged. In 1920 *The Literary Digest*, a prominent periodical of the day, said in an illustrated article, ". . . one would think it more appropriate to 'give her to the god of waves, the lightning, and the storm,' as Oliver Wendell Holmes proposed for *Old Iron-*

sides. . . ." There were newspaper items galore, and as late as 1925 a Boston paper carried in its gravure section a picture of the remains of the *Mary Powell* as they then appeared, which indicates the continuing interest in the passing of the vessel. The late Sophie Miller, who for many years wrote a column on local history for the Kingston *Daily Freeman,* lamented the fact that the steamer had not been preserved as the nucleus of a living marine museum at Kingston Point.

But of course she was not preserved. As Mr. Fischer commenced the dismantling he found that he had a ready market for many parts of the *Mary Powell,* which people were interested in acquiring for sentimental reasons, or which tempted the antiquarians from the common collector up to Henry Ford. This market lasted long after the supply was exhausted, and it is safe to say that there are today many treasured "relics" of the *Mary Powell* that never had the slightest connection with the vessel. During the course of the dismantling the steamboat was moved from the wharf and put on the mud flat directly above it. There the work was completed, and the hulk settled down to a long career of slowly rotting away.

The tall smokestacks lay on the wharf until 1938, when they were sold for use as conduits. The walking beam, which had fallen into the mud, was not removed until 1947, when the lighter *William S. Keeler,* then engaged in recovering junk metal, hauled it out. Over the years the last resting place of the *Mary Powell* was marked by a near-by cottage, built from her woodwork and adorned by the name from the front of her pilot-house. In 1957 sparks from a bonfire accidentally ignited the dry wood and the little building was destroyed.

Still today, one who knows the area may visit the Anderson family plot in Montrepose Cemetery, Kingston, where Captain Absalom Lent Anderson and his sons Captain Jansen H. and Captain A. Eltinge Anderson, are buried. After a walk of but a few minutes the visitor will come to a spot on a hill overlooking what little remains of the *Mary Powell's* hull. Not even death has separated her by far from those who loved her well.

Appendices

APPENDIX A-1

Basic Data

For quick reference, here are some figures on the measurements and equipment of the *Mary Powell*.

Statutory dimensions —

As built (1861): 267' length, 34'6" breadth of beam, 9'2" depth of hold.

After lengthening (1862), in revised measurements: 288' length, 34.6' breadth of beam, 9.2' depth of hold.

Tonnage, after lengthening and under present system: 983 gross, 877 net tons.

Engine (vertical beam) —

Cylinder (original): 62" diameter, 12' length of stroke.

Cylinder (enlarged 1874-75): 72" diameter, 12' length of stroke.

Boilers, two on guards: *Mary Powell* had six sets; the following years indicate seasons between which new boilers were installed, then the construction material and the contractor.

Original — iron — Fletcher, Harrison & Co., New York, N. Y.

1866-67 — iron — John Dillon, Rondout, N.Y.

1872-73 — steel — Alexander Cauldwell, Newburgh, N.Y.

1880-81 — steel — McEntee & Dillon, Rondout, N.Y.

1890-91 — steel — McEntee & Rodie, Rondout, N.Y.

1903-04 — steel — Townsend-Downey Shipbuilding Co., Shooters Island, N.Y.

The method for taking statutory dimensions, as prescribed by law, is as follows: "The length from the fore part of the outer planking on the side of the stem to the after part of the main stern-post of screw steamers, and to the after part of the rudder-post of all other vessels measured on the top of the tonnage-deck shall be accounted the vessel's length. The breadth of the broadest part on the outside of the vessel shall be accounted the vessel's breadth of beam. A measure from the under side of the tonnage-deck plank, amidships, to the ceiling of the hold (average thickness), shall be accounted the depth of hold." Therefore, the statutory length and breadth were not the same as the overall length and breadth.

Besides the data given above, there were many sources of information, both correct and erroneous, on the *Mary Powell*. For the reader seriously interested in such matters, some are included in Appendix A-2.

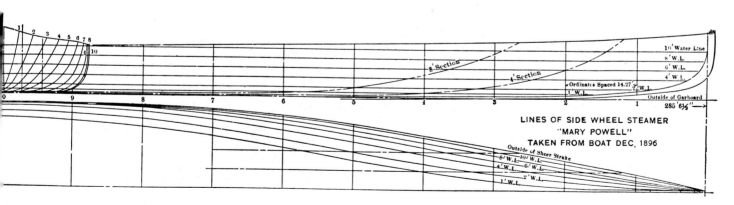

LINES OF SIDE WHEEL STEAMER
"MARY POWELL"
TAKEN FROM BOAT DEC. 1896

183

(*—Hudson River Day Line collection, Steamship Historical Society of America, Inc.*)

Various Measurements of the MARY POWELL

Theron Skeel, M.E., in the 1870s had occasion to make a number of trips on the *Mary Powell* between Newburgh and New York, and he took the opportunity to make a detailed study of the vessel. This information he set down in a paper entitled "An American River Steamer — Performances of the *Mary Powell*," which appeared in *The Iron Age* for May 23, 1878 (vol. 21, no. 21, pp. 1 and 3). Skeel, described in the number as a "clever young engineer," had died a short time before. His article began:

> The following paper contains the results of some experiments made on the steamer *Mary Powell*, running on the Hudson River between Rondout and New York.

> The *Mary Powell* is acknowledged to be one of the fastest, if not the very fastest boat upon the river. The details of the following experiments should be of particular interest to the engineer, as they are the first that have ever been published with any pretension to accuracy.

Skeel briefly described the essentials of his subject in a few sentences.

> The hull is built in the usual style of the North [Hudson] River boats — that is, a shallow hull stiffened by immense hog-frames and masts and stays. The whole hull is as light as possible. No freight is carried. Passengers are carried on the main deck and on the next deck above. The upper [hurricane] deck is only of 5/8-inch pine and serves as a roof. The steward's department is in the hold.

> The boat is propelled by one beam engine of the ordinary river boat style. . . . This engine is condensing, the condenser being under the cylinder, and the air pump is worked from the main beam.

Amongst the army of figures which Skeel marshaled for his paper are these:

Hull:

Length on waterline	286'0"
Length overall	294'0"
Beam at waterline	34'3"
Beam overall	64'0"
Depth of hold	9'0"
Height from main deck to promenade deck	10'0"
Height from promenade deck to upper deck	8'0"
Draft of water with mean load of passengers and coal	6'0"
Square feet midship section (estimated)	200'0"
Cubic feet displacement (estimated)	28,000'0"
Projected area of surface resisting head wind, square feet	2000'0"

Engine:

Diameter of cylinder	72"
Stroke of piston	144"
Diameter of air pump	40"
Stroke of air pump	62"
Diameter of shaft	15"
Diameter of paddle wheels over tips of buckets	31'0"
Length of each bucket	10'6"
Width of each bucket	1'6"
Number of buckets to each paddle wheel	26
Greatest immersion of outer edge of bucket at mean draft	3'6"

Boilers (two, direct flue and return tubular type, built of steel stamped 72,000 pounds):

Length overall	26'0"
Length of cylindrical shell	16'1"
Length of firebox	9'0"
Width of firebox	11'0"
Diameter of cylindrical shell	10'0"
Diameter of steam drum	5'10"
Height of steam drum	12'0"
Width of each furnace (two in each boiler)	4'10"
Length of furnaces	8'0"
Length of direct flues	9'1"
Number of direct flues in each boiler, and diameter	two, 9"
	two, 14"
	six, 16"
Diameter of tubes, external (80 in each boiler)	4½"
Length of tubes	16'6"
Grate surface (two boilers)	152'0"

Comparative data for three years:

	1875	1876	1877
Number of observations	—	12	27
Running time in minutes from Newburgh to New York or return	185½	187½	182
Revolutions per minute from Newburgh to New York or return (by counter)	—	21.80	21.77
Statute miles per hour from Newburgh to New York or return (The decline in 1876 was thought to have been due to the heavy traffic generated by the Centennial Exposition of that year.)	19.3	19.2	19.8

Comparative data for three years (con't)

	1875	1876	1877
Revolutions per round trip from Rondout to New York and return	—	13,100	12,190
Coal per round trip, in long tons	23.79	22.85	24.25

Specific mean data for 1877:

Number of revolutions of engine per hour	1306
Pounds of coal consumed per hour	5970
Pounds of combustible (ashes 16⅗%)	4870
Steam pressure in boilers, pounds per square inch above atmosphere	28
Vacuum, inches of mercury	25

Indicator card data, steam pressure in cylinder, in pounds per square inch above zero —

Initial pressure at beginning of stroke of piston	40.0
At point of cut off of steam	31.2
End of stroke of piston	16.4

Power —

Total horsepower	1899
Indicated horsepower	1540
Net horsepower	1446

Chief Engineer B. F. Isherwood, U. S. Navy, in preparing "The American River Paddle-Wheel Steamboat *Mary Powell*," which appeared in *The Journal of the Franklin Institute* for July, 1879 (vol. 108, whole no. 643, pp. 18-27), used information supplied to him by Skeel and stated, ". . . my friend, the accomplished engineer, Mr. Theron Skeel, having occasion to make many trips in the *Mary Powell* during the summer of 1877, kept for me an accurate record. . . ." But many of the figures which Isherwood set down differed from those presented by Skeel in his own paper or had not been included by Skeel. The following data is taken from the Isherwood article.

Hull:

Length on load waterline from the forward edge of the rabbet of the stem to the after edge of the sternpost	290′
Extreme breadth on load waterline	34′
Depth of hold from top of floor timbers to underside of deck plank	9⅓′
Depth from load waterline to lower edge of rabbet of keel	6′
Depth of keel below lower edge of its rabbet	6″
Area of greatest immersed transverse section to load waterline	198.5 sq. ft.
Displacement to load waterline	881 tons
Weight of machinery with appurtenances, including boiler water	approx. 210 tons
Weight of coal embarked	approx. 30 tons
Total weight in engineer department (27.24% of displacement)	approx. 240 tons

Boilers:

Extreme length, exclusive of projecting steam drum	25′½″
Projection of steam drum forward of boiler shell	1′3½″
Extreme height, exclusive of steam drum	10′9″
Extreme breadth	11′
Height of steam drum above boiler shell	12′

Anthracite of small nut size used as fuel.

Isherwood described the engine: "There is one overhead beam-engine with a wooden gallows-frame. The cylinder is vertical and has four balanced poppet-valves, two for admitting and two for exhausting the steam. The steam-valves function also as expansion valves by means of the mechanism known as Stevens' cut-off. The condensation of the steam is effected in a jet-condenser. The air-pump is vertical and single-acting. The cylinder is not steam-jacketed; its ends, its valve-chests and its side-pipes have no protecting covering, but its cylindrical portion and all the steam-piping connecting it with the boilers were well covered with asbestos felting."

For many years the guidebook published annually by the Mary Powell Steamboat Company gave dimensions for the steamer. These are from the 1896 number.

Length on waterline	288′9″
Length overall	300′0″
Breadth of beam, molded	34′4″
Breadth of beam over guards	64′0″
Depth	10′3″
Draft of water	6′0″

After the overhaul between the seasons of 1903 and 1904, *Marine Engineering* of August, 1904 (vol. 9, no. 8, pp. 378-379), ran a feature on the *Mary Powell* from which the following is taken.

Hull:

Length between perpendiculars	286′0″
Length on load waterline	288′9″
Length overall	300′0″
Beam, molded	34′4″
Beam, over guards	64′0″
Draft, mean	6′0″
Midship section	170.5 sq. ft.
Displacement, approximately	800 tons

Paddle wheels:

Outside diameter (previously 33′)	31′9″
Number of buckets	26
Length of each bucket	10′6″
Face area of each bucket	15½ sq. ft.

185

Boilers (tubular):

Length	27'0"
Width of front	11'6"
Diameter	10'8"
Length of flues	10'10"
Number of flues in each boiler, and diameter	two, 12"
	two, 15"
	four, 16"
	two, 18"
Diameter of tubes (80 in each boiler)	5"
Length of tubes	19'
Grate surface (two boilers)	156 sq. ft.
Indicated horsepower:	1560
Number of passengers:	1700

This data is from Hudson River Day Line records, some years after the 1903-1904 overhaul.

Length overall	300'
Length, keel	285'
Beam	34'
Beam overall	64'
Boilers, working pressure, pounds	45
Bunker capacity, tons	35
Fuel consumption, buckwheat coal, 12 hours, in tons	20
Fuel consumption, 200 miles, in tons	25
Horsepower	2400
Passenger capacity	1800

Apparently when the *Mary Powell* was under Day Line control and running regularly on the Rondout route, she carried a crew as large as 45 when necessary. This was later cut to 39, to include one master, two pilots, one mate, eight deckhands, one chief engineer, one assistant engineer, four firemen, one watchman and twenty in the steward's and other departments as needed.

The certificate of inspection in 1914 shows the passenger capacity still as 1800, but on the temporary certificate of inspection for 1915 it was given as 1550 and this figure appears on the 1918 certificate, issued after the last inspection, which took place on May 13 of that year.

In *List of Merchant Vessels of the United States — 1902*, the first one in which the number in the crews of vessels was included, the figure for the *Mary Powell* was given as 35 and so continued.

The figure of 2400 for indicated horsepower, cited above, was likewise shown in the *List*. The 1903 volume was the first in which this information was included for the *Mary Powell*. In the 1916 through 1919 volumes, as the result of a typographical error, the horsepower was given as 400.

Johnson's Steam Vessels of the Atlantic Coast, 1917, and *Johnson's Steam Vessels of the Atlantic, Gulf and Pacific Coasts, 1920*, for which data was often supplied by the owners or checked by them, gave this data for the *Mary Powell:*

Length	288'
Breadth	34.6'
Depth	10.3'
Indicated horsepower	1560
Return tube boilers, length	27'
Boilers, diameter	10.8'
Boilers, working pressure	45

The *Mary Powell,* since she plied between United States ports on waters under federal jurisdiction, had to be enrolled to meet statutory requirements. This was done at a customhouse, after which a copy of the certificate of enrollment, describing the vessel in brief and setting forth ownership, was issued. Any changes in these areas called for a new enrollment.

The accompanying table shows all the enrollments of the *Mary Powell,* from the files in the National Archives, Washington. The discrepancies between them are not unique and point up some of the problems which confront any marine historian who goes searching for "facts."

For the first enrollment, the tonnage is set down as 819 87/95. Many years ago the National Archives supplied the author with a figure of 819 81/95, which was used thereafter. A recent and close study of the document itself indicates that the "81" stemmed from a very understandable misreading of the longhand figure and should have been "87." Also on the first enrollment, John L. Hasbrouck's last name was misspelled "Hasbrook" and on the second, "Harbeck."

On the third enrollment (number 117) decimals rather than fractions were used in the figures for measurement and tonnage, and the tonnage was computed by a different formula than had been used previously. This was a result of new legislation, by which vessels also had to be readmeasured. On enrollment number 117, too, the date built was incorrectly entered, probably by a nodding clerk, and became 1862 instead of 1861.

On the sixth enrollment (number 2), another clerical error completely changed the dimensions; two enrollments later (number 5½), the length was farther increased by a tenth of a foot and at the same time the tonnage was expanded slightly. This latter error was rectified another two enrollments later (number 99).

Net tonnage came into being for vessels of the United States by an act of 1882, and the net tonnage for the *Mary Powell* was first entered across the face of enrollment number 22 (January 29, 1883).

The clerical errors in the year built and in the dimensions persisted down through the years and onto the last enrollment (number 65). On the surrendered copy of this document in the National Archives, the year built has been corrected in pencil from 1862 to 1861, and the dimensions from 288.9 x 34.4 x 9 feet to 288 x 34.6 x 9.2 feet. Apparently some meticulous soul unofficially made the corrections to bring the year

built into agreement with the original enrollment, and the dimensions into agreement with enrollment number 117 of May 8, 1865, issued after the vessel was readmeasured.

The National Archives has advised by letter, "We have no means of determining when these changes were made on the document. There is no reference on either the front or back of any document issued for the *Mary Powell* after May 8, 1865 that refers to a readmeasurement or change in description. . . ."

In the government's annual *List of Merchant Vessels of the United States* during the 1880s, when the date a vessel was built was added to the information furnished, the *Mary Powell* was shown as having been built in 1869. Dimensions of vessels were first incorporated into the *List* for the year ending June 30, 1885, and those for the *Mary Powell* were set down as 288.9 x 34.4 x 9.0 feet, the same as on the the then current enrollment, number 30. In the 1886 *List* the depth was inadvertently increased to 9.9 feet, and these figures continued through the 1896 *List.* However, in the 1890 *List* the date built had been "corrected" from 1869 to 1862 so that it agreed with the date on the enrollment.

At last, in *List of Merchant Vessels of the United States — 1897,* the entry for the *Mary Powell* was completely and rightly corrected to give the date built as 1861, and the dimensions as 288.0 x 34.6 x 9.2 feet. The tonnage figures had been valid and, except for the dropping of the decimal portion of them in the 1898 *List,* when this was done with all vessels, there were no further changes to the entry. Consequently, it remained correct through the *List* for 1919, the last volume in which the *Mary Powell* was carried.

A final comment on enrollments in general is perhaps in order. The date of a re-enrollment does not always correspond to the date possession of a vessel changed, nor does it necessarily indicate when alterations affecting measurements took place. The *Mary Powell* was lengthened in the fall of 1862, but was not re-enrolled with the new measurements until April 30, 1864.

As an example in the case of ownership change, the bill of sale when Alfred Van Santvoord and J. McB. Davidson bought the *Mary Powell* was executed in February, 1869, but they did not have the vessel enrolled in their names until July, 1869. Again, when they sold her to Captain A. L. Anderson in January, 1872, the captain did not complete the payments until June, after which he had the vessel enrolled with himself as sole owner.

ENROLLMENTS OF THE MARY POWELL

Official Number 16982

Date	Port	Enrollment Number	Owners	Shares	Date Built
1862, Apr. 25	New York	44	Absalom L. Anderson John Ketcham John L. Hasbrook	1/2 1/4 1/4	1861
1864, Apr. 30	New York	105	Absalom L. Anderson John Ketcham John L. Harbeck	1/2 1/4 1/4	1861
1865, May 8	New York	117	A. L. Anderson John Ketcham John L. Hasbrouck	1/4 1/8 5/8	1862
1865, Oct. 17	New York	353	Thomas Cornell	Sole	1862
1865, Oct. 17	New York	354	Thomas Cornell Daniel Drew	1/2 1/2	1862
1867, Feb. 26	Albany	2	Thomas Cornell	Sole	1862
1869, July 12	Albany	9	Alfred Van Santvoord J. McB. Davidson	1/2 1/2	1862
1872, July 2	New York	5½	A. L. Anderson	Sole	1862
1873, June 10	New York	233	A. L. Anderson	Sole	1862
1879, June 17	Albany	99	A. L. Anderson	Sole	1862
1883, Jan. 29	Albany	22	Thomas Cornell	Sole	1862
1885, May 12	Albany	30	Mary Powell Steamboat Co. (Wm. H. Cornell, Vice-President)	Sole	1862
1886, Feb. 23	Albany	11	Mary Powell Steamboat Co. (A. Eltinge Anderson, Secretary)	Sole	1862
1912, May 16	Albany	65	Mary Powell Steamboat Co. (A. Eltinge Anderson, Gen. Mgr.)	Sole	1862

65 Surrendered, Albany, March 31, 1920; vessel abandoned.

Length	Breadth	Depth	Tons		Reason Issued
267'	34-6/12'	9-2/12'	819-87/95		First document
288	34-6/12	9-2/12	889-78/95		Vessel rebuilt; readmeasured; tonnage increased
288	34.6	9.2	983.57		Readmeasured (Act of 1864 and 1865 amendment)
288	34.6	9.2	983.57		Property changed
288	34.6	9.2	983.57		Property changed in part
288.8	34.4	9	983.57		Property changed in part
288.8	34.4	9	983.57		Property changed
288.9	34.4	9	983.59		Property changed
288.9	34.4	9	983.59		Original of prev. enrollment lost
288.9	34.4	9	983.57		District changed
288.9	34.4	9	Gross 983.57	Net 877.16	Property changed
288.9	34.4	9	983.57	877.16	Property changed
288.9	34.4	9	983.57	877.16	Managing owner changed
288.9	34.4	9	983	877	New form issued

APPENDIX B
Landings and Schedules

Landings of the *Mary Powell* —

Rondout: Always the northern terminus of the route, on Rondout Creek, which flows into the Hudson on the west side. Rondout became part of Kingston in 1872, but the waterfront area continued to be known as Rondout.

Rhinecliff: East bank, opposite the mouth of Rondout Creek. Experimental northbound landing during a short time in the summer of 1862, for discharging passengers for that side of the river.

Esopus: West bank. Substituted for Hyde Park as a summer landing, 1902-04.

Hyde Park: East bank. Added in the 1870s; in later years, only a summer landing. Discontinued after 1901 season.

Poughkeepsie: East bank. Always a landing.

Milton: West bank. Always a landing.

Marlborough: West bank. A landing on Saturday northbound trips only, June 26 to August 28, 1886.

New Hamburg: East bank. (Usually spelled New Hamburgh on *Mary Powell* timetables.) Not a landing during the 1871 season.

Newburgh: West bank. Always a landing.

Cornwall: West bank. Always a landing.

Cold Spring: East bank. A landing from 1862 to 1864; possibly in closing weeks of 1865 season.

West Point: West bank. For a number of years, no landing was made after mid-September.

Cozzens': West bank. The landing for Cozzens' Hotel. After the property changed hands, in 1882, the landing became Cranston's, although the apostrophe was not used consistently. Eventually Cranston's Hotel was sold and converted into a school, Ladycliff Academy, under the direction of the Franciscan Sisters. Then, during the 1901 season, the landing was redesignated Highland Falls, which was the name of the village there. Discontinued after 1915.

Bear Mountain: West bank. A northbound landing in 1915, July 7 to September 4; regular landing, both ways, 1916-17.

Grassy Point: West bank. A landing in 1862 for a short time.

Yonkers: East bank. Added as a northbound landing during the 1913 season; summer landing, northbound, 1914-15; regular landing, northbound, 1916-17.

New York terminus: Jay St., 1862-64; Desbrosses St., 1865-69; Vestry St., 1870-89; Desbrosses St., 1890-1917.

"Up-town" landing: West 34th St., September 19, 1870, until end of that season; West 24th St., 1880; West 22nd St., 1881-1904; West 42nd St., 1905-17.

Additional New York landing: West 129th St., northbound landing, Saturdays and holidays only, commencing during 1902 season, and in 1903-04; regular landing, both ways, 1905-17.

————————

Changes in time —

Rondout departure: Usually in September, as the days grew shorter, the 5:30 a.m. sailing time was put back one-half hour to 6 a.m., with these exceptions: 1866-68, New York sailing time advanced one-half hour instead; 1869, 6:30 a.m.; 1870, New York sailing time advanced one-half hour instead; 1871 and 1883-87, no change; 1888, 6:30 a.m.; 1900-03, 6:30 a.m. In the period 1904-14, the Rondout sailing time was 6:00 a.m. throughout the season, and in 1915-17, 7:00 a.m. Early season sailings for a short time in 1871 were made from Rondout at 5:15 a.m.

New York arrival and departure: From 1862 to 1866, arrival time was advertised as 11:00 a.m. Thereafter it varied (10:30, 10:45 and 11:00 a.m.) through 1879. Sailing time, 1862-79, was 3:30 p.m., with late season exceptions noted above. Changes then became effective as follows:

1880: Arrive West 24th St. (West 22nd St., 1881 and following), 10:30 a.m.; Vestry St., 10:40 a.m. (later, 10:50 a.m.). Leave Vestry St., 3:10 p.m.; West 24th St., 3:30 p.m.

1881: Leave Vestry St., 3:20 p.m.; West 22nd St., 3:30 p.m.

1882: Leave Vestry St. (Desbrosses St., 1890 and following), 3:15 p.m.; West 22nd St., 3:30 p.m.

1886: Commencing June 19, with the growing popularity of the Saturday half-holiday, Saturday sailings were advanced one hour.

1888: Arrive West 22nd St., 10:45 a.m.; Vestry St. (Desbrosses St., 1890 and following), 11:10 a.m.

1890: Saturday sailing time again advanced, to 1:45 p.m. from Desbrosses St. and 2:00 p.m. from West 22nd St.

1902: West 129th St. added as a New York landing, northbound, Saturdays only, with a departure time of 2:20 p.m.

1904: Arrive West 22nd St., 11:15 a.m.; Desbrosses St., 11:40 a.m.

1905: Arrive West 129th St., 11:00 a.m.; West 42nd St., 11:20 a.m.; Desbrosses St., 11:45 a.m. Leave Desbrosses St., 3:10 p.m. (Saturday, 1:45 p.m.); West 42nd St., 3:30 p.m. (Saturday, 2:00 p.m.); West 129th St., 3:50 p.m. (Saturday, 2:20 p.m.).

1907: Saturday sailing time made regular sailing time, Monday through Saturday.

1915: Arrive West 129th St., 11:55 a.m.; West 42nd St., 12:15 p.m.; Desbrosses St., 12:45 p.m.

Rondout arrival: Since there was no set schedule on the northbound run until the early years of this century, the Rondout arrival time for decades was qualified as average. It was considered to be 8:20 p.m., then 8:30 p.m. and 8:45 p.m. through 1906, by which time "average" had been eliminated. In the years 1907-17 it was 7:45 p.m. During the period of early Saturday sailings, the Rondout arrival time was, of course, earlier on that day.

NOTE: Service on the route was provided on Monday through Saturday, but never on Sunday.

The *Mary Powell's* sternboards are owned by Roger W. Mabie of Port Ewen, grandson of Captain William H. Mabie, a prominent master and pilot on the Hudson. Posing with the boards is the owner's son, William H. Mabie, named for his great-grandfather.

191

Fast Runs

Over a long period of time, the *Mary Powell* made a number of excellent runs. All of these fast trips were northbound, when the *Mary Powell* was not required to hold to a timetable and could be pushed the entire distance from New York to Rondout, if desired. All were made with favorable tidal conditions.

1863, June 11: Jay St. to Poughkeepsie, 3 hours 40 minutes elapsed time (7 landings); 3 h. 20 m. running time. To a point off Rondout Lighthouse, 4 h. 30 m. elapsed time (8 ldgs.).

1864, September: Jay St. to off Caldwells, at the southern gateway to the Highlands, 1 h. 47 m. running time. To Cozzens', the first landing, 2 h. 6 m. running time. To Newburgh, 2 h. 36 m. running time.

1867, June 10: Desbrosses St. to Newburgh, 2 h. 50 m. elapsed time (3 ldgs.). To Poughkeepsie, 3 h. 40 m. elapsed time (6 ldgs.). To Rondout Lighthouse, 4 h. 23 m. elapsed time (7 ldgs.); 4 h. running time. Poughkeepsie to Rondout Lighthouse, 39 m. running time. Total number of passengers discharged at 7 ldgs., about 250.

1873, June 18: Vestry St. to Newburgh, 2 h. 49 m. elapsed time (3 ldgs.). To Rondout Lighthouse, 4 h. 26 m. elapsed time.

1874, August 6: Vestry St. to Newburgh, 2 h. 47 m. elapsed time (3 ldgs.). To Poughkeepsie, 3 h. 39½ m. elapsed time (6 ldgs.); 3 h. 19 m. running time.

1879, May 30: Vestry St. to Newburgh, 2 h. 50 m. elapsed time.

1881, June 7: Vestry St. to Newburgh, 3 h. 1 m. elapsed time (4 ldgs.); 2 h. 53 m. running time. To Poughkeepsie, 3 h. 47 m. elapsed time (7 ldgs.); 3 h. 33 m. running time. To Rondout Lighthouse, 4 h. 32 m. elapsed time.

1881, June 20: West 22nd St. to Newburgh, 2 h. 44½ m. elapsed time (3 ldgs.). To Poughkeepsie, 3 hr. 33¾ m. elapsed time (6 ldgs.). To Rondout Lighthouse, 4 h. 19½ m. elapsed time; 3 h. 53½ m. running time.

1882, May 26: West 22nd St. to Newburgh, 2 h. 41 m. elapsed time. To Poughkeepsie, 3 h. 28 m. elapsed time; 3 h. 13 m. running time. To Rondout Lighthouse, 4 h. 14 m. elapsed time; 3 h. 54 m. minimum running time.

Following the courses of the *Mary Powell,* these are the approximate distances in statute miles from the original New York terminus at Jay Street to various points on the route: off Piermont, 23.88; off Caldwells, 41.90; Cozzens', 49.20; Newburgh, 59.55; Poughkeepsie, 74.35; and off Rondout Lighthouse, 89.35. For distances from the terminus either at Desbrosses Street or Vestry Street, deduct one-third of a mile; from West 22nd Street landing, deduct another 1 5/6 miles.

Using these distances and selected runs, the average speeds are:

Vestry St. to off Piermont — 23.95 m.p.h. (see below)

Jay St. to off Caldwells — 23.50 (September, 1864)

Jay St. to Cozzens' — 23.43 (September, 1864)

Jay St. to Newburgh — 22.90 (September, 1864)

Jay St. to Poughkeepsie — 22.31 (June 11, 1863)

Desbrosses St. to off Rondout Lighthouse — 22.25 (June 10, 1867)

West 22nd St. to Poughkeepsie — 22.44 (May 26, 1882)

West 22nd St. to off Rondout Lighthouse — 22.40 (June 20, 1881)

While the actual mileage covered by the *Mary Powell* on any or all of these runs may have varied slightly from the distances given, the averages are felt to be a fair indication of her top speed to the points named. They were, of course, computed on running time, after landing deductions had been made. This allowance was generally considered to be the time between the ringing of the engine-room bell to slow upon approaching a landing and the ringing of the bell for full speed ahead upon leaving.

For short spurts, one can find claims for a run between Newburgh and New Hamburg at 26¾ m.p.h. and for others at even greater speed. Nevertheless, Andrew Fletcher, of the firm that built the engine, estimated 25 m.p.h. as a maximum for a short distance under completely advantageous conditions, and this would appear to be just.

Relative to the first average on the list, there are several trips of record on which the *Mary Powell* ran from the New York terminus to a point off Piermont with times ranging from 59 to 62 minutes. Fifty-nine minutes was used to compute the average of 23.95 miles per hour.

A few words are in order about the 1881 and 1882 trips, which were timed from West 22nd Street rather than the New York terminus. These were made during the intense and well-publicized rivalry with the *Albany,* so one would be led to expect a slight exaggeration, but the landing allowances claimed do not indicate this. And, as for the June 7 and June 20, 1881, trips, it is reasonable to assume that Captain Anderson would have wanted to test the capabilities of his steamer after the rebuilding of the hull, regardless of the *Albany.*

On the June 20, 1881, trip, on the basis of published timings, the *Mary Powell* would have bettered her average speed of June 10, 1867, from New York to Rondout Lighthouse by about two-thirds of one per cent, with the 1881 average from West 22nd Street rather than the terminus, as it was in 1867. Incidentally, the 1867 trip was one to which Captain Anderson never referred. Being human, he would hardly have pointed with pride to something that happened when he was in no way connected with the steamboat.

After the close of the 1881 season, Captain Anderson was quoted by the Kingston *Daily Freeman* (October 21) as saying, ". . . one trip . . . we beat the fastest time on record. We left New York at 3:30 o'clock and arrived at Rondout light house at 7:45. This was making eighty-seven miles in four hours and fifteen minutes." No record of this trip has been found and about it the captain was properly vague.

Again, after the run on May 26, 1882, on which the *Mary Powell* left West 22nd Street at 3:33 p.m. and arrived off Rondout Lighthouse at 7:47 p.m., the claim was made that this beat the previous record by 10 minutes.

Later on the Mary Powell Steamboat Company was to describe in its guidebooks a trip, said at first to have been run in 1882, as ". . . her fastest trip between New York and Rondout, far outdoing any previous steamboat record over that course. She left her pier in New York at 3:32 P.M., and reached Rondout at 7:45 P.M. During this trip she made eight stops, landing 450 passengers before reaching her destination. The length of the route is one hundred miles, and the *Mary Powell's* speed on that day was twenty-five miles an hour."

Subsequently the year was changed to 1881, the time of departure to 3:33 and the statement about a speed of 25 miles an hour deleted. Next the year was omitted, but the claim marched on through the annual guidebooks, that the *Mary Powell* on her fastest trip covered 100 miles in 4 hours 12 minutes and made eight landings — something much easier done in print than on the river!

(*—R. Loren Graham collection*)

APPENDIX D
Poems

The *Mary Powell* probably inspired more lines of rhyming verse than any other steamboat. Usually the rhyme was the important thing; what went in between was of little moment.

An early effort told of the arrival of the *Mary Powell* at Cornwall on a Saturday evening and, if nothing else, caught the spirit of a high spot of a summer vacation in 1871.

SATURDAY EVENING LANDING OF THE *MARY POWELL* AT CORNWALL

The sun is setting in the Heaven,
  The carriages all do flock
On this, the last day of the seven,
  To Cornwall's spacious dock.

The sight is goodly to the eyes;
  The ladies' costumes gay;
Horses of every color and size,
  Brown, white, black and grey!

Team after team, in fine array,
  Comes dashing down the hill,
Until you cry out in dismay,
  "Why, what place can they fill?"

But hush! hush! hush! Hark! hear that bell?
  How changed the busy scene:
All quickly to each other tell
  The *Mary Powell* is seen!

Hark! what a change! See! all is still;
  Eyes on the river meet!
Hearts all with expectation thrill,
  Their loved ones soon to greet!

The grand old Highlands frowning down
  Upon the Hudson blue!
The sunset's brilliant, golden crown,
  Makes up this lovely view.

Around the river's graceful turn
  The *Powell* appears in sight;
She seems the water's aid to spurn,
  She glides along so light.

How, like a swan, she proudly glides
  Over the water's clear!
The crowds that throng her ample side
  Wave, for she now draws near.

Majestically, as if to rest,
  At Cornwall now she stops;
Upon the noble Hudson's breast
  Reclines she by the dock.

Free waves her streamer on the wind;
  She passes out of sight,
Leaving the merry scene behind
  Her whistle cries, "Good night!"

Husband and wife exchange embrace;
  The mother, on the dock,
Gazing once more in her son's face,
  Finds all her fears forgot.

Joyfully little children press
  Around their father dear,
Tell him their frolics, great and less,
  With voices ringing clear!

Light, girlish forms, are flitting round,
  And faces fresh and sweet,
By their admirers are found,
  With welcome smiles to greet.

At last, in carriages and stage,
  They all are closely stowed;
The horses willingly engage
  To pull their merry load.

And winding slowly up the hill,
  Bathed in the sunset's light,
Their joyous voices the air fill,
  As they pass out of sight.

— Julia Bayard Cummings, August 26, 1871

The passing of the *Mary Powell* brought forth a rush of sentimental tributes in a period when sentiment had to be expressed in poetry. Regardless of how we evaluate the results, we must admit that only a steamboat with an extraordinary hold on the affections of the Hudson Valley could motivate people to spend the time, the pencil biting and the soul searching that went into the composition of such outpourings as these.

Farewell, thou Queen of the Hudson!
Tho' thou wilt be gone
From those dear waters
That were to thee as home
Thou shalt not go
From the hearts that loved thee,
As a living thing.
But through shadows gray and ghostly
Methinks thy graceful form
Will speed all silently
Along the river's quiet shores.
And in the evening softness

194

The silvery notes of thy clear-toned bell
Will call the echoes from the hills around.

— Attributed to a descendant
of the Anderson family

Our *Mary* is going to leave us
  If she's not already gone
The vandals are going to scrap her
  And leave us all forlorn.

No more will we hear her bell
  In the early morn
When the welkin rings with music
  Right after she's blown her horn.

No more will little foot prints
  Go pattering through the saloon
No more will little children's pants
  Go sliding down the stairs.

With sadness we will think of her
  When she is torn apart
The eagle's flight from the pilot house
  Will almost break our hearts.

Goodby, dear *Mary Powell*
  Your work was done so well
That surely if you had a soul,
  It would find its place in heaven.

— John Bright, Esopus, N.Y.

THE SWAN-SONG OF THE *MARY POWELL*

Good-by to the *Mary Powell*, to
  The fast old river boat
That used to show a foaming wake
  To everything afloat.
For she has reached her final dock,
  And nevermore will glide
In white and swanlike grace upon
  The Hudson's silver side.

Oh, where the brooding Highlands throw
  Deep shadows on the sheen
Of dancing waves, for many a year
  We'll miss the River Queen,
And long in fancy we shall hear
  Her whistle's cheery blast
In greeting to the rival boats
  She sped so proudly past.

Her engine's scrapped, her timbers wrecked,
  Her funnels fallen, she
From Troy to New York City now
  Is but a memory,
But half a century of brides
  Who took the Hudson trip
In sprays of withered orange flowers
  Embalm the little ship.

— Minna Irving, in the New York *Sun*

How sad to now take this boat apart.
Long has she waved on high.
And many an eye has been delighted to see,
Her sailing over the tide.

Around her were the traffic's shout,
The deep, blue river's roar.
The beauty of the Hudson,
Shall sail the tide no more.

She has served the common public.
Served them long and well;
Like a beautiful furnished palace,
In a quiet, lowly dell.

Her career has been found faultless,
Her crew they were always true;
And never a life has she lost,
While she sailed the Hudson's blue.

But at last she must be torn apart,
This boat with the wondrous pride,
That was called "The Queen of the Hudson,"
In days and years gone by.

So give her the praise that is due her,
Praise her for beauty and grace,
Praise her for safely carrying,
Her cargo of human race.

And let us always remember,
That *Mary Powell* was the name,
Of the boat that plied the Hudson,
The boat of beauty and fame.

None knew her but to admire her,
None knew her but to praise;
So we will think of her as anchored,
Safe in the distant haze.

— Mrs. Irving Jansen, Stone Ridge, N.Y.

The old *Mary Powell* lies in her grave,
  Stripped of all that made her beautiful and great,
Save the memory and pleasure she gave,
  To the millions that mourn her sad fate.

Mr. Junkman, handle her timbers with care,
  We ne'er shall see her like afloat again;
Lay them aside with a sigh and a prayer,
  And sing a song of the glory of her reign.

O, thou wondrous thing of beauty and grace,
  Thou beloved "Queen of the Hudson," without a peer;
None can hope to claim thy crown nor place
  In the hearts of those who hold thy memory dear.

— Almet S. Moffat, in the *Home County Magazine*,
February, 1924 (vol. 2, no. 7)

QUEEN OF THE HUDSON

O, *Mary*, dear old *Mary*, you too have
    passed away
To join the loving memories of a happy
    yesterday,
The faithful crew who worked on you are
    many gone before
You were their pride, their life, their pal
In the dear days of yore.

All spotless white, they named you right
You were the river's "Queen"
Like a diamond sparkling from above
You shone far down the stream
Your decks with crowds were always bowed
Your service far renowned.
Though time may come and time may go
Your like can ne'er be found.

Your whistle stilled like a loving voice
Its echoes heard no more.
Have phantom hands reached out for you
From that eternal shore?
Though you've passed away like yesterday
In thoughts we will e'er be true
A wreath made of tender memories
We dedicate to you.

            — Florence A. Maines

IN MEMORIAM

Among the Hudson's wondrous fleet
    No vessel ever won such fame,
And carried through the passing years
    Such widely known and honored name.

For many a year you filled the hearts
    Of thousands here, both old and young,
And by thousands more your fame was known
    Thru songs the poet's lore has sung.

In days gone by the waiting throng,
    On river docks along the shore,
Welcomed the sound of your silvery bell,
    Which hailed your coming in sight once more.

Your wheels no more the waters churn,
    The throbbing engine's pulse is still,
The helm no longer guides your course
    In answer to the pilot's will.

Good-bye old boat, your work is done,
    And now we shed the parting tear,
And pay a tribute here in prose,
    To you, who all old friends hold dear.

            — Fletcher DuBois, June, 1921, in
            A Memorial of the Mary Powell, *1862-1918*

The steamboat lies at the wharf on the south side
of Rondout Creek, where the dismantling began.

As the work progressed, her stacks, boiler covering, links on the after end of the walking beam, and paddle-box centerpieces were gone by 1921. Then, at left, the paddle boxes too. (*—Above, Eldredge collection, courtesy of The Mariners Museum; left, Captain William O. Benson collection*)

The above picture was taken with a panoramic camera, which accounts for the great curve in the creek. Of the near buildings in the lower left, the one farthest right is Fischer's hotel. At left is a portion of the Island Dock, connected to the mainland by causeway. Opposite is the hamlet of Connelly and its shipyard. At the extreme right of the picture is the West Shore Railroad bridge.

By 1924 the stern portion of the *Mary Powell* was almost down to the keel as the dismantling went on.

Elwin M. Eldredge took the photograph below of the *Mary Powell's* remains on July 5, 1926.

Taken in late 1931 or early 1932, the above picture shows the engine
bed, with the walking beam in the mud. Below, we look forward over
the hulk of the *Mary Powell*.

The stacks of the *Mary Powell* were still lying on the wharf on May 11, 1938. The walking beam, below, had settled even deeper into the mud by 1947.

The lighter *William S. Keeler* works near the hulk in June of 1947.

The engine bed in the picture above, was overlooked by the cottage built from the steamer's woodwork, on the hill in the background.

At left is the bow of a *Mary Powell* lifeboat owned by Mr. and Mrs. Chester B. Glunt. Mrs. Glunt — Ruth Reynolds Glunt — is the author of *The Old Lighthouses of the Hudson River*.

The *Mary Powell* cottage was adorned with the name from the front of the pilot-house. The steamer's landing bell, below, went to Indian Point Park. (—*Below, photograph by William H. Ewen, Jr.*)

At the left we look aft from the engine bed in 1947.

The centerpiece, or lunette, from a paddle box of the *Mary Powell* is in the Senate House Museum, Kingston. The top of the window, directly beneath it, gives an idea of the size.

The wheel of the *Mary Powell*, in the Senate House Museum, was a gift of Robert S. Rodie. Draped on it, at left, is the flag she flew on her last trip with passengers. In front of the window sits one of the ornaments that decorated the tops of the spars.

The sternboards belonging to Roger W. Mabie are here arranged as they were on the vessel.

Above and at left are the national colors flown on September 5, 1917, the *Mary Powell's* last revenue-producing trip. The flag is folded in the traditional method allowing it to be raised without touching the deck.

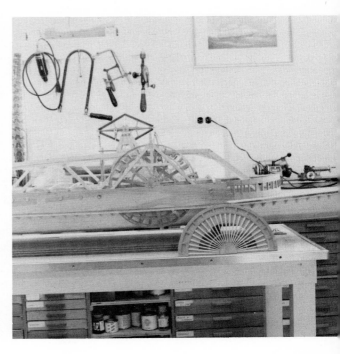

The model of the *Mary Powell's* engine is at Mystic Seaport, Mystic, Conn. Above right is one stage in the construction of a model of the steamboat by famed modelmaker Bernhard Schulze at the Storm King Art Center. Below, a model by F. Van Loon Ryder is now in the West Point Military Museum. The view looks up through the Highlands towards Newburgh. (*—Below, courtesy of F. Van Loon Ryder*)

The model at right was built by Pilot Guernsey B. Betts. Immediately below is another model of the vessel by F. Van Loon Ryder, presented to the Historical Society of Newburgh Bay and the Highlands by Mrs. W. Clement Scott. (—*Right, Herman F. Boyle collection; below, courtesy of Walter A. Tuttle*)

Captain William O. Benson built this lively model of the *Mary Powell* to show her in the later years of her life.

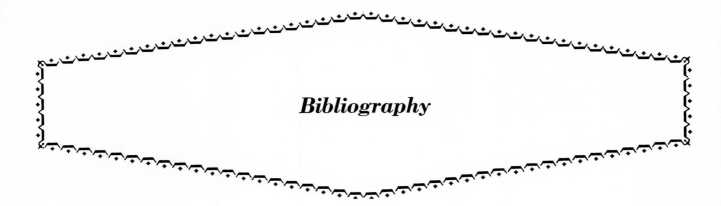

Bibliography

Barnes, William H. *The Fortieth Congress of the United States.* New York: George E. Perine, 1869.

Beers, F. W. *County Atlas of Ulster, New York.* New York: Walker & Jewett, 1875.

Briggs, Harry T. *"Mary Powell,* 'Queen of the Hudson.'" Year Book, Dutchess County Historical Society, vol. 38, 1953. Copyright, 1955.

Century of Progress: History of the Delaware and Hudson Company, 1823-1923, A. Albany, N.Y.: J. B. Lyon Co., printers, 1925.

Commemorative Biographical Record of Dutchess County, New York. Chicago: J. H. Beers & Co., 1897.

Commemorative Biographical Record of Ulster County, New York. Chicago: J. H. Beers & Co., 1896.

De Lisser, R. Lionel. *Picturesque Ulster.* Parts 1-3. Kingston, N.Y.: The Styles & Bruyn Publishing Co., 1896 and ff. Republished, eight parts in one volume. Cornwallville, N.Y.: The Hope Farm Press, 1968.

De Witt, William C. *People's History of Kingston, Rondout and Vicinity.* New Haven, Conn.: Tuttle, Morehouse & Taylor Co., printers, 1943.

Dictionary of American Naval Fighting Ships. Washington: U. S. Government Printing Office. Vol. 1, 1959; vol. 4, 1969.

DuBois, Fletcher. *A Memorial of the* Mary Powell, *1862-1918, with Interesting Recollections of Hudson River Steamboats.* Booklet. Philadelphia: Fletcher DuBois, c. 1921.

Elliott, Richard V. *Last of the Steamboats: The Saga of the Wilson Line.* Cambridge, Md.: Tidewater Publishers, 1970.

Ewen, William H. *Days of the Steamboats.* New York: Parents' Magazine Press, 1967.

Gazetteer of the State of New-York Including the Census of 1840, A. Albany, N.Y.: J. Disturnell, 1842.

Hickey, Andrew S. *The Story of Kingston: First Capitol of New York State, 1609-1952.* New York: Stratford House, 1952.

Holdcamper, Forrest R. "Registers, Enrollments and Licenses in the National Archives." *The American Neptune,* vol. 1, no. 3, July, 1941.

Hudson River Day Line Collection. The New-York Historical Society, New York, N.Y. This includes records and publications of the Mary Powell Steamboat Co., which became a subsidiary of the Hudson River Day Line.

Hudson River Day Line Collection. The Steamship Historical Society of America, Inc., reference library, Staten Island, N.Y. Also includes Mary Powell Steamboat Co. material.

Hungerford, Edward. *Men of Erie: A Story of Human Effort.* New York: Random House, 1946.

Husted, Mary Irving. *Hudson River Children.* Boston and New York: Bruce Humphries, Inc., 1943.

Isherwood, B. F. "The American River Paddle-Wheel Steamboat *Mary Powell.*" *The Journal of the Franklin Institute,* vol. 108, whole no. 643, July, 1879.

Kelley, Elizabeth Burroughs. *John Burroughs: Naturalist.* New York: Exposition Press, 1959.

List of American-Flag Merchant Vessels that Received Certificates of Enrollment or Registry at the Port of New York, 1789-1867. 2 vols. Compiled by Forrest R. Holdcamper; introduction by Kenneth R. Hall. Washington: The National Archives, 1968.

List of Merchant Vessels of the United States, 1868-1919. Annual list. Washington: U. S. Government Printing Office.

Lossing, Benson J. *The Hudson, from the Wilderness to the Sea.* New York: Virtue & Yorston, c. 1866.

Lyman, John. "Register Tonnage and Its Measurement." *The American Neptune,* vol. 5, no. 3-4, July and October, 1945.

Morrison, John Harrison. *History of American Steam Navigation*. New York: W. F. Sametz & Co., Inc., 1903.

National Archives and Records Service, General Services Administration, Washington. Files of documents of American vessels.

New York State Illustrated: or, the Tourist's Guide through the Empire State. Albany, N.Y.: edited and published by Mrs. S. S. Colt, 1872.

Newspapers. Files of newspapers of Rondout and Kingston in the Kingston City Library, Kingston, N.Y.; of Poughkeepsie in the Adriance Memorial Library, Poughkeepsie, N.Y.; of Newburgh in the Newburgh Free Library, Newburgh, N.Y.; of these same places and of New York and Albany in the New York State Library, Albany, N.Y.

Portrait and Biographical Record of Orange County, New York. New York and Chicago: Chapman Publishing Co., 1895.

Ruttenber, E. M. *History of the County of Orange with a History of the Town and City of Newburgh*. Newburgh, N.Y.: E. M. Ruttenber and Sons, printers, 1875.

Schoonmaker, Marius. *The History of Kingston, New York*. New York: Burr Printing House, 1888.

Shaughnessy, Jim. *Delaware & Hudson*. Berkeley, Cal.: Howell-North Books, 1967.

Skeel, Theron. "An American River Steamer — Performances of the *Mary Powell*." *The Iron Age*, vol. 21, no. 21, May 23, 1878.

Smith, Townsend J. "Hudson River Steamboat *Mary Powell*." *International Marine Engineering*, vol. 25, no. 5, May, 1920.

Stanton, Samuel Ward. *American Steam Vessels*. New York: Smith & Stanton, 1895.

Sylvester, Nathaniel Bartlett. *History of Ulster County, New York*. Philadelphia: Everts & Peck, 1880.

Tourist's Guide through the Empire State, The. Albany, N.Y.: edited and published by Mrs. S. S. Colt, 1871.

Tuttle, Walter A. "Temple Hill, 1783-1966." Historical Society of Newburgh Bay and the Highlands, publication no. 42, 1966.

Wakefield, Manville B. *Coal Boats to Tidewater*. South Fallsburg, N.Y.: Steingart Associates Inc., printers, 1965.

Whitman, Walt. *Specimen Days & Collect*. Philadelphia: Rees Welsh & Co., 1882-83.

Willis, Nathaniel Parker. *Out-Doors at Idlewild; or, the Shaping of a Home on the Banks of the Hudson*. New York: Charles Scribner, 1855.

Index of Vessels

General Index